The Fluid Frame
in Cinema:

Collected Essays

The Fluid Frame in Cinema:

Collected Essays

Pradipta Mukherjee

Cambridge Scholars Publishing

The Fluid Frame in Cinema: Collected Essays

By Pradipta Mukherjee

This book first published 2021

Cambridge Scholars Publishing

Lady Stephenson Library, Newcastle upon Tyne, NE6 2PA, UK

British Library Cataloguing in Publication Data
A catalogue record for this book is available from the British Library

Copyright © 2021 by Pradipta Mukherjee

All rights for this book reserved. No part of this book may be reproduced, stored in a retrieval system, or transmitted, in any form or by any means, electronic, mechanical, photocopying, recording or otherwise, without the prior permission of the copyright owner.

ISBN (10): 1-5275-6790-7
ISBN (13): 978-1-5275-6790-0

CONTENTS

Acknowledgements vii

Introduction viii

Part 1. Ruminations on Indian Cinema

Chapter 1 2
Framing Partition in the Films of Ritwik Ghatak and M. S. Sathyu

Chapter 2 15
Romancing Transgression: Representation of Gender by Post-Millennial Women Film-makers

Chapter 3 30
Media Constructions of Women's Sexuality in Indian Cinema

Chapter 4 44
Women as Desiring Subjects in *Devdas* on Screen

Chapter 5 59
Reflections on Masculinity and Popular Romance: *Jaane Tu Ya Jaane Na*

Chapter 6 64
Irrfan Khan: An Understated Genius

Chapter 7 69
Revisiting Mumbai Gangster Flicks: *Maqbool* in Perspective

Chapter 8 85
Negotiating Indian Tradition and Modernity: Globalisation and Hindi Cinema

Part 2. At the Crossroads of Adaptations

Chapter 9 100
Classic Shakespeare Cinema and Auteur Directors

Chapter 10 113
King Lear on Redemption or Apocalypse Road: Kozintsev, Kurosawa, Brook, and Levring

Chapter 11 121
A Metafictional Detour: Appropriating John Fowles's *The French Lieutenant's Woman* on Screen

Chapter 12 136
Dialectics of Exchange in William Wyler's and Luis Buñuel's Adaptations of *Wuthering Heights*

Chapter 13 145
"Ceaselessly into the Past"—In Search of Fitzgerald's Gatsby and the American Dream on Celluloid

Part 3. Unlocking the Troubled Mind: Aesthetics of Hitchcock and Kubrick

Chapter 14 156
Vertigo's Afterlife: A Travel through Six Decades

Chapter 15 161
Crosswinds of Fear and Desire: Hitchcock's Adaptation of *The Birds*

Chapter 16 171
A World unto Itself: Hitchcock's Mastery of Suspense

Chapter 17 178
From Gothic Romance to Horror Text: Problematising Genre in *Rebecca*

Chapter 18 183
Chaos and Collapse: Forty Years into the Magnificent Enigma of *The Shining*

Index of Film Titles 189

General Index 196

ACKNOWLEDGEMENTS

This book is dedicated to my late mother-in-law, Ila Mukherjee. Her consistent encouragement and understanding through all these years made everything I did possible. My heartfelt gratitude to the late Prof. Subhabrata Bhattacharyya who initiated me into cinema studies early in my career.

This book is the result of several years of research, writing, reading, viewing, and importantly, constant dialogue with mentors and friends, to whom I owe a great deal of thanks for their insights. My heartfelt indebtedness and appreciation to Prof. Douglas Lanier for his excellent suggestions and constant encouragement, particularly on the section on Shakespearean cinema.

Special thanks to Prof. Mark Thornton Burnett for inspiring me to develop a project on Shakespearean cinema for future years. My exchanges with Prof. Lanier and Prof. Burnett helped create the kind of stimulating academic ambience that makes good work possible.

Love and heartfelt thanks to my family—their solicitude and kindness made the years before I wrote this book easier to bear. Ananda, Atreyo, and Asmi supported all my endeavours and offered much needed humour through the long process of researching, writing, and publishing. Without the technical expertise of Atreyo, this book would never have seen the light of day.

Additional thanks to Debasish for conceptualising and making this a better book than it would otherwise have been. Gracious enough to read rough drafts of chapters, he offered good editorial suggestions that helped strengthen key portions of the book.

Last but not least, I would like to express my gratitude to my publisher, Cambridge Scholars Publishing, and its editors and support staff, for their invaluable assistance. My heartfelt thanks to Edward Crooks for going through rough drafts of this project and giving the book its final shape.

Introduction

The essays in this collection inhabit a fluid frame of critical inquiry. These essays are the milestones of my journey with cinema over the last ten years. They chart my progress from being fascinated by the medium to striving to make sense of that fascination. The collection may thus be best described as reflections, explorations, and meditations on cinema. In the writing of this book, which has lasted for over a decade, I tried to begin by recording my impressions of motion pictures, a sequence of individual pictures, but I experience it quite differently—as a steady stream of sensations.

The desire to write a book on cinema, the most collaborative of art forms, came with the realisation that films are a highly complex act of communication. As one takes a closer look into the very strategies of film-making, the primary purpose is to understand the language of cinema, the codes and signs through which this dynamic art form interacts with and engages its audience. The success of a film depends on how effectively the images projected on screen allow its audience to make meaning.

When we talk about films we usually refer to characters, action, and dialogue. Yet a film is also a vast outpouring of signs and signs are the most fundamental units of meaning in cinema. My critical manner has been to "read" films as advocated by the critical practice that emerged out of the Birmingham Centre for Contemporary Cultural Studies. From language, semiotics, and the study of cinematic signs to gender, subjectivity and discourse—they have been my zones of inquiry in every essay.

Of singular interest is the encoding and decoding of the film text, the nuances that necessitate elaboration. I remain firmly in awe of the artwork's independence and it remains my first and final point of reference. My experience of a film remains empirical to me. I am as interested in what is left "in frame" as I am interested in what is left out. Diegetic sound, the music of the frame, frame-making to frame-breaking, and freeze frame to fluid frame intrigue me. I embark upon processes of decoding such artistic signatures in several of my essays.

Not limited by genre, technique, or film history, my essays in the first section are dedicated to Indian cinema. Critical rigour, arising out of my passionate engagement with Indian cinema of every genre—both Hindi cinema emanating from Bollywood and vernacular Bangla films—

attempts to revamp any critical hierarchy that may exist in academic readings of Indian cinema. The worldview of directors like Ritwik Ghatak and M. S. Sathyu exists besides those of Mira Nair or Aparna Sen. Popular cinema can be a formidable tool of empowerment in the hands of intelligent film-makers. This book is an inquiry into the uneasy relationship between art and entertainment. The book also challenges the idea that popular cinema, whose reach is phenomenal, only entertains. Rather I look at how commercial cinema has gradually become more accommodating of a wider range of ideas and harbours new imaginations. My inquiry aims to see whether commercial cinema—the films I have read closely—also realises its potential of transformation. Whether the producers and financiers of cinema have taken the responsibility of being agents of emancipation. That has been the nature of my inquiry.

Issues like the role of the media in constructions of gender in modern Indian society are highlighted in the unearthing of such films as *Fashion* and *Iti Mrinalini*, which were given short shrift by the critical establishment. I include an essay on the role and new artistic provenance of the work of women directors in recent times where I look in depth at several films and try to, perhaps, read the emergence of a new film aesthetics. This essay is expected to fill the void of a major critical omission in this regard.

Of particular interest to me has been the area of adaptation studies and the interface between literature and cinema. The book has an entire section dedicated to this subject. The section, I hope, will offer fresh approaches to the art, theory, and cultural politics of film adaptations. Cinematic adaptations of Shakespeare in the West, and in India, have always fascinated me. This section includes two essays on Shakespearean cinematic appropriations and an essay on John Fowles's *The French Lieutenant's Woman*. An essay each on turning fiction into film in adaptations of *Wuthering Heights* and *The Great Gatsby* round off this section.

The essays in the final section are passionate recalibrations of the oeuvres of Alfred Hitchcock and Stanley Kubrick. The essays explore the auteur directors as master manipulators and as great craftsmen. This section hopefully will help readers understand how films communicate by considering the stories they tell, the sign systems they deploy, the interpretive contexts the viewer is invited to place them in, and the range of aesthetic elements that contribute to the cinematic image. This final section concludes with a case study of *The Shining*.

Several of the essays in the collection germinated at various international conference presentations in India and abroad. Certain earlier drafts have been published in leading dailies. Coupled with some unpublished material, they make up a representative palimpsest of my inquiries in cinema. I hope my readers will find walking down the trails I have taken pleasurable and perhaps instructive.

PART I

RUMINATIONS ON INDIAN CINEMA

Chapter 1

Framing Partition in the Films of Ritwik Ghatak and M. S. Sathyu

In the weeks leading up to the apocalyptic event of Partition, both on the Eastern and Western frontiers, massive populations of Hindus and Sikhs moved into India, as Muslims moved in the other direction, into Pakistan in search of a home. The birth of two sovereign states, India and Pakistan, out of the flames of unprecedented violence and trauma in 1947 etched itself, in indelible character, upon the psyche of Ritwik Ghatak, an individualist genius film-maker from Bengal. A refugee from East Bengal, which had become East Pakistan, Ghatak, like innumerable other traumatised souls, relocated to Calcutta in West Bengal from East Pakistan as Partition unexpectedly turned him into a foreigner in his homeland.

The Partition that tore "Mother Bengal" apart, with unspeakable barbarity lacerating both sides of the border, forced twelve million people to embark upon hazardous and perilous journeys to find a home and shelter elsewhere. While Jean-Luc Godard was obsessed by the events in Paris in May 1968 and the Vietnam War, Ritwik Ghatak found the cataclysmic event of the Partition of the Indian subcontinent equally compelling.

The pioneer of the experimental and avant-garde in Indian film-making, Ghatak was indeed himself a migrant out of erstwhile East Pakistan. Such agonisingly traumatic historical circumstances shaped his preoccupation with Partition on the eastern frontier: its searing pain and unbearable wound blazed in his work. As the revolutionary chronicler of postcolonial South-Asian national disintegration and individual displacement, Ghatak's position remains unique and unparalleled.

Among directors who concentrated on social and political conflict to reveal dystopian tendencies in the postcolonial nation-state whilst also rekindling hopes of a different future, Ritwik Ghatak was a pioneer. With his strident authorial voice and positioning as an iconoclast, Ghatak emerged as the great contemporary of Satyajit Ray. Both Ray and Ghatak were torchbearers for Indian alternative cinema. They were the lifeblood of what may be called the parallel art cinema movement in India.

Both Ghatak and Ray set themselves apart from commercial, mainstream cinema and inspired other innovative talents from India like Adoor Gopalkrishnan, Mrinal Sen, Girish Kasarvalli, Kumar Shahani, and Mani Kaul. These film-makers were either inspired by Ghatak or emboldened by him. Ghatak's Partition trilogy, *Meghe Dhaka Tara*, *Komal Gandhar*, and *Subarnarekha*, which voices the saga of the refugee community from East Bengal, migrating across the border from Bangladesh (formerly East Pakistan) to West Bengal in search of shelter, has sealed his reputation as perhaps the most emphatic narrator of rootlessness. Ghatak, so much beyond parochialism, so much at home in the world, under the duress of Partition carved out a new uncharted trajectory for Indian parallel cinema.

In *Subarnarekha,* the refugee searching for an identity or home is the focus of the narration, while in *Meghe Dhaka Tara* it is the tale of the economically deprived middle class with bourgeois aspirations that comes to the fore. Ghatak's plots effectively render the cultural and historical memory of Partition. They are driven by a nostalgia and yearning that many Bengalis had for their pre-Partition way of life.

Brecht-inspired epic narratives blend with Tagorean romanticism, modernist expressionism co-exists with traditional or new archetypes and myths. They constitute the hallmarks of Ghatak's discursive approach to film-making, as Rajadhyaksha notes, where "competing epistemologies intertwine" (56). Replete with Indian classical music—the *ragas* and *aalaps*—and Tagore songs, Ghatak's soundscape did not preclude the use of folk music. These varied aural signatures allowed him to meld popular Indian aesthetics with Jungian psychology in his films in order to explore the human subconscious through Soviet style sound-image montage. This was the inception of a new semantics of cinema. The evolution of a discursive film aesthetics through Ghatak's innovative reworking of Hindu mythology, archetypes, and epic structures led to a new dawn.

1

Neeta, Geeta, and their mother in *Meghe Dhaka Tara* (*The Cloud-Capped Star*, 1960), Ghatak's seminal work on Partition, represent archetypal symbols embodying three traditional but contrasting aspects of femininity. The symbology of ruthlessness or outrage surrounding the Hindu goddess Kali, or the malevolence and destructive demeanour of another of her female avatars, Chandi, inheres in the figure of the mother, whereas Neeta, the breadwinner, assumes the role of a provider or nourisher deriving from the munificence of a Mother Goddess (Rajadhyaksha 53–54; Bhaskar 36).

The sensual woman Geeta, with her seductive wiles, finds a parallel in the *femme fatale* of Western cinema, of which she may be seen as an Eastern counterpart. Such archetypes come to the fore right from the beginning of the film.

Ghatak is rather careful in his construction of the *mise en scène* in the opening shot of *Meghe Dhaka Tara*. A train in the background becomes pivotal, signifying motion without direction or any particular arrival or departure. This train that seemingly journeys to a proverbial nowhere is very unlike the train in Satyajit Ray's *Pather Panchali* (1955) where it represents the call of the unknown and the possibilities of reaching out to a wider world. The train in Ghatak's film becomes an artefact, a symbol of machine-made culture—characterless, fashioned out of the mechanical forge of modernity: signifying the mundane.

In the opening sequence of *Meghe Dhaka Tara*, Neeta is introduced as the human incarnation of natural forces or as an archetype. Shankar, Neeta's brother, an aspiring classical singer, is framed on the left rendering *Raga Hansadhwani* in an unstinting, untrained voice. A pond in the mid-ground reinforces the provider image. Neeta is seen in profile in the foreground of the same frame, with a warm smile of satisfaction and understanding of her brother's clumsy but earnest efforts, fortifying the idea of a tolerant, benignant female godhead. The tall, exfoliating tree presides over the scene, suggesting abundance and security. The relationship between the compassion and grace of the female protagonist and the motherly nurture of the sylvan scenes from Bengal is stitched together by Ghatak, inimitably, by his use of Indian classical music. Combined, they set the undertone for a new utopian and/or dystopian homeland.

The characters in *Meghe Dhaka Tara* and the precarious nature of their existence in a refugee colony are all captured by Ghatak's camera, while the last notes of the song die out and Neeta enters her neighbourhood. Gradually Neeta's image comes to be invested with the characteristics of an idealised Bengal, the nation as mother—the benevolent nurturer and universal sustainer. As Ghatak gives concrete shape to the self-effacing character of Neeta, he builds on the iconic and archetypal possibilities contained in it. Neeta is gradually magnified into a larger-than-life figure in her family courtyard. She is almost deified as the Great Mother who is tranquil, caring, and succulent. However, in a complex matrix of human portraiture, Ghatak also frames the calm, affectionate, and self-sacrificing Neeta as the eternally unwed bride.

The post-Partition female subject and especially the iconic figure of Neeta are framed innovatively by Ghatak's camera through ideal representations of the woman—as compassionate, caring, and all-giving—against the grain of brutality, discord, and inhumanity that gather like a storm around a poverty-stricken refugee family. Neeta is also the sole breadwinner of this displaced family. In Ghatak's film, Neeta gradually comes to signify the goddesses Jagadhatri (The Bearer of the World) and Uma (Tranquility), the other name for the goddess Durga in Hindu mythology. With Neeta's birthday coinciding with the day set apart for the worship of the goddess Jagadhatri, she is made to stand symbolically as the Mother Goddess walking the earth. As Ghatak turns on the magic lantern with his cinematic eye, the shades of the divine are subtly superimposed on Neeta's persona.[1]

The poise of a powerful female deity is compared with the ragged bewilderment of her exhausted and distraught alter ego; this great act of juxtaposition of archetypal images and the inversion of gender roles within the family are brought into sharp focus in the character of Neeta. This coming together of contrasting socio-cultural registers is also testament to the contradictory demands placed on women in everyday life. The tallying of the sacred and secular in terms of themes by Ghatak can thus be taken as a telling commentary on the unifying potential of Partition sagas.

With the Bengal Famine of the 1940s, the communal riots of Noakhali, and Partition itself as the three foundation stones of his attempts to make sense of these tempestuous times in film, Ghatak fortified his women protagonists with the powerful archetype of the Great Mother. It was his way of instilling in his female protagonist—educated, working, yet repressed—some measure of agency in a feudal-capitalist world.

Social dislocation produced in the wake of Partition enabled women to emerge into the public sphere as breadwinners. We are aware of how the trauma and violence of a divided Bengal destroyed the lives of a whole generation of women. However, as working women who were the principal source of income for their families, they came to occupy spaces in the public arena denied to them in more secure and sheltered times.

Post-1990s Indian Partition films, like *Train to Pakistan*, *Earth*, *Hey Ram*, and *Pinjar*, portray tropes of rape, abduction, and murder as the bodies of women become prized possessions of their captors and violators. These films demonstrate insistently how the conflict between communities is played over the bodies of women. *Meghe Dhaka Tara*, in turn, questions this univocal language of Partition by focusing on the idea that there are

---

[1] For Ghatak's ideas on Neeta as Jagaddhatri or Uma see Ritwik Ghatak, "Manab Samar, Amader Aitihya, Chabi kora o Amar Prachesta," in *Chalachitra Manush Ebong Aro Kichu*. Kolkata: Dey's Publishing, 2007, 19–20.

other realities of which one needs to be cognisant beyond the tragic consequences of mindless violence, the sufferance of Bengal, or just the victimhood of women. The evolving nature of female roles—the emergence of women as part of the new labour force—became a symptom of a world turned upside down. This was a genuine blow to the social feudalism of patriarchy although this essentially conservative male worldview was in part shared by a certain class of women.

Here the power and provenance of Ghatak's non-representational aural register, its burgeoning influence, must give us pause. Throughout the film, classical ragas, Rabindrasangeet, Baul songs, and several forms of folk music fuse together to strengthen the dramaturgy of the visuals. Together, they function as building blocks of a visual register carefully used by the film-maker in the construction of the *mise en scène* of individual film sequences.

Rabindranath Tagore's lyrical oeuvre provides Ghatak with the grist for his creative mill as he crucially uses the song *Je raate mor duwaar guli bhanglo jhore* (That night when the storm beat down my doors) as the soundscape of protest made by Shankar, Neeta's brother, against her blatant exploitation by the family. The bond between the twin Bengals and the bond between the two siblings are analogous (Rajadhyaksha 72) here. Ghatak borrows the repertoire of images from Tagore's song that stands for the reassertion of hope amidst despair, thus suturing together romantic and religious imagery. In Ghatak's film, the song becomes the voice of Neeta's perturbation, her turmoil, and the violence she has suffered: not overt sexual violence but the predictable violation of the private by public life, in making public the disgrace of "the private."

The harmonious closure of Tagore's song is disrupted, however, by the discordance of a whiplash. This extra-diegetic aural refrain in the soundtrack insistently subverts any association with romanticism. The sonic disruption or whiplash here insistently subverts the narrative's systematised termination. Any hopeful suggestions of *Mukti* (salvation) made by the Tagore song are permanently erased as Neeta cries her heart out with the tragic strains of a bewailing sarod. Neeta's body, psyche, and consciousness being the embodiment of Bengal, the whiplash returns as historic memory and trauma bearing down upon her as an individual and as the symbolic motherland. Ghatak's film aesthetic is defined in this song by the positioning of the camera at high and low angles and the dramatic lighting composition. The adoption of an expressionist acting style, the camera angles, innovative but minimal lighting techniques, and the *gestus* further illustrate Ghatak's artistic principles.

On several occasions, Ghatak makes extra-diegetic use of Bangla folk songs that lament the departure of Uma (another name for the goddess Durga) from her familial home to the abode of her husband, the lord Shiva, on Mount Kailash in the Himalayas: "Come my daughter Uma, to me/ Let me garland you with flowers," the song longingly intones. Used contrapuntally, the song also suggests how Neeta, the Mother Goddess, although unwed, is symbolically sacrificed and allowed to leave like the goddess of myth. Such reworking of Indian cultural myths and archetypes within a melodramatic context allows Ghatak, for whom the Partition was mishandled and ill conceived, to explore the degradation of post-Independence Bengal.

There is a play of forms in Ghatak's assemblage of modernist subjective expression and distinct Hindu archetypal myths. In his *Komal Gandhar* (1961), the camera comes to a halt with the jerk and jolt of a train grinding to a stop, confronted with the prospect of a railway track that has been abruptly cut off at the border between two nations. The gaze of the camera is petrified at the point where the road trails off into East Bengal signalling a journey that has now become a taboo. This was a sight meant to raise a "searing cry in Anasuya's heart" (Ghatak 50). Ghatak's search for an idyllic and mythic homeland continues in *Subarnarekha* (1962). The spatial outsider remains the quintessential melodramatic trope in Ghatak's films as he fuses two antithetical practices—"realist art cinema and the melodramatic popular tradition" (Biswas 48)—from the 1950s and carries the fusion forward in his films of the sixties.[2]

Ritwik Ghatak's timeless historicity did not move away from the legacy of his cultural roots, although it never cloistered his international, almost planetary, humanism and sensitivity. Old and new archetypes are at violent odds with each other in *Subarnarekha* as they push to the limit the tenuous boundary of the epic structure employed to keep them in. Despite this, the film ends, as it began, in a utopian vein, searching for and creating the idyll of a mythic homeland. Ghatak fuses two antagonistic practices from 1955—"realist art cinema and the melodramatic popular tradition"[2] (Biswas 48)—and carries them forward in his films of the sixties.

In *Subarnarekha*, a dark film on the post-Partition scenario, Iswar Chakraborty, a refugee from East Bengal, migrates to the west with his young sister Sita. Victims of Partition, compelled to leave their native land, East Bengali refugees set up squatters' colonies in West Bengal.

---

[2] Biswas regards Nimai Ghosh's *Chinnamul*, the first Partition film, as seminal for its Italian neo-realist influences. It is a film, he corroborates, that foregrounds the "country–city dualism . . . unknown to Indian cinema till then" (40).

Ghatak's film opens with homeless migrants uprooted from the district of Pabna, in erstwhile East Pakistan, collectively building a colony on marshland owned by a *zamindar* (feudal landowner) on the outskirts of the city.

Ghatak explained his methodology in *Subarnarekha* thus: "What I have tried to say in this film is about the present socio-economic and political crisis in Bengal, the demonic form it has assumed from 1942 to 1962." This is exactly what he stated: "By the word refugee or uprooted I don't mean only the uprooted people from East Bengal. I have tried to give it another dimension, a different nuance to lift it a bit from its geographical constraints" ("Subarnarekha Prasange" 152–54).

Uprooted and driven from his home, Iswar takes upon himself the responsibility of looking after an orphan boy, Abhiram, hailing from Dhaka (erstwhile East Pakistan) whose mother was abducted while both were searching for shelter in West Bengal. This boy is later, crucially, revealed to be a low-caste person in the film. Iswar takes a job at the local foundry and moves to the scenic banks of the river Subarnarekha as he manfully tries to shoulder the responsibility of bringing up both Abhiram and Sita. The significance of this move in Ghatak's semiotic universe is not lost upon us, as Iswar, representative of a people who have lost almost everything, moves tentatively forward towards the river called Subarnarekha, meaning the line drawn in gold, the ray or beacon of hope in the dun smoke of the realities of Partition.

Now settled by the scenic river, Abhiram and Sita on one of their childish jaunts come across an abandoned airstrip and the decrepit remains of an aeroplane. Ghatak brilliantly triggers a spatio-temporal ferment in this sequence as the realities of the Second World War and the dropping of atomic bombs on Hiroshima and Nagasaki are made to collide with the innocent, guiltless childhood wonder that permeates the frame. Quite unaware of the momentous nature of the ground on which they play, the children tread on space interdicted by the violent history and horrors of war.

Interestingly, it is on this abandoned airstrip that Sita later, transfixed with fear, encounters the Kali impersonator or *bohurupi*, whose masquerade is a form of folk entertainment. According to Ghatak:

> this is one archetypal image that has been haunting us from [the] remote past, [and] is today confronting us all over the world. You may call it by many names: The Hydrogen Bomb, or Strategic Air Command, or De Gaulle, or Adenauer, or some other name you would not like to mention. It is the power of annihilation, the ability to destroy, and perhaps like little

Sita we have suddenly found ourselves confronted by it. ("Chalachitra Chinta" 33)

In the epic *Ramayana*, Sita is the very epitome of self-sacrifice. Plumbing the depths of our religious consciousness, Ghatak visualised the terrible aspect of the "Primordial Mother Image" confronting Sita to bring into focus the decadence of post-Independence partitioned Bengal. For Ghatak it was an encounter with the "Mahakaal" or the great circle of Time ("Chalachitra Chinta" 32–33). As a concept it leads back to the destroyer of the universe in the trinity of Hindu divinity, the lord Shiva. It refers to the end of time, a vortex into which everything is sucked and which is thus beyond the realms of mortal living.

In a dramatic reversal of the archetypal image later in the film, Iswar encounters his own sister, Sita, driven to prostitution out of poverty, in a brothel. Ghatak's grip on our sensibilities allows us no escape from the realisation that the decaying, fractured Bengal we are getting to see daily is like our Sita who has descended into the dark abyss of modern society, stripped of all her emblematic value as a paragon of virtue and sacrifice, devoid of its rich tradition of Puranic portraiture. Iswar's progress, from being a liberal-minded refugee who would have denounced casteism to being one of the new bourgeoisie, is closely documented in the film.

To better appreciate Ghatak's work one needs to delve deeper into his mental conditioning in a Marxist socio-cultural and political milieu during his upbringing. To reveal the decadence of post-Partition Bengal, Ghatak successfully fused Stanislavski and Brecht—an epic approach and the alienation effect—with the cinematic influence of Eisenstein, Pudovkin, Godard, and Buñuel. Sergei Eisenstein's use of landscape and the collision of montage and musical abstraction in his work and Federico Fellini's use of music in *La Dolce Vita*—which Ghatak borrowed for *Subarnarekha*'s nightclub sequence—had a deep impact on his films.

The archetypes drawn from Indian mythology, traditional images from the epics and the symbolism of belief structures have their origins in the *shastras* and *puranas*. Such allegorical associations, embedded deep in people's psyches and inside India's collective unconscious for centuries, were deployed in the making of Ghatak's film aesthetics. The complex symbology deployed by him in his experimental films stems from and absorbs the influence of such sources. Thus, working in tandem with his iconoclastic views, Ghatak's cinematic practice had a huge impact on the growth of the art cinema movement in India. The process of appropriation for Ghatak was a process of reinvention: even when he was appropriating the music of Fellini in *Subarnarekha*.

2

Ghatak was a member of the IPTA (Indian People's Theatre Association), the cultural wing of the communist party of India. Ismat Chugtai, the Urdu writer, Kaifi Azmi, Balraj Sahni, the veteran actor, and M. S. Sathyu were all Marxist intellectuals who came to cultural prominence in the 1950s as members of the Progressive Writers Association. M. S. Sathyu, the director of *Garam Hawa*, was involved with the IPTA. These film-makers and writers were united by their desire to see the emergence of a new nation in India that would move beyond sectarian divisions and focus on economic, political, and social justice.

Partition was a repressed issue in society as the wounds and scars of Partition were still strongly felt in the Indian psycho-social matrix, as noted by the Indian director Gulzar. Hindi films of the 1970s gave vent to these concealed emotions by dealing with repressed issues in society.

Garam Hawa (1973), based on an unpublished short story by Ismat Chugtai, narrates the plight of the minority community in India, to be more specific a Muslim family in Agra who decide to stay back in India after Partition. In terms of Indian new wave Cinema, or what one may term as the Indian *nouvelle vague*, *Garam Hawa* is quite exemplary. Like Shyam Benegal's *Mammo* (1994), which problematises notions of nationality, and Govind Nihalani's *Tamas* (1987), Sathyu's work foregrounded a revolutionary consciousness. Along with M. S. Sathyu's *Garam Hawa* (1973), *Tamas*, the television miniseries, is the most trenchant and sustained rumination on this cataclysmic event in Indian history.

When Govind Nihalani graduated from his long apprenticeship as the cinematographer to Shyam Benegal and set about making his mark in the world as a director in his own right, *Tamas* was his first magnum opus. A graphic, searing, unromantic, brutally honest, and tenebrous account of what man did to his fellow human and to what humanity descended to during the days and weeks of Partition in Punjab—*Tamas* leaves us gasping and reeling for light and air. It seemed all vices in the nation's collective subconscious and its memories have been vivified in the flesh, afresh. There are no convenient escape routes to Utopian or ivory tower reflection. All the paths reek of human fear, confusion, and suffering. Every imaginative exit is scored in the blood and guts, mire and detritus of inhumanity, opportunism, and political expediency. The long nightmare opening sequence of the killing of a pig remains a dark refrain that returns to haunt and terrify, like Vanraj Bhatia's insidiously dark music that returns like swelling nausea or creeping apprehension in the *mise en scène* of each of Nihalani's frames. That cracked, tuneless death rattle to a deaf, unaiding divinity that starts off the television series ("Hai Rabba!" or O Almighty!) signals the futility of any escape from the viciousness of the darkness descended upon man that was Partition.

Controversy has necessarily dogged *Tamas* from its very first screening on the national government-owned television channel, Doordarshan. The fact that the entire series was produced by Doordarshan shows that the courage and artistic foresight of those in decision-making roles had not been affected by political short-sightedness or mindless religious hysteria. This would be unthinkable in a modern day scenario. *Tamas* was at the heart of a culture war, interrogating concepts like civility, humanity, religion, communal hostility, and legitimacy, and articulating discourses of community honour, sexuality, and gendered violence during the Partition era. No wonder, then, that it rekindled sectarian passion and reopened old wounds. The complexities of mass-scale mediations of social trauma are foregrounded in the representation of a mass suicide of women in the series and its several interpretations.

Spatial cartographies of belonging become the very signifiers of displacement in *Garam Hawa* as space emerges as a significant discursive motif. The film's portrayal of the essentially Muslim character of the cultural space of the city of Agra is informed by the spatial politics and aestheticisation of space that reflect contemporary politics in post-Partition India. The film's focus also brings to the fore postcolonial histories of national fragmentation.

The emotional world of Salim Mirza, one of the film's protagonists, the owner of a shoe factory, played by Balraj Sahni, is the initial focus of Sathyu's work. Despite India being his country, post-Partition, Mirza is ostracised as banks and moneylenders refuse him business loans believing that he too like his friends and family will migrate to Pakistan. The municipal authorities evict his family from their ancestral *haveli* (mansion) in the wake of the sudden departure of his brother, the politician Halim Mirza, to Pakistan.

Salim's son Sikander fails to secure a job in a climate of growing unemployment in society. Salim Mirza's tale of woe does not end there, however. He is harassed on false charges of espionage and his factory is set on fire. Mirza's perfectly ordered life unravels before his eyes as his daughter Amina, in love with Kasim, is left in India with promises of Kasim's return from Pakistan to wed her. Disastrously, however, Kasim on arrival is caught and deported to Pakistan. The litany of misfortune and faithlessness reaches the proportions of a saga as Amina succumbs to the romantic overtures of Shamsad, who too migrates to Pakistan realising his bleak future in India. Amina keeps waiting for Shamsad, hoping he will come to fetch her.

More mishaps stalk the Mirza family, however. Amina is devastated by the news of Shamsad's engagement in Pakistan and unable to bear the betrayal commits suicide. This tragedy shatters Salim's resolve and he decides to migrate to Pakistan. In a rousing reversal in the final sequence of the film, however, he and Sikander, realising they are not alone in their struggle for existence in India, decide to stay back.

Amina's grandmother vehemently refuses to leave the family's ancestral *haveli*. It is symptomatic of an emotional and familial attachment to place "downplayed by official narratives, while concerns about property rights, political gain, potential spouses, college degrees and Salim Mirza's business foreground the (im)practicalities of leaving India" (Rijneveld 18).

After the departure of Kasim and his family to Pakistan, Amina, alone on the porch, is shown knitting for her beloved Kasim, with a pensive look in her eyes. The close-up image of the locked door appears on screen at this point, an effective use of *mise en scène* in the shot. The iconography of the locked door raises a cry in the heart of Amina, who now has to wait for Kasim's arrival.

The camera's movement and pace is handled in the sequence to parallel the movement of a train pulling out of a station. The inexorable sound of a train departing in the soundtrack and its juxtaposition with the final still image of the lonely Amina, almost static with grief in the foreground, is effectively constructed to highlight the fragmentation of a family: the impossibility of an uncomplicated return. The threat of historical separation in the aftermath of Partition is localised in the pain of the separation of lovers.

The splendour of Mughal architecture and the grandeur of Mughal lore fill the scenes of courtship between Shamsad and Amina. Islamic cultural markers are foregrounded in the music, with the qawwali song sequences harking back to the glory of Mughal heritage. However, a syncretic Indianness permeates the iconography of these scenes and invests the religious and cultural signifiers with a wider range of acceptance.

The romantic scenes in the film are shot at famous historical sites associated with the Mughal empire, namely the Taj Mahal and Fatehpur Sikri, with specific references to Dargah Salim Chisti. In fact, the Taj Mahal is foregrounded as a site where the legend of eternal love may find its true abode. These lovingly undertaken shots are an ironic reminder of Sathyu's own personal religious identity, which is incongruous with the city that he is so passionate about as the city is decorated with Islamic monuments, art, and artefacts. However, such secular and humanistic approaches to art and life uphold the glory of India and its national pride.

In the suicide sequence of Amina, the scenes of courtship are revisited in flashback. Inside the monument, the lovers walk on a floor with precise shapes and geometric patterns etched on it while a rapturous qawwali song resonates the diegetic frame. The camera takes in everything with a high-angle shot. The possible violence of historic rupture looms large over this scene of the consummation of Shamsad and Amina's love.

In the microcosmic reflection of larger tensions and contradictory movements in the discursive categories of nation or state, in its daily minutiae, the private world brings the real complexity and violence of the issues home to us. Amina's private despair has its social parallel. The nexus between the see-saw of union and separation in the private realm of the lovers, and even a fatal estrangement, and the trauma that attends the sundering of nations are brilliantly upheld in *Garam Hawa* through its visuality, aural landscape, and iconography. Truly, in Sathyu's film, the invasion of the private by the political is complete.

Works cited

Bhaskar Ira. "Myth and Ritual: Ghatak's Meghe Dhaka Tara." *Journal of Arts and Ideas*. Screen Unit, 1983.

Biswas, Moinak. "The City and the Real: *Chhinnamul* and the Left Cultural Movement in the 1940s." *City Flicks: Indian Cinema and the Urban Experience*, edited by Preben Kaarsholm. Seagull Books, 2004.

Bhattacharya, Nandini. "Nation (De)composed: Ritwik Ghatak, Guru Dutt, Saadat Hasan Manto, and the Shifting Shapes of National Memory." *The Indian Partition in Literature and Films: History, Politics and Aesthetics*, edited by Rini Bhattacharya Mehta and Debali Mookerjea-Leonard. Routledge, 2015.

Ghatak, Ritwik, director. *Komal Gandhar*. Performances by Supriya Choudhury, Abanish Banerjee, and Bijon Bhattacharya, 31 March 1961.

—, director. *Meghe Dhaka Tara*. Performances by Supriya Chowdhury, Anil Chatterjee, and Gita Ghatak, 14 April 1960.

—. *Rows and Rows of Fences: Ritwik Ghatak on Cinema*. Seagull Books, 2000.

—, director. *Subarnarekha*. Performances by Madhabi Mukherjee and Abhi Bhattacharyya, 1 October, 1965.

—. "*Subarnarekha* Prasange." *Chalachitra Manush Ebong Aro Kichu: A Collection of Essays by Ritwik Kumar Ghatak*. Dey's Publishing, 2018, 152–54.

—. "Chalachitra Chinta." *Chalachitra Manush Ebong Aaro Kichu*. Dey's Publishing, 2018, 31–33.

Rajadhyaksha, Ashish. *Ritwik Ghatak: A Return to the Epic*. Screen Unit, 1982.

Rijneveld, Cornelis. "Hindu Heroes and Muslim Others: An Analysis of the Portrayal of Partition in Kamal Haasan's *Hey Ram* (2000), Rakesh Om Prakash Mehra's *Bhaag Milkha Bhaag* (2013), and M. S. Sathyu's *Garam Hawa* (1973)." *South Asianist* 3, no. 2, 2015, www.southasianist.ed.ac.uk.

Sarkar, Bhaskar. *Mourning the Nation: Indian Cinema in the Wake of Partition*. Orient Blackswan, 2010.

Chapter 2

Romancing Transgression: Representation of Gender by Post-Millennial Women Film-Makers

Two decades into the new millennium, women directors in India are still few in number. Quite surprisingly, the number of women who have been able to advance into positions of power and decision-making is minuscule compared to the number of men. The percentage of women in influential, decision-making roles in India is still appalling.

This article tries to revisit certain controversial issues, such as, does representation always reflect the point of view of creators? Or, shall we ever be in a position to claim that the film-maker's female gender produces a different genre of film, or different perspective on a film genre? Is it that women directors always want to produce films on themes that are different from the content produced by men? Or, is it that if there are greater numbers of women directors they will not be able to challenge prevailing practices and ideologies? Time and again, these issues have resurfaced and undoubtedly they elicit further elaboration.

We have often seen how media images make women invisible, something that results in a "symbolic annihilation of women" (Tuchman 150). However, some post-millennial Indian women film-makers have chosen not to portray women in the stereotypical roles of victims and/or consumers. Nor are female characters in their films defined in terms of their relationships with men—suggesting that women are capable of leading their own lives without male "guidance" and are, in the end, independent. It is interesting to review therefore how women film-makers are moving beyond dominant stereotypical bodily figurations or representing bodies that are challenging stereotypes. It is necessary to ascertain whether these films are challenging normative spectator–screen relations in their entirety.

The 1980s was a significant decade for the development of pioneering women film-makers in India and the decade witnessed the development of a disciplined feminist historiography. Women directors who challenged and resisted dominant male cultures had evolved. Women pioneers of Indian cinema in the eighties include Sai Paranjape (Hindi cinema), Arundhati Devi, Aparna Sen (Bangla cinema), Prema Karanth (new wave Kannada cinema), Vijaya Mehta (Maratha cinema), and Vijaya Nirmala (Telegu cinema).

As far as regional cinema is concerned, the availability of resources is limited. Often, translation and subtitles for regional literature and cinema are unavailable, but any larger study of Indian cinema should refocus the history and development of regional cinema in India. The cultural context of Indian cinema demands pluralistic approaches to film historiography and the absence of these would have serious consequences for comprehending women's cinema.

When we think of women film-makers in Indian cinema, film-makers like Aparna Sen, Zoya Akhtar, Reema Kagti, Farah Khan, Nandita Das, Meghna Gulzar, and Tanuja Chandra and diasporic Indian film-makers such as Mira Nair and Deepa Mehta immediately come to mind.

Acting's gendered impact on women

In order to understand women's cinema in India, it is imperative to also look beyond Mumbai cinema and rearticulate this history via the multiple flows between region and nation, including questions of language and regional cultures. I begin my reading of films with a film-maker from Bengal, Aparna Sen, who achieved critical acclaim for directing films such as *36 Chowringhee Lane* and *Sati*. *Sati* (1989) speaks of gender reforms in colonial Bengal and *Iti Mrinalini: An Unfinished Letter* (2010) looks at acting's gendered impact on women's careers. The film is a meditation on a star's public recognition, fame, and glamour, and also personal failures. It is about the crisis that confronts ageing actresses like Mrinalini when they are replaced by younger rivals.

Growing old negatively affects the careers of both men and women, but age affects the careers of actresses far more than their male counterparts. Given acting's gendered impact on women's careers, women face a double jeopardy in sustaining acting careers relative to men. The woman "actor" is often valued most for her youthful looks, so roles disappear particularly in middle age, until old age, when looks are of less concern. It is interesting to watch how Aparna Sen performs ageing, compared with her youthful counterpart Konkona Sen Sharma in *Iti Mrinalini*. In a recent interview in *The Telegraph* T2 (Screen Bollywood) of 24 September 2020, Konkona Sen Sharma in her interview, following the release of her film *Dolly Kitty Aur Woh Chamakte Sitare*, states:

It's true that I don't get so many parts, primarily because there aren't many interesting characters being written for women who are older. The bulk of women characters on screen are in their 20s, aren't unmarried [*sic*] . . . and the funniest thing is that such decisions are being taken by producers and directors who are men in their 40s and 50s (laughs), because that's what they want to see! (T2, Screen 8)

Few women manage to survive this gendered impact on their careers. From the world of Western cinema, we have witnessed how Meryl Streep's career dipped. Very few women actors have achieved fame later in their lives like Dame Judi Dench; in Bengali cinema, Suchitra Sen's phenomenal decision to fade into oblivion from the public eye, on the verge of ageing, is a case that may be cited. In *Iti Mrinalini*, the ageing actor, unable to cope with the crisis of ageing decides to end her life. In real life, Aparna Sen's position as a woman director and as an ageing actor who decides to engage and end a socially transgressive relationship (in the film) contributes to the woman auteur's vision. Sen's musical *Arshi Nagar* (2015) foregrounds communal rivalry, revisiting Shakespeare's *Romeo and Juliet*.

Performativity of gender in women's cinema

This essay will now look at the performativity of gender in relation to cinema. I take Joan Scott's definition of gender as a constitutive element of social relationships based on perceived differences between the sexes, and as a primary way of signifying relations of power, to capture the inclusive nature of this concept. The significance of gender, therefore, hinges on this very basic idea of imposing definitive disciplinary categories on the sexed body. This perception naturalises and governs gender identities.

As I look at the performativity of gender in cinema, I further argue how I would consider the ways "performance" has been appropriated to describe gender identities, which includes Judith Butler's notion of "performativity." By closely looking at cinema's construction of the performativity of gender, through which I seek to approach a greater understanding of the relationship between gender identities and performance, in terms of gender as both an act and a social construction, which thereby analyses representations of roles played by film actors in the construction and circulation of such acts, I seek to examine the specific signs that comprise such performances.

It is necessary to take into account, for instance, codes that constitute manliness, that valorise certain qualities while stigmatising others, and the contextual meanings of difference between femininity and masculinity, or how patterns of social relationships are determined based on this imposed identity. One may look at performance as a socially embedded experience, not just as a series of actions performed in isolation.

Firstly, I would begin with how such films reconstruct gender and how the performativity of gender is foregrounded in Hindi popular cinema. In the present article, I explore the director's construction of femininity and masculinity, studying the representation of transgressive sexuality and reading how such acts of transgression lead to the subversion of societal norms.

In the process, I attempt to tease out the nexus of tropes around visuality, femininity, and desire to examine the problematic relationship between women and desire. The objective is to see the central representational tropes in the figuring of the woman and how women film-makers adopt several representational tropes for the expression of female desire. I shall explore how the camera in the hands of the woman film-maker looks at the woman's desiring gaze, and how desire in society is problematised because of the conflict between societal and cultural restraints due to the normativity of society that finds female desire a disquieting phenomenon.

Case study 1: Reema Kagti's *Talaash* (2012)

Performing masculinity

Masculinity represents not a certain type of man but, rather, a way men position themselves through discursive practices. Since what constitutes "masculinity" is always already constructed (masculinity is constructed in discourse), normative masculinity is itself an image and only conceptions or representations of normative masculinity exist. Thus, the concept of performance examines its usefulness as a term in considering masculinity as a social and cinematic construct.

Masculinity is something to have or to lack. Certain films foreground that to "be a man" is a performance, something to be proved and acted out, and also depict the varying ways male identity is defined and performed. It would therefore be interesting to read films that do not reinforce traditional notions of masculinity but concurrently underscore the notion of masculinity as performance—how in Reema Kagti's *Talaash* (2012) the role of Surjan Singh Shekhawat (Aamir Khan) as a tough cop with a hard exterior is actually a mask to hide his profound sense of melancholy and regret.

Surjan is a lone and distressed hero/figure in crisis, who exists within the larger discourse of "masculinity in crisis"; in the psychological thriller *Talaash*, such crises and male angst are performed. The term "crisis" here includes male insecurity, instability, and uncertainty in a broader sense, while "angst" relates to the specific manifestations, performances, and presentations of such masculinity.

My concern in this essay is not the defining of male crisis or arguing for its existence, but in considering the performativity of this male angst that is projected by such heroes. Three identifiable shades of performing masculinity become evident: firstly, by specific analysis of the performance of masculinity on screen; secondly, reading the performance of masculinity in relation to specific social and historical contexts; and, thirdly, the relationships fostered in the performance of masculinity off screen (social roles, gender discourse, and popular culture). This would entail multiple iconicities that are performed both on and off screen.

The distressed male hero, the central protagonist of *Talaash*, leads us to the conclusion that visual texts offer emotionally powerful portraits of men that often complicate the view that representations of masculinity in cinema are overwhelmingly about men's violence and power over others. Kagti's film complicates the frequently heard claim that the performance of masculinity reinforces traditional notions of patriarchy and men's power over women, because the film refuses to set up an ideal type of masculinity.

Given the hero's role in the film as an inspector having to deal with criminals and local thugs, Surjan's performance of masculinity does not have recourse to performing male codes of violent masculinity or its manifestation in violent action. Nor does the film's narrative trajectory lead us to a depiction of the binary of violent masculinity as opposed to passive rescued femininity.

We see Surjan performing paternity in *Talaash* as a guilt-ridden father who suffers from the guilt of killing his own son. Interesting here is the lone male as a figure of crisis or distress. However, the presence of such distressed males is not necessarily new. Hollywood cinema is littered with "wild" male figures that women wish to "tame" (the brooding heroes of film noir, the mythology of the cowboy, James Bond, who may get shaken but are never stirred). What characterises these figures is their silence, rarely speaking of some unknown trauma they have suffered. Their emotional reticence somehow makes them all the more alluring.

My interest in Kagti's film is to see whether such depictions are now shifting in a more nuanced, narcissistic, and complex direction. Surjan's passive subjective world—because he is very active professionally—

becomes all the more mysterious. Gradually *Talaash* showcases the repressed semiotic *chora* that disrupts the rational order of the paternal-symbolic and challenges the masculine subject's apparent stability.

The construction of the *femme fatale* or the troubled gender

Gender in cinema is always relational when we see patterns of masculinity emerging that are socially defined in contradistinction to certain models of femininity (real/imaginary): for example, the idea that women are non-violent and peaceful has long been used by patriarchal ideology to control women.

Talaash belongs to a genre that appeals to the audience's repressed fears and desires. As such, women directors are less likely to direct films in the horror or thriller genre. The abject in Kagti's film, the desiring woman (Rosie), later revealed to be a member of the living dead, does not terrify us, but her appeal fascinates us all the same. Drawing on Julia Kristeva's notion of the abject, I define the abject as that which "disturbs identity, system, order" and "does not respect borders, positions, rules" (Kristeva). The abject both fascinates and horrifies: it thrives on ambiguity and transgression of taboos and boundaries.

My interest in Kagti's film lies in the depiction of the abject: firstly, it allows the spectator to indulge vicariously in taboo forms of behaviour; secondly, in the hands of a woman director, there is innovation in the treatment of the trope of the fallen woman. In a way, the film challenges stereotypical feminine images. She is not the monstrous "other" but a highly sexualised object: the reinvented *femme fatale*. She reminds us of Kim Novak in *Vertigo*, Glenn Close in *Fatal Attraction* and *Dangerous Liaisons*, and Eva Marie Saint in *North by Northwest*.

The *femme fatale* of Hollywood cinema is the sexual seductress; *femmes fatales* have a very long international lineage and the alterations in her representation continue in Bollywood cinema to the present day. We have seen how the "Westernised vamp" existed as a contrary image to the virtuous, virginal Indian woman in Hindi cinema of the 1970s and 80s. By the time we reach the 1990s, the vamp disappears making way for more blurred feminine identities in cinema.

Neither the deadly dame nor entirely the lethal seductress, Rosie's positioning in *Talaash* continues to serve as a barometer of cultural repression, desire, victimisation, and reification. She is a disruptive temptress who has a destabilising effect on the hero. The woman director's camera, though, captures the visual objectification of the woman that concurrently problematises the male gaze. There is no sexual greed that characterises Rosie; the potentially dangerous woman who apparently poses a sexual threat is ultimately revealed to be a victim of circumstances.

In *Talaash*, the *femme fatale* is a performatively constituted construct through the trope of the fallen woman. She is the "Other," the troubled gender, and in so being she challenges hegemonic gender and sexual roles. Being the "troubled Other," she is likely to cause a crisis of masculinity and social anxieties. The virtuous and devoted housewife Roshni (Rani Mukherjee) and the *femme fatale* become dichotomies in the film and it is the presence of the *femme fatale* that poses a threat to the patriarchal family model.

The presence of the dangerous woman throws into question theories of spectatorship. Here the male character is not aligned with the active controlling gaze and the woman despite being the eroticised other is not the object of the male gaze. Rather the active nature of the female gaze is more operative here. Rosie continuously switches her allegiance between being abject, a female castrator, and a victim (she particularly holds appeal for the female spectator, who perhaps feels "empowered" by identifying with the female castrator); the filmic codes encourage our varying degrees of identification with either figure. But then her positioning in the film as a female desiring subject is problematised by also showing her probable conformity to a wider stereotype of femininity in cinema. We start questioning—is she playing the love interest of the male hero?

In an interview on a film she had recently directed, *Qarib Qarib Singlle* (2017), Tanuja Chandra was asked:

> Q: You directed your first film, *Dushman* in 1998 and almost two decades later, there are only a handful of female directors . . .
> A: Which is a tragedy. At least half our directors need to be female, otherwise you can't call this an equal playing field. When I started out, there were four-five female directors and now the number is in double digits, but it needs to be more. We need more women making movies . . . as directors, producers, writers, cinematographers. . . . I really believe that will make a difference in the kind of movies we make. (*The Telegraph*, T2, 1 Nov. 2017, Screen 5)

The male hero of *Qarib Qarib Singlle*, Yogi (Irrfan Khan), with his uncouth, flirtatious manner is initially unimpressive to the heroine, Jaya (Parvathy Thiruvothu), yet later she finds him very attractive for his quick wit, repartee, and self-deprecating humour. When they decide to undertake a journey to revisit places associated with their pasts, they also escape their restrictive immediate surrounding.

Motifs and bodily figurations

A recurring motif that distinguishes Gauri Shinde's debut film or the films of Zoya Akhtar is the recurring motif of escape. Such an escape takes a variety of narrative forms: a foreign holiday in the form of a bachelor's trip to Spain in *Zindagi Na Milegi Dobara* (2011), henceforth *ZNMD*; a family holiday with friends and business partners on a star cruise in *Dil Dhadakne Do* (2015), or a trip to Manhattan to attend a family wedding in Gauri Shinde's *English Vinglish* (2012).

The motif of escape is perhaps best understood in such films as a movement through a realm of possibility where their lives take on a different course. Both Shashi (Sridevi) in *English Vinglish* and Jaya in *Qarib Qarib Singlle* respond to their space from their predetermined cultural and sexual positioning. Shashi and Jaya undergo a redefining and re-empowering transformation of identity or rite of passage.

Case study 2: *Zindagi Na Milegi Dobara* (2011)

Laila in *ZNMD* is already in possession of that realm—an independent world of her own—when the film begins. She has already crossed the threshold and positioned herself in that liminal territory. Laila is a character who has distanced herself from the demands and entrapment of everyday life. Akhtar has given the fiercely independent-minded Laila (Katrina Kaif) a stable standpoint to signify the ushering in of a new emancipated woman in Hindi cinema. Laila, often viewed through the point of view of men like Imraan (Farhan Akhtar) and Arjun (Hrithik Roshan), is highly desirable; therefore it is through Laila that the female actress's desirability is enacted.

The woman director's camera exhibits her "to-be-looked-at-ness" and concurrently looks at how she performs her desirability (rather than allowing the camera only to objectify her and treat her as the object of the male gaze). She performs the role of the desiring sexual subject who has achieved a sense of self assurance, power and sexual autonomy by actively choosing to represent herself in a seemingly objectified manner, a mode of self-depiction that may be termed "subjectification" (Rosalind Gill, "From Sexual Objectification to Sexual Subjectification" 100–106).

Laila's redefining of her sexuality is volitional and empowering, particularly in the scene in which she rides the motorbike (in India motorbikes are used almost exclusively by men; in films like *Dhoom* and *Dhoom 2*, the motorbike is an iconic vehicle for projecting male aggressiveness and male prowess; a motorbike is often the vehicle used by the macho male). With her characteristic élan, the woman in *ZNMD* races a car with a borrowed motorbike to reach her romantic partner.

Laila performs a transnational, dynamic, globally empowered femininity and *ZNMD* is a pivotal film reclaiming the female body as a site of women's own pleasure—a film where the woman director changes the essence of representation of womanhood in post-millennial Hindi cinema. Akhtar's film is also iconic in reconsidering the metaphorical dimension of the sea (or associated imagery of underwater scenes) as signifying woman's sexuality. Underwater sequences filming women's bodies prior to *ZNMD*, in films like *Thoda Pyaar Thoda Magic* (2008), *Blue* (2009), and *Kites* (2010), directed by Kunal Kohli, Anthony D'Souza, and Anurag Basu, respectively, all objectified the female body for voyeuristic pleasure.

The depiction of the visual spectacle of the underwater world in *ZNMD* goes for a systematic erasure of the stereotyped representation of the fetishised woman's body. The change of element allows the release of the power in the woman's corporeal presence. A sea change truly occurs. The sea is projected as a fearful domain, particularly through sound effects; Laila as a diving instructor is shown to be highly capable from years of training and experience to handle such oceanic depths fearlessly, which even men fear and consider a challenge. Breaking the stereotype of the docile mermaid, the woman assumes the archetypically male role of Neptune, the tamer of the sea. Thus with the advent of globalisation, it is not just the "attitudes" but also the "body" of the Indian woman that has been reimagined.

It is essential to eliminate any fixed, trans-historical model of hegemonic masculinity. Rather one needs to see masculinity as a fluid category and gender as a historical category, because social definitions of masculinity are subjected to change. In this connection, let me also bring to light the construction of Arjun's metrosexual masculinity in *ZNMD*. His sculpted masculine features, six-pack abs, chiselled waistline, and dreamy eyes and that he is super rich are highlighted. What emerges through the character of Arjun is a new transnational business masculinity, which is the new emerging "hegemonic masculinity" in Hindi cinema. The question of course now is, who is hegemonically masculine? It is questionable whether it is the sensitive new age urban youth who can enact hegemonic practices. Secondly, does such enactment lead to the subordination of non-hegemonic masculinity?

Contesting the body or performativity through citationality

From a different perspective, we see how Hindu and Muslim women in *Firaaq* (2008) contest the body (the film again shows how bodies are discursively constructed), that is, they are performative bodies, and women in *Firaaq* relate performativity to the social constructedness of gender identities. They reclaim the body by reversing roles to appropriate identities based on religion (the Muslim woman appropriates the body of the Hindu woman to earn money)—here her transgression is a subversion of normative sexuality and by appropriating the markers of a Hindu woman's body, the Muslim woman's transgressive act disrupts normative gender identities. She asserts her sexual agency by reclaiming the body. Nandita Das's *Firaaq* is a critique of fixed gender and sexual identities based on religion.

Farah Khan's *Om Shanti Om* (2007) rethinks performativity by parodying gender roles, bringing into play citational complexities. The *Dhoom Taana* song and dance sequence composed of four verses fuse four different genres and eras in Indian film music. The first sequence is a homage to the Amrapali classical song and dance number from the 1966 film *Amrapali* starring Sunil Dutt; the second sequence is a cabaret number from a 1970s film, *Sachaa Jhutha* (1970) with Rajesh Khanna; the third is a romantic comedy duet from a 1970s film; and the fourth is an archetypal gypsy number evoking a courtesan dance sequence from *Jay Vejay* (1977). The entire song and dance sequence is a tribute to Indian film music of the past and heavily borrows and simultaneously parodies gender roles from 1960s and 70s Hindi films.

Meghna Gulzar's spy thriller *Raazi* (2018) focuses on the relationship between the cinematic figure of the woman and the nation state. *Raazi* offers tantalising possibilities for the articulation of a new, complex female subjectivity. Through the patriotic yet duplicitous Sehmat, Gulzar almost attempts to reorient the war film narrative of Hindi cinema.

Gulzar's earlier film *Talwar* (2015) is based on the infamous 2008 Noida double murder case—in which fourteen-year-old Aarushi Talwar and her family's domestic help, Hemraj Banjade, aged forty-five, were slain. Rather than focusing on sensationalism, Gulzar tries to objectively analyse facts and experiments with multiple points of view in her film narrative.

Gender intersecting with class/caste identities

We may now look at gender as an analytical category (I am refusing to look at women as a homogenous category), which is informed by global and local culture and in the Indian context is further problematised through the intersection of class and caste identities. Again, Nandita Das's *Firaaq* is interesting because gender intersects with class, religion, and nation. Created in the aftermath of the 2002 Gujarat communal riots (the film was criticised for its pro-Muslim stance), it shows the highly abused traditional middle-class Hindu housewife as the victim of gender violence. My reading of the film is that in doing so, the film erases the off-screen violence done to Muslim women in Gujarat. Anusha Rizwi's *Peepli Live* (2010), a documentary-style drama based on farmer suicides, shows gender intersecting with class and nation.

Case study 3: *Dil Dhadakne Do* (2015)

Gender as an analytical category is informed by global and local culture and in the Indian context is further problematised through the intersection of class identities, as we get to witness in the film *Dil Dhadakne Do*, directed again by Zoya Akhtar; interestingly, the screenplay is also by women, Akhtar and Reema Kagti. The film highlights relationship issues, marital conflict, issues related to divorce, and societal reaction and heteronormative responses to divorce.

Ayesha (Priyanka Chopra) despite being an upper-class woman, has set up her own business by selling off her own jewellery. With good entrepreneurial skills, Ayesha is shown to be more capable of handling her father's (Kamal Mehra) business than her brother Kabir (Ranveer Singh). Her father Kamal however does not acknowledge his daughter's abilities; instead, he attempts to promote his unwilling son, Kabir, and tries to rope him into the family business. Class conflict becomes apparent when Kabir falls in love with a Muslim bar dancer (Anushka Sharma).

Ayesha faces gender inequality even after her marriage to Manav (Rahul Bose) and soon realises she cannot love her husband. I will now analyse the scene where Sunny (Farhan Akhtar), a journalist who was Ayesha's first love, and Manav, Ayesha's husband, pick a fight on issues related to journalists who according to Manav publish fabricated news to earn their living. Shortly after, Manav takes pride in saying that he has broken all past traditions of his family by "allowing" Ayesha to work or set up her own business. As he tries to reify traditional stereotypes of femininity or narrow down definitions of womanhood, he is snubbed by

Sunny who objects to Manav's stance. When the altercation ensues, the woman (Ayesha) is in a realm of silence. However there is a politics of silence operating here as Ayesha is on the verge of freeing herself from an overwhelming patriarchal structure (dominated by both father and husband) by deciding to divorce her husband.

What is interesting in this scene is not that a man—here Sunny—speaks up for a woman or that Sunny appropriates the voice of Ayesha. The Western feminist Toril Moi despises the effort made by men to speak out in women's defence: "Since this is precisely the ventriloquism patriarchy has always done: Men have constantly spoken for women, or in the name of women" (Moi 67–68).

Then the question becomes whether Sunny will speak in Ayesha's defence. If he speaks, this may entail he can be attacked as the ventriloquist of patriarchy. It is problematic either way. In the film, such a treatment of patriarchy is even more interesting because the dialogue is here more nuanced and narcissistic, as one man is trying to gain an edge over another. Manav is here performing patriarchy and Sunny is performing masculinity; Sunny is trying to assert his superiority over another (Manav) and is performing hegemonic masculinity by positioning himself within a discursive practice.

What the film here does not overtly show is that perhaps Sunny wants his power to return, particularly over Ayesha, or what Hélène Cixous would define as "the insistence on the proper, . . . which leads to masculine obsession with classification, systematization and hierarchization," or what she calls "the pervasive [Indian] masculine urge to judge, diagnose, digest, name. . . . If a man spends it's on condition that his power returns" (Cixious, 38).

But Akhtar's feminist stance will not allow that return. She wants her woman to fracture this unjust economy because it clearly functions only to men's advantage, allowing women to be deprived and stripped of their identity. Ayesha although partly deprived never loses her identity. She establishes herself as a successful entrepreneur and her decision to seek a divorce from Manav is therefore a way to regain agency.

The interstitial space in romance and representation from the diaspora

Several diasporic and pivotal films in the NRI genre since 1995 have depicted traditional fathers with varying degrees of sternness through whom the Indian patriarchal values of such communities are demonstrated (e.g., Baldev in *Dilwale Dulhaniya Le Jayenge*, or the father figure in

Pardes, *Kabhi Khushi Kabhi Gham*, or *Namastey London*). These films were directed by male film-makers like Yash Chopra, Subhash Ghai, and Karan Johar. Their films focus on intra-family relationships, the trope of marriage to the right partner in the belief that this partner will uphold Indian values and Indian virtues, and the traditional Indian father who is only willing to give up his daughter in marriage to an Indian bridegroom. These films end with marriage to the right (Indian) partner and the assumption that the couple live happily ever after. Class-consciousness and intersections of gender with ethnicity complicate identity formations in the diasporic space represented in these films.

The diasporic Indian fiction film *The Namesake* (2006) by the expatriate Indian woman film-maker Mira Nair deviates from the standard representation or treatment of this interstitial space in romance. In her film, this space makes room for a woman's transgression. Significant in the film is the construction of women's sexuality in Nair's take on post-marital complications.

The Namesake focuses on first and second-generation Indian immigrants living in the United States. Gogol does marry Moushumi after falling in love with her, but this match is also desired by his Bengali mother, Ashima (Tabu), because Moushumi (Zuleikha Robinson) is a diasporic Bengali. In the film, the diasporic space that the characters inhabit emerge as a site of contestation with an underlying consciousness of conflicts.

Diasporic film-maker Deepa Mehta's *Fire* (1996) and *Water* (2005) show male Hindu hegemony and patriarchal Hindu attitudes to women and sexuality in dire need of reform. Mehta's films may be read as globalised India's representation and negotiation of new and more liberated female sexualities. As a result, it is interesting to consider the social, cultural, and historical context in which performances take shape and how contemporary Indian films by women film-makers engage with and respond to the changing social positioning of masculinity and femininity.

Unwarranted binaries such as male/female, Black/White, male as active/female as passive are so hard to escape or to move beyond even today that a focus on women film-makers and films by women is still warranted. The constraints that women are under in society remain different to those on other groups. Compared to how male directors have fared, women still lag behind in terms of access to funding and resources as well as in terms of distribution. Still there is much to achieve in the sphere of gender equality particularly in a gender-stratified society such as India.

Women film-makers from around the world are challenging heteronormative ways of being women, resisting prevailing discourses, institutions, and socio-political practices that continue to oppress women of all colours. Indian women film-makers are building on the struggles of prior generations. The story of women, and women's transgression, resistance, and film-making have just begun.

Works cited

Akhtar, Zoya, director. *Dil Dhadakne Do*. Performances by Priyanka Chopra, Anil Kapoor, and Farhan Akhtar, Eros International, 5 June, 2015.
—, director. *Zindagi Na Milegi Dobara*. Performances by Hrithik Roshan, Abhay Deol, Farhan Akhtar, and Katrina Kaif, Eros International, 2011.
Butler, Judith. *Gender Trouble: Feminism and the Subversion of Identity*. Routledge Classics, 2006.
Cixious, Hélène. "Castration or Decapitation?" *Signs: Journal of Women in Culture and Society* 7, no. 1 (Autumn, 1981): pp. 36–40.
Chandra, Tanuja. "Interview: Screen 5." *The Telegraph, T2*, 1 November 2017
Das, Nandita, director. *Firaaq*. Performances by Naseeruddin Shah, Deepti Naval, Shahana Goswami, and Nawazuddin Siddiqui, Percept Picture Company, 2008.
Gill, Rosalind. "From Sexual Objectification to Sexual Subjectification: The Resexualisation of Women's Bodies in the Media." *Feminist Media Studies* 3, no. 1: pp. 100–106.
Kagti, Reema, director. *Talaash*. Performances by Aamir Khan, Kareena Kapoor, and Rani Mukherji, Reliance Entertainment, 2012.
McCabe, Janet. *Feminist Film Studies: Writing the Woman into Cinema*. Wallflower, 2005.
Mehta, Deepa, director. *Fire*. Performances by Nandita Das and Shabana Azmi, Zeitgeist Films, 1996.
—, director. *Water*. Performances by Lisa Ray and John Abraham, Fox Searchlight Pictures, 2005.
Moi, Toril. *Sexual/Textual Politics: Feminist Literary Theory*. Routledge, 2003.
Nair, Mira, director. *The Namesake*. Performances by Tabu, Irrfan Khan, Kal Penn, and Zuleikha Robinson, Fox Searchlight Pictures, 2006.

Scott, Joan Wallach. "Gender: A Useful Category of Historical Analysis." *Gender and Political History*. Columbia University Press, 1999, pp. 28–50.

Sen, Aparna, director. *Iti Mrinalini.* Performances by Aparna Senand Konkona Sen Sharma, Shree Venkatesh Films, 29 July 2011.

Tuchman, G. "The Symbolic Annihilation of Women by the Mass Media." *Culture and Politics*, edited by L. Crothers and C. Lockhart. Palgrave Macmillan, 2000. https://doi.org/10.1007/978-1-349-62397-6_9.

CHAPTER 3

MEDIA CONSTRUCTIONS OF WOMEN'S SEXUALITY IN INDIAN CINEMA

Contemporary Indian films on women resituate gender within a wider network of power relations. There are social technologies involved in the construction of gender or "technologies of gender" (de Lauretis, *Technologies* 86) and the social construction of gender is what Althusser calls "ideological state apparatuses," two of which happen to be the media and family (56).

The institutions of media and family produce discourses that have the power to produce and promote representations of gender that are then accepted and internalised by subjects. The social process of gender construction and reconstruction in contemporary films from the commercial Indian film industry is an act of reworking and reproducing women's own gendered representations.

Women in *Fashion* (2008), *The Dirty Picture* (2011), and *Heroine* (2012) are exemplary exhibitionists cast as fashion models and actresses. They are perfectly reconstructed products whose body—stylised, aestheticised, often eroticised, and fragmented by close-ups—is the content and theme behind such media attention, of their on-screen presence, and they are the direct recipients of the spectator's look.

The underlying feminist discourse is how women understand such mindless constructions of the "body" or resist such overemphasis on the corporeality of the body. At the subjective level, or at the level of self-representation, they form a resistance to such dominant representations. In performance, female protagonists like Shonali (*Fashion*), Meghna (*Fashion*), and Silk (*The Dirty Picture*) all inhabit the space of the frame that is defined by male points of view, while the real women remain outside. These films also represent a view of women from elsewhere: from the blind spots or the "space-off" of its spaces of representation.

"Space-off" is a term I borrow from Teresa de Lauretis (*Alice Doesn't* 25) to designate space that cannot be seen within the frame yet that can be inferred from it. In these films the space-off is not absent: it is felt outside or behind the stage. In the case of Aparna Sen's *Iti Mrinalini*, the space and the space-off converge as the performing woman enacts a scene that voices her own pain and sorrow.

The films discussed in this essay are a constant negotiation in the space of the frame—how media images construct and/or deconstruct representations of women and the concomitant space-off in cinema that voices women's resistance. The essay further explores what is at stake here: the image of women and how the conflict is resolved by the woman's destruction or reterritorialisation.

I argue that the task of cinema is to foreground rather than resolve the duplicity of the media. As a cultural text, the film and its discourse comply and themselves subvert such stereotypes. What they foreground along with women's resistance is a disruption of the way in which meaning and pleasure are constructed in an entertainment industry dominated by men. The focus lies in a paradox—that of women, who are simultaneously absent and present in the dominant culture, in a world overpowered by the media.

More than in other countries, because of the popularity of the Hindi film industry and the strong fan culture that exists, actresses are not merely performers but celebrities whose aura is defined, produced, maintained, and constantly negotiated by the media. This essay highlights women in performance as actors, fashion models, or superstars whose lives are constantly guided by the media. The ways in which female stars' bodies are often scrutinised and discussed, as if they were a public good, is incredibly problematic. In the films to be discussed, the body of the female actress is a text where the body has been stigmatised by gendered and sexualised significations.

The prevailing issue is one of control—the means whereby the female subject is "embodied" in society through agencies external to itself. How such external agencies attempt to control her body and its representations are the subject of the discussion. This external agency is symbolised by the media. Paradoxically, such women while often being "constantly spoken of" remain "inaudible," displayed as a spectacle and yet unrepresented. This essay is therefore a discussion on how women in performance express resistance in a world dominated by the media.

Case study 1: *Fashion*

In Madhur Bhandarkar's *Fashion*, Meghna Mathur is a small-town aspiring model who wants to become a supermodel. The film shows the darker aspects of the fashion world and what lies behind the glamour and façade of this spectacular branch of showbusiness. The media predetermines how women are to be looked at. Women in the fashion world or entertainment industry are put in an impossible position—they are held to insanely high beauty standards, and in other cases they become spokespersons for a certain kind of bodily image. They are then trapped in their own prison, one that vigilantly guards a female star's bodily image as the ultimate measure of her worth and the standard by which she may be judged or undermined. The media also writes about men's bodies but the level of scrutiny is minuscule compared to women's bodies.

Do Meghna (Priyanka Chopra) and Shonali (Kangana Ranaut) as supermodels in *Fashion* resist such an embodiment or commodification? Are they successful? The fashion world that Madhur Bhandarkar's film projects is one of flamboyance and frivolity. Before Meghna's rise to stardom, Shonali is the etherealised "image" that Meghna aspires to. Shonali's fetishisation by the media is a constructed image.

Meghna's desperate survival strategy as an aspiring model in a fiercely competitive world is to be photographed by the famous photographer Kartik Suri, for Meghna has realised that photography will reinscribe her sexually and create the privilege of looking desirable. Photography in the film therefore acts as a power mechanism that reinscribes both Shonali and Meghna's success. Subsequently, Kartik, through photography, reconstructs an image of Meghna that she desires consciously: the wish to resemble a supermodel, in Meghna's case, Shonali. Photography therefore in *Fashion* may be read psychoanalytically, which is beyond the scope of this essay.

Gradually this distance between Meghna as a spectator and Meghna's identification with Shonali's image is erased. As a struggling model, Meghna initially identifies with the supermodel Shonali on stage and page; she aspires to be like her and ultimately usurps her position in the fashion world.

Shonali's image is a media construct of her success story compounded by processes of globalisation. Focus is always on the increasingly public and easily commodified nature of her star persona. But behind the spectacle of glamour of this supermodel lies a tumultuous story of her disturbed personal life, of which the media tries to steal a glance. As we get a sneak peek into Shonali's undisciplined personal life, we learn she is an alcoholic who is addicted to drugs. There are scenes between Shonali and her partner indulging in petty fights, taking recourse to domestic violence. At times, Shonali is even physically abused by her partner; she ends up with a bruised lip, a mark that has the potential to tarnish her media-constructed etherealised image.

On the other side, the success behind Panache, the brand Shonali and then Meghna work for, glorifies and reinstates Shonali and later Meghna's constructed image. Hence when Anisha, instructed by Mr. Sarin, terminates Shonali's contract to hire Meghna for Panache, it is alleged that Shonali is not able satisfactorily to converge the persona she plays on screen—that of a diva—with her "real"-life personality. Her actual life was at odds with her constructed image on stage. Her personal life gradually comes into the public eye because of an indiscreet media. This, the owner fears, will consequently defame Panache's brand image.

Here, Panache emerges as a symbol of the same patriarchy that disciplines and regulates women's sexuality. Meghna's desire to be like Shonali is therefore fraught with irony. Yet, in both cases, Meghna loses herself in the "image." Her endeavours to save Shonali from ruin are therefore an attempt to rediscover her own lost self.

When Meghna replaces the reigning supermodel Shonali, she is declared the "new face of Panache." Yet it is Shonali who warns Meghna that in the ever-changing, transient world of fashion, fame and success are short lived. Here everything changes so fast that we remain unaware of its pitfalls and dangers. When Meghna becomes the "new face" that the fashion world has embraced, the subtext and the social message that the film gestures towards are pretty glaring. For Meghna is now Shonali, or Shonali is repackaged as Meghna. She has stepped into her shoes and her identification with Shonali is now complete, though up to this point the identification has not reached full circle.

In this glitzy, glam world of fashion, Meghna herself, like Shonali, embarks on a journey of self-discovery. Meghna's life becomes a story of betrayal: betrayal by the owner of Panache, the sophisticated and polished Mr. Sarin (Arbaaz Khan), with whom Meghna indulges in an unsuccessful, illicit affair.

Motherhood represents a new dangerous territory for men, for motherhood functions to define the female body, and denying Meghna motherhood is in some ways to deny the would-be mother her identity. In both Shonali and Meghna's life, Panache reproduces the same patriarchy that endeavours to predetermine and control women's bodies. The frustrated and lost Meghna fails to identify her own image in the mirror. Her mirror image tells her that she has dissociated herself from her identity. She fails to "see" her own self in the mirror. In Meghna's image invisibly lurks the shadow of Shonali who had once suggested to Meghna that it is easy to lose one's own self in the fashion world and that everything changes in the blink of an eye. Midway through the film, Meghna's identification with the lost Shonali comes full circle.

In Mumbai, Meghna is rejected everywhere. Yet she refuses to be a loser and fights her own battle despite several adversities. In Rahul Arora's fashion show, she freezes on stage in front of the camera as she remembers her recent past experiences with the fashion industry and the men who control it. Shattered, she believes she will never be able to perform again. On the other side, Shonali, like Meghna, is doomed to frustration because of the sudden decline in her career. Like Meghna, she becomes a victim of clinical depression; the case becomes more extreme in Shonali's case because of her addiction to drugs. Meghna rushes to her rescue as her identification with Shonali reaches full circle.

The media deconstructs its own constructed image to focus on a woman (Shonali) who has lost her mind but was once a supermodel. Earlier, the media made the most of a fashion disaster in which she accidentally stripped off her outfit, speculating whether it was a publicity stunt on Shonali's part. The same media now cashes in on her mentally derailed image. It becomes Meghna's task to revive Shonali; this task she takes up as a challenge. Her actions have their roots in Meghna's psychoanalysis of her own guilt and fear. Shonali too gives her a lot of emotional support and revives her lost confidence.

To rediscover Meghna and to give Meghna her own identity, Shonali has to die. News of Shonali's death reaches Meghna just as she is about to come on stage for a spectacular, gorgeous fashion event. Despite all adversities and the grief of Shonali's death, she puts on a stunning performance. Her postures and gestures and the female gaze directed towards the onlookers—Mr. Sarin, Anisha, Rahul Arora, and Janet amongst others—reflect her new found confidence and unvanquished spirit.

In this scene, Meghna effectively erases Mr. Sarin's (the male) gaze. Therefore, despite the bodily construction of her image in the traditional exhibitionist role, Meghna is not consumed or overtaken by the grand fashion show that predetermines her role. Her capability to perform again, now with regained confidence, subverts patriarchal definitions of her incapability as she successfully transcends her assigned status as a "failed supermodel."

The more sombre Meghna who gazes at the camera, at the audience, and at us is the new Meghna who has undergone a journey of self-discovery and who has rebuilt herself by countering the vices and injustices of the fashion world. She is the new Meghna who has for the second time through strength of mind carved a niche of her own in the male-dominated fashion world. Consequently, there is no overt flamboyance in her outlook, style, and poise.

The last sequence of *Fashion* may be read as Meghna's statement on how women need to assert themselves. The glamour world too has to learn to appreciate and give real worth to a woman's inherent talent. For Meghna's resistance is to men who treat women merely as commodities, cheapened in status by focusing on their physicality, making a spectacle of their bodies and sexuality. Her fashion statement is one that discards the frivolous; rather, it is now all about restraint, confidence, and elegance. Her fashion no longer remains primarily related to outfits, embellishment, jewellery, hairstyles, or make up. It is more about her rediscovery of the self, a style that now is reflected in her attitude.

In the last grand fashion event, held in India and then in Paris, there is a shift in perspective accompanied by the recognition that supermodels like Meghna do not just passively absorb pre-given meanings "forced" upon them by the media, but learn to actively create their own meanings.

Case study 2: *Heroine*

Madhur Bhandarkar says *Heroine* is a "contemporary film which reveals the underbelly of the movie industry and its well-kept secrets" (Interview, Rediff). The film is a glamorous and scandalous behind-the-scenes account of the reality behind the celebrity world that our film stars inhabit. Behind the screen, famous female actor Mahi Arora is shown to be battling depression and popping anti-depressants. Like Shonali in *Fashion*, Mahi (Kareena Kapoor) in *Heroine* fails to find a satisfactory convergence between the characters she plays on screen and her "real" personality through various media outlets. Media images of Mahi's stardom are constructed and we see how the media fictionally constructs this aura of glamour.

In real life, superstar Mahi Arora is easily upset, very emotional, confused, insecure, and vulnerable; Pallavi, her mentor, tells her, "You have to stop playing the victim." She tells Mahi that as she is a star she need not try to become an actress; however, Mahi is unhappy with her star persona image. She has been taunted for being a star and not an actress in public. In her real life, her priorities keep changing: from Aryan she seeks commitment (which Aryan refuses); when Angad, the other man, proposes, she becomes more career-oriented; and Rashid Bhai, her secretary, warns her "Heroine ka waqt bahut kum hota hai" (the life of a heroine is short-lived).

In *Heroine*, film politics become integrated with personal politics—it shows the life of a rising female star and, again, the darker side of the film industry. As a failing actress, Mahi takes recourse in cheap publicity stunts for her upcoming film, degrades herself, and consequently is tormented by the media. She ultimately is shown to have quit the film world and found happiness in ordinary life.

In the film, formulations of "the feminine" are completely consonant with traditional derogations of women, such as the claim (here represented in the character of Mahi, a character suffering from bipolar disorder and depression) that she is irrational, speaks incoherently, cannot concentrate on one thing at a time, is closer to her body, or is more oriented towards pleasure than men. Mahi resists such personality traits/disorders in her character. Mahi succeeds in overcoming depression and ultimately rises in her career as a highly desirable star.

Both *Fashion* and *Heroine* depict women who rewrite their bodies to move into uncharted, unexplored, non-gendered territory. They prove a point that iconicity is beyond the petty constructions of gender. The reductive role of the media is flouted by these women of substance who have had to go through physical and emotional extremes to emerge in their own light as truly admirable characters.

Case study 3: The Dirty Picture

Milan Luthria's *The Dirty Picture* may be treated as a discourse on women's sexuality. It is based on the real lives of actors Silk Smitha and Disco Shanti, depicting the meteoric rise and sudden downfall of such screen sensations. The film portrays real-life character Silk Smitha as a sexual icon who was used and exploited by the South Indian film industry of the 1980s. It showcases the strategies of resistance or attempts to subvert hegemonic norms of Indian womanhood through the character of Silk: the cult of the female star, Silk Smitha, whose star status revolves around her overtly sexualised persona.

The public display of sexuality also binds Silk's career within the roles she procures or generates. The apparently decent and respectable society and its norms create the new Silk (played by Vidya Balan) out of an ordinary woman, Reshma. Silk uses her sexual allure to her benefit, firstly to cope with poverty, and, secondly, to benefit her own real life. Gradually the glamour of the star is emphasised and becomes pleasurable in itself, a perfect streamlined image of femininity and sexuality. She poses a threat to the reigning male superstar Suryakant's stardom (played by Naseeruddin Shah) who consequently decides to make her subservient to him.

There is a subtext that nurtures the film throughout. It is about the inner turmoil and the psyche of the female protagonist who is disgraced by a society that has played a major role in constructing her as a sex icon. Silk's power lies in her sexuality and, significantly enough, her sexuality is not repressive, not does it succumb to limits and taboos. Her power incorporates resistance. Silk resists, embraces sexuality, and refuses to conform to hegemonic and patriarchal social structures.

With increasing globalisation, films, print media, and fashion magazines all inform one another in terms of style and presentation and depend on one another to perpetuate a consumerism of aspiration among the public. *The Dirty Picture* shows how celebrity journalism culture emphasises representations of female sexuality. Technologies and media are also discourses of power and Silk's life is entirely guided by the amount of attention she receives from the media for being a sex icon. A man like Abraham (played by Emraan Hashmi), a film-maker in the film, condemns her and believes film-making is an art, abhorring the idea of inserting item numbers or a steamy song and dance as crowd-pullers. In one particular scene, Silk says there are only three factors in any film that can ensure its success: "Entertainment, Entertainment and Entertainment." Taking the film industry by storm, she unabashedly fulfils her dreams of becoming a highly successful star by emphasising her sexuality, which makes her desirable to a youthful male audience. But she soon realises that the society in which she lives thrives on double standards.

The men who construct her as an icon—as an object to be looked at—and men on screen and in her real life are the agents of that look; they are whom the spectators identify with to enjoy vicarious control and possession of the woman. They are even wary of giving her social respectability. Therefore, the witty dialogue she utters is often candidly critical of the men who dominate the entertainment industry, with whom women like Silk are compelled to work. When rejected by society she turns into a rebel and raises her voice against the mechanisms of voyeurism and fetishism that underlie the patriarchal unconscious of such films.

What the film with reverence celebrates and simultaneously criticises is the use, consumption, and circulation of women's sexualised bodies. Silk's character defies the commonly held attitude to women's sexuality that sees them as being either a pure woman or a whore. At the same time, because she has to play highly sexualised roles in the films in which she appears, which almost makes her a porn star in the 1980s film industry, Silk's personal life, in particular her involvement with the married Suryakant and others, is used by the media to erase the boundary between Silk as an individual and the roles she plays. Her comfort with her image as a sex icon on screen is exploited by the media to construct the same image of her personal life, purposely degrading her. Silk throughout her life counters such an image through her own constructed image of sexual bravura in her personal life, which is potentially transgressive and daring.

The Dirty Picture candidly exposes the duplicity of a world that craves sex and excitement but is fearful or simply ashamed to acknowledge this basic human need. The film exposes the hypocrisy of men like the successful big shot Suryakant, who desire passionate women like Silk but only behind closed doors. Silk is treated as dirt and everyone's "dirty secret." The daring Silk at the zenith of fame and success is disgusted by the double standards of society, and the same society continues to relentlessly criticise and reject her for her sexually explicit roles.

The media outlet that Naila, a journalist works for—a fashion magazine—sets itself up as a site for sexual regulation and surveillance; the women, here Silk, who provide subject matter must in turn act within that space as self-regulators of their sexualised images. Silk never negotiates her sexuality with the media. The sense of rejection by society and the media gradually and quite painfully overpowers her. As a result, her liberatory attitude borders on the reckless and she is driven to the verge of destruction.

Passing through disastrous love affairs, consuming alcohol, and drowned in debts, Silk never finds social respectability even in the eyes of men she has truly loved. Her lusty co-star Suryakant, with whom she is in love, is especially critical of her and disgraces her in every way. Drowned in sorrow she encounters failure and ruin. She is the victim of a society that once made a star of an ordinary woman by highlighting her aggressive sexual presence on screen and her embracing of sexuality in real life. This same society and state apparatus—media—once constructed her as an object to be looked at, coded for strong visual and erotic impact (Mulvey 26).

The scene showcasing Silk's alluring performance that seduces her fan base and fan culture (dominated by men) explicitly demonstrates her understanding of and resistance to the media's construction of the image of her sexuality as being unacceptable, her performance a playful mockery of the duplicity that both utilises and disavows her sexualised body.

Now disgraced and almost ostracised by society, the same media frames her roles as disgraceful. The film understands that there is an element of coercion inherent in producing or creating a person such as Silk for physical commodification. By the time Abraham (Emraan Hashmi) accepts her, she has already been disembodied, penalised, and made into a non-entity. The same film industry, media, and camera that once perfectly fetishised her body converted her into an object of erotic spectacle and overvalued it. Failing to find respect and true love in society, she ends her career by committing suicide in this hegemonic, patriarchal world that never appreciates her talent.

The double conflict in Silk's case is resolved by the woman's destruction of her own body. Silk in her departure gloriously drapes herself in a red saree that perfectly adorns her lifeless yet desiring female body. Her death is a symbol of the "Indian mediascape's patriarchal codings of women's sexuality," to quote Govindan and Dutta's article ("Global Bollywood" 185), a commentary on how society thrives on the fake, of how a spirited, bold woman seeks sustenance in a world dominated by men. Further, the film exposes the darker, exploitative side of the 1980s South Indian film business.

Treated as a symbol of "wanton female sexuality," the media tries to tame Silk in the name of "discipline." In the 1980s, in the Indian public sphere, actresses had to locate themselves strategically within limited sexual identities, as either the "vamp" or the "virgin" or some blurring of the two. Silk was neither a virgin nor a vamp and the necessity of having the identification label of an actress was one of the prerogatives of the existing Bollywood film industry at that time. Thus, when an actress like Silk attempts to resist such categorisation within the field of media representations, her "rebellion" is subverted and recuperated within patriarchal definitions of sexuality. Silk's suicide is symbolic of the same patriarchy that disciplines and regulates women's sexuality.

Case study 4: Iti Mrinalini

In *Iti Mrinalini* (2010), a film by Aparna Sen, we are drawn into the film through its leading protagonist, an aging Bengali actress, Mrinalini (Aparna Sen), as we share her experiences, seeing the situations within the film from her point of view. There are constant cuts to Mrinalini's past and the embodied female voiceover maintains narrative continuity. In a film within a film, Mrinalini plays the role of Laila/Radha, (played by Konkona Sen Sharma, the younger Mrinalini) to reflect on her character within the frame in a costume drama that she is acting in.

Here her own plight and situation is reflected. Her screen persona represents significant elements of the real person, Mrinalini. The process of film production is never hidden: we see repeated shots of film-maker Siddhartha Sarkar directing a film within a film, the cast and crew with Mrinalini as an actor/performer. The narrative of the aged Mrinalini is designed as a self-contained world, understandable in itself.

Iti Mrinalini, works in a different style altogether, prioritising the spectator. Here Mrinalini the person works upon the spectators. The past is visualised for the spectators in an extended flashback. The female speaker (Mrinalini) tells her story through an embodied voice-over. The voice-over is autobiographical and confessional, with extended flashbacks revealing how the speaker arrived at this present state of contemplating suicide. She narrates how throughout her life she has been a victim of media attention; therefore, in death she wishes to be spared it. As a performing actor, timing has always been important to her. If her coming into this world exhibited no choice, she believes she has the right to choose the moment of her exit. Before ending her life, she decides to destroy her memorabilia—letters, photos, and newspaper clips—lest they again fall into the hands of the media.

As the film progresses, we become entirely aligned with the character of Mrinalini and acquire a privileged perspective as a viewer into her private world. We see the entire story through this fictional character. As she reviews her past life, we see how memories keep haunting her on the last night of her life. Unravelling as a journey down memory lane, Mrinalini's reflections on her life of relationships and betrayals, of agonies endured, of awards cherished, unfurl.

The film is a meditation on a star's public recognition, fame, glamour, and personal failures. It is about the crisis aged actresses like her endure when they are replaced by upcoming young actresses. Much later in her life, with Imtiaaz, the Bengali Muslim director of *Born of the Sun*, the aged Mrinalini shares a romantic relationship in real life. Yet what she represents is a maternal image as she plays the role of Kunti, the mother of Karna (played by Imtiaaz). The young actress, Hiyaa, plays the role of Draupadi, the one who is romantically inclined towards Karna. The young Hiyaa acts as a threat to Mrinalini's chances of playing Nandini in *Red Oleanders*, who is an "embodiment of youth," as Mrinalini herself believes. In a media event, Hiyaa is announced as the star who is to play the role of Nandini. Gradually Hiyaa, replacing her as Nandini, also disrupts Mrinalini's personal relation with Imtiaaz.

As we have more access to Mrinalini's point of view and the subjectivity of the character, we become dependent on her for our "take" on the film as a whole; in the process, we form a particularly close bond, an "identification," with her. The disembodied voice-over in the form of a poem at the end of the film, too, is a reflection of life in general, and again Mrinalini's life in particular. As spectators, our role becomes passive, for the spectator in this film is never simultaneously "inside" and "outside" the fictional world of the film. We somehow tend to surrender completely to the film experience through a form of imagining that can only be compared to some sort of infantile regression. Had we been made active spectators, we would have been able simultaneously to be inside and outside the film.

In this film, once we enter Mrinalini's world, we are never given the scope to come out of it. Such a scope or possibility only comes as glimpses in the form of a male character/friend named Chintan, who develops a strong bonding with Mrinalini and looks at her and also speculates objectively about her world and love life. As spectators, we never share Chintan's objective point of view for we are sutured into Mrinalini's world and share her subject position.

Conclusion

In the films discussed in this essay, I think, women/female protagonists are displayed as spectacle and yet do not remain unrepresented. The possibility of a paradox grounded in real contradiction is negated. Women, as real social beings, are not the same as the "Woman" represented by the media, yet they are "caught," experientially and conceptually, between the two. This is what happens to Meghna, Shonali, and Mahi, who are bombarded with cultural fantasies of the "Woman" in the media and advertising and are expected to live up to those images.

In *Fashion, Heroine,* and *The Dirty Picture* there are complex negotiations at work between the female protagonists as credible persons and our familiarity with the image of a star persona. The image takes us into broader areas of cultural study. This interrelationship of real person–role–persona–image may be further studied by exploring how stars are "constructed."

When stars are projected as stars in a film, their image is more than just a visual image. The persona (the mix of star image and the character role) engages our interest, producing meaning. The characters of Meghna, Shonali, Mahi, Mrinalini, and Silk demonstrate a powerful mixture of strength and vulnerability. These films present the paradox of stardom: the stars seem knowable, accessible, ordinary, and yet, at the same time, extraordinary and only attainable in the everyday world of the spectator in the forms of desire and fantasy.

At the heart lies a paradox. We spectators temporarily are lured into imaginary or illusory identification with this media-reconstructed world of glitz and glamour. We as spectators are aware that the female body has been stereotyped, stigmatised by gendered and sexualised significations while the spectacle of glamour is just a façade, an illusion. There are things that the frame hides from our hearing, gaze, and understanding.

In these women-centric films of resistance by Indian directors, the hidden frame is also exposed and made visible by uncovering what lies behind this façade. Consequently, a feeling of lack and disempowerment becomes dominant that overcomes our pleasure at the spectacle. Cinema, the most powerful medium of the modern age, has not been turned into an odd commodity for the entertainment business in India. It has definitely not created more insecurities than confidence. Cinema in India is not lost, nor is it stuck between a highly personalised and subjective art form and an extremely crude and mindless enterprise.

Works cited

Althusser, Louis. "Ideology and Ideological State Apparatuses (Notes Towards an Investigation)." *Mapping Ideology*, edited by Regina Schulte. Verso, 1970.
Carter, Cynthia, et al., eds. *The Routledge Companion to Media and Gender.* Routledge, 2015.
Chandra, Tanuja. "Interview: Screen 5." *The Telegraph, T2*, 1 November 2017
De Lauretis, Teresa. *Alice Doesn't: Feminism, Semiotics, Cinema.* Indiana University Press, 1984.
—. *Technologies of Gender: Essays on Theory, Film, and Fiction.* Indiana University Press, 1987.
Fashion. Directed by Madhur Bhandarkar, performances by Priyanka Chopra, Kangana Ranaut, and Arbaaz Khan. UTV Motion Pictures, 29 October 2008.
Govindan, Padma, and Bisakha Dutta. "From Villain to Traditional Housewife: The Politics of Globalization and Women's Sexuality in the 'New' Indian Media." *Global Bollywood*, edited by Kavoori and Punathambekar. Oxford University Press, 180–202.
Iti Mrinalini. Directed by Aparna Sen, performances by Aparna Sen, Konkona Sen Sharma, and Rajat Kapoor. Shree Venkatesh Films, 29 July 2011.

Heroine. Directed by Madhur Bhandarkar, performances by Kareena Kapoor, Arjun Rampal, and Randeep Hooda. Bhandarkar Entertainment, 21 September 2012.

Mulvey, Laura. "Visual Pleasure and Narrative Cinema." *Visual and Other Pleasures*, edited by Laura Mulvey. Palgrave Macmillan, 2009.

Dirty Picture, The. Directed by Milan Luthria, performances by Vidya Balan, Naseeruddin Shah, and Emraan Hashmi. Balaji Motion Pictures, 2 December 2011.

CHAPTER 4

WOMEN AS DESIRING SUBJECTS IN *DEVDAS* ON SCREEN

The eminent Bengali novelist Sarat Chandra Chatterjee's *Devdas* (1917) has enjoyed immense popularity since its publication, first in Bengali and eventually in a number of other Indian languages. Subsequently this phenomenally successful romance had an afterlife through various Indian film adaptations made over eight decades.[1]

---

[1] There are at least ten different translations in Hindi. Significant film versions of the novel in Bengali, Hindi, Telugu, Tamil, and Assamese include:
Devdas (1927 film), directed by Naresh Mitra, starring Phani Sarma as Devdas, Tarakbala as Paro, and Niharbala/Miss Parul as Chandramukhi.
Devdas (1935 film), directed by P. C. Barua, starring himself as Devdas, Jamuna as Paro, and Chandrabati Devi as Chandramukhi.
Devdas (1936 film), directed by P. C. Barua, starring K. L. Saigal as Devdas, Jamuna as Paro, and Rajkumari as Chandramukhi.
Devdas (1937 film) (in Assamese), directed by P. C. Barua, starring Phani Sarma as Devdas, Zubeida as Paro, and Mohini as Chandramukhi.
Devdas (1953 film) (also known as *Devadasu*) (in Tamil and Telugu), directed by Vedantam Raghavaiah, starring Akkineni Nageswara Rao as Devdas and Savitri as Paro.
Devdas (1955 film), directed by Bimal Roy, starring Dilip Kumar as Devdas, Suchitra Sen as Paro, and Vyjayantimala as Chandramukhi.
Haath Ki Safai, a song in the film is about the play Devdas with Randhir Kapoor as Devdas and Hema Malini as Chandramukhi.
Devdas (1979 film) (also known as *Debdas*), directed by Dilip Roy, starring Soumitra Chatterjee as Devdas, Sumitra Mukherjee as Paro, and Supriya Choudhury as Chandramukhi.
Devdas (2002 Bengali film), directed by Shakti Samanta, starring Prasenjit Chatterjee as Devdas, Arpita Pal as Paro, and Indrani Halder as Chandramukhi.
Devdas (2002 film), directed by Sanjay Leela Bhansali, starring Shah Rukh Khan as Devdas, Aishwarya Rai as Paro, and Madhuri Dixit as Chandramukhi.
Dev D (2009 film), a modern take on the classic novel *Devdas*, directed by Anurag Kashyap, starring Abhay Deol as Dev, Mahi Gill as Paro, and Kalki Koechlin as

Despite the fact that the classic renouncer figure, the enduring archetypal hero Devdas, has almost acquired a mythical status, this essay looks at the female characters, Parvati and Chandramukhi, and the nature of the female gaze. Exploring the representations of the female gaze in the two major Bollywood[2] adaptations of *Devdas*, the classic adaptation by Bimal Roy (1955) and Sanjay Leela Bhansali's *Devdas* (2002), the essay analyses the positioning of female characters as desiring subjects and their varying degrees of acceptance or refusal to conform to accepted gender roles of femininity.

The notion of the "female gaze" in my essay is an alternative to the "male gaze" proposed by Laura Mulvey in her classic film essay "Visual Pleasure and Narrative Cinema" (1973). Mulvey argues that the controlling gaze in cinema is always male. Spectators are encouraged to identify with the look of the male hero, which makes the heroine a passive object of erotic spectacle. My paper will focus on two questions. First, is there a male gaze, or rather an active female gaze, in the two Bollywood adaptations of *Devdas*? Second, what is the nature of the gaze, what does it essentially signify, and how does it contribute essential meaning to gender roles?

The narrative of *Devdas* has come to represent itself as a "mythological reference point for Hindi melodrama" (Rajadhyaksha and Willemen 244). "The aristocratic, lovelorn, politically disengaged and ultimately tragic hero" (Arora 1) of *Devdas* is perhaps the most enduring icon of the Indian film oeuvre. The pathos of this doomed hero was

---

Chanda. The uncoy heroines in *Dev D* represent a very liberated female sexuality where Paro is not shy about her desires. Paro and Lenny (Chandramukhi) are bold, sensuous, angry, aggressive, and refuse to be stereotyped into the limited definitions of sexual identities.
Devdas (2010 Pakistani film), directed by Iqbal Kasmiri, starring Nadeem Shah as Devdas, Zara Shaikh as Paro, and Meera as Chandramukhi.
Devdas (2010 Bangladeshi film) directed by Chachi Nuzrol Islam, starring Shakib Khan as Devdas, Apu Biswash as Paro, Moushumi as Chandramukhi.
Guru Dutt's *Pyaasa* (1957) and *Kaagaz Ke Phool* (1959) appropriate the *Devdas* legend. Shakti Samanta's *Amanush* (1975) and Prakash Mehra's *Muqaddar Ka Sikandar* (1978) have been successful as versions of *Devdas*. These films are not direct adaptations but appropriations of *Devdas*.
[2] This essay does not intend to examine contestations surrounding the term "Bollywood." The rise to prominence of this term is undoubtedly a cultural symptom whose meaning requires further exploration. For further discussion on the hybridity of the term and disputes over the name, see M. Madhava Prasad "Surviving Bollywood," in *Global Bollywood*, ed. Anandam P. Kavoori and Aswin Punathambekar. Oxford: Oxford University Press, 2008.

captured by Indian cinema; as Eric Barnouw and S. Krishnaswamy, in the first edition of *Indian Film* (1963), observed, "virtually a generation wept over Devdas" (80).

Set in a feudal Bengali milieu, Chatterjee's novella is the story of a doomed love between an affluent *zamindar's*[3] son and his middle-class neighbour's daughter Parvati who is also known as Paro. The two had been childhood friends, but Devdas's family opposes their growing attachment. Devdas is unable to stand up to his tyrannical father who sends him to Calcutta for higher studies and to acquire sophistication. Devdas is unhappy but, in a weak moment, writes to Parvati disavowing his love for her. Consequently, Paro's parents arrange her marriage to a rich old widower. Devdas returns to the village to prevent the marriage, but in vain.

Parvati marries the elderly widower with grown-up sons, takes up her duties as mistress of his estate, and discharges her responsibilities with earnestness. Yet Parvati stays in her new family merely physically and in her mind she has taken Devdas as her husband. Devdas too is unable to contend with this turn of events. Back in the city, he takes to drink, and finds solace in the company of a courtesan, Chandramukhi. Parvati, learning of Devdas's lapse, comes to see him and pleads with him to give up drinking. He promises, instead, to come to her once before he dies. Devdas wastes away despite Chandramukhi's unflinching devotion and care. He stays with Chandramukhi but lives only to suffer from his love for Parvati.

Torn as Devdas is between Paro and Chandramukhi, unable to claim one, unwilling to accept the other, he journeys inexorably to his doom and death. Hopelessly ill, but anxious to keep his promise to Parvati, he journeys all night to get to her village and dies at her doorstep.

In both Roy's and Bhansali's films, Parvati is constructed as the epitome of Indian womanhood by focusing on her chastity, devotion to her lover as a future husband, later fidelity to her husband, and, most importantly, her suffering and forbearance. The mythological underpinnings of this ideal can be traced to the Indian epics and the virtue of their main female characters. Yet one must not lose sight of the fact that representations of Parvati vary significantly in the two films and the difference may be studied in relation to their female gaze.

---

[3] In India the term "zamindar" denotes a holder or occupier (*dār*) of land (*zamīn*). In the late eighteenth century the British government made these zamindars landowners, thus creating a landed aristocracy in Bengal and Bihar that lasted until Indian Independence (1947).

I shall now refer to a sequence in Bimal Roy's film when Devdas returns from the city after a long time and goes to meet Parvati; I will study how the female gaze directed towards the hero is an indication of the devotional nature of her desire. Ravi Vasudevan claims in "Addressing the Spectator of a 'Third World' National Cinema" that the "strategy of narration indicates that Parvati's point of view is used to underline the desirability and the authority evoked by Devdas's image" (304).

In this sequence, Devdas calls from outside and from this moment Parvati's point of view dominates the narration. As Devdas enters the house and asks for Paro, the shot shifts to Paro as she hurriedly climbs the stairs in anticipation of Devdas and we withdraw with her to her room upstairs. As she begins to hear Devdas's footsteps, she hurriedly lights the devotional lamp. Vasudevan, interestingly, notes how Parvati's attempt to light the lamp before Devdas enters her room is caught by a suspenseful intercutting between her lighting of the lamp and shots of the empty doorway.

The doorframe in the sequence is symbolic of the shrine in which the divine idol is housed. Devdas's entry is shown in a highly deifying way: first his feet are shown in the doorway, followed by a cut to the lighted lamp. Finally, his face is revealed. There follows a cut to Parvati and her gaze. What I claim here is that in this scene Roy shows Parvati lighting the devotional lamp and that the extra-diegetic sound of the conch shells (used in Hindu idol worship) highlight the devotional nature of the desire and also the desire to be desired by Devdas.

As Parvati's look in this sequence inscribes Devdas as an image, I extend Vasudevan's claim further by adding that Paro's point of view upholds a double desiring position—her desire for Devdas, and the desire to be desired by Devdas. This leads to identification on the part of the female spectator with the romantically unfulfilled woman character (Paro). It further makes way for the female spectator to identify with Paro's female gaze at once—she is a doubly desiring spectator whose desire is simultaneously "desire for the other, and desire to be desired by the other" (De Lauretis 143).

However, it is still necessary, as Vasudevan insists, "to acknowledge the framework of masculine authority within which female desire is finally held" (305). But it should be noted that in the Bimal Roy film, as Devdas emerges from the shadows, we see Paro not with downcast eyes but with the direct and romantic gaze of an adoring lover.

I study a corresponding scene in Sanjay Leela Bhansali's film from 2002, in which it is staged in part as a devotional prayer to the goddess Durga (an incarnation of Devi or Parvati) and a simultaneous reference to her expected future husband as a deity. The 2002 version of this scene is in the context of a song and dance sequence and clearly departs from the 1955 version. Bhansali's digital version with its Rs. 500 million budget was the most expensive film ever made in India at that time. Its elaborately choreographed song and dance sequence apparently adheres to the expectations and "formula" of the popular Bollywood romance genre. In this scene, the lyrics narrate an affair the flame of which has never been extinguished and that remains the visual conceit of the song. The choreography shows Parvati fondly protecting a devotional lamp in the palm of her hand, a lamp she has never allowed to be extinguished, constantly keeping its flame burning since her childhood until Devdas returned, signifying her undying desire and passion for Devdas. Furthermore, she is anticipating Devdas's arrival any day.

In the sequence, the worship is directed in part at the goddess, rather than simply at Devdas. Parvati is dressed as the goddess Durga as she symbolically defies the class barriers of society (the curtains shown here act as a signifier of such fetters), ignores the mockery of her friends, and re-enacts the effort with which she keeps the flame burning through all possible adversities and impediments (the rain, wind, and dazzling pirouettes are signifiers of such adversity). The lyrics state, "Silsila yeh chahat ka maine na bujhne diya, oh piya, yeh diya . . . mere chahat ka diya" (I did not let this affair of desire grow cold/ My love, this flame has not died, nor will it/ My desire's flame.) (*Devdas*)

Bhansali deploys an active camera, with a number of pans and angles, continuous 360-degree shots, and rhythmic movement to suggest such a deification. Towards the end, as Parvati in a dance rhythm repeatedly whirls around, vermillion[4] explodes in bursts of reddish haze (Shreshtova 252), suggesting the devotional nature of the desire and the worshipping gaze.

Two modes of representation of femininity unlike the Roy film are at work here. First, Parvati's desire for Devdas in the sequence marks her as a desiring subject. Second, the commodification of her femininity, the camera's gaze at her suggestive sexuality through her dance rhythms, postures, and longing for Devdas mark her objectification as female. She is also the object of desire, a clear departure from Roy's version.

In both Roy's and Bhansali's films, the child Parvati's gaze at Devdas reflected her love and longing for Devdas. Evidently she was

---

[4] A mark of vermillion or Indian sindoor on a woman's forehead denotes that she is married. Wearing sindoor is customary and considered auspicious (therefore it is used in weddings, festivals, and Hindu religious worship). Traditionally, it holds a great degree of significance for married Indian women.

much more mature than Devdas in her early realisation of love, in almost all its dimensions. Parvati's childhood gaze of love defined what subsequently developed into Parvati and Devdas's narrative of love. Therefore, the song sequence in Bhansali's film cuts to a short flashback to the child Parvati and her sorrowful gaze at the lighted diya, after Devdas's departure.

I will now refer to a scene in Bimal Roy's film in which Devdas tries to apologise for his betrayal and the slighted Parvati accuses him of being arrogant and narcissistic for thoughtlessly rejecting her marriage proposal. Devdas writes a letter to Parvati deliberately rejecting her and stating: "It has never crossed my mind that I desire you." (*Devdas*) Parvati, of course, reads this as a callous rejection and has no choice but to agree to the match her parents have arranged. Paro claims that if Devdas's parents have their sense of dignity then her parents too are not lacking their own self-esteem. She asserts that her parents have been wise in arranging her marriage to a rich and older man, one who is not impetuous and fickle like Devdas.

Parvati's gaze of agony and pride remains central to the situation. Devdas is incensed by Parvati's comments. As he fails to break the shackles of familial feudal fetters and marry Parvati, Devdas realises that he has lost her forever. "And this was the point: losing the girl, he wins the audience" (Ahmed 304). Accusing her of supreme pride that needs to be tamed, and comparing her beauty to that of a full moon that is marred by a scar on its face, he hits Parvati on the forehead with a fishing rod intending to leave a similar indelible mark on her otherwise flawlessly beautiful face. This scar he claims would remind her of him and the wound almost deflowers her.

The sexual undercurrent of the scene, implicit in the wound and in Parvati's bleeding forehead, remains unmistakable. Parvati's gaze reveals that Devdas has again exercised his claim over her (he had been hitting Paro when they were children and Paro had loved and worshipped Devdas since she was a child). Parvati is immediately subdued and after a tender reconciliation the lovers part. The construction of Parvati's femininity and sexuality is significantly negotiated in the sequence as a powerful woman and a devoted mistress. Suggestions abound in the film that the scar will remain symbolic of her defilement or perhaps a violation of her chastity.

In both Roy's and Bhansali's films, if Parvati's desire for Devdas may be viewed as a psychical construct, Chandramukhi's desire may be viewed as both a psychical and a social construct. Chandramukhi's articulation of desire for Devdas to Chunilal and her plea that Chunilal should bring him back to her *kotha* (brothel) are dynamically interwoven with relations of power in her society. Her social positioning as a courtesan relegates her to the margins and Devdas at the centre detests her for her "traditional exhibitionist role," her "to-be-looked-at-ness" (Mulvey 19).

We now move to the sequence in Bimal Roy's film where Chandramukhi has saved Devdas from the clutches of the city and has restored this violently sick man to life. When asked whether he still despises her, Devdas acknowledges her goodness and his love for her. From this point, the camera follows the point of view of Chandramukhi to her room, where the close up of her face indicates her happiness at securing Devdas's affection. The camera is gazing at her in this scene and her gaze is overtly suggestive of how Devdas has been transformed from hatred towards Chandramukhi's profession—the feudal-domination subordination ethics—to that of love. The camera sustains our focus on her gaze, and thus her feelings about him and herself. The audience here shares Chandramukhi's point of view, her happiness.

That Paro and Chandramukhi share the same emotional domain where love is able to transcend all boundaries is subtly communicated by Bimal Roy through the unifying nature of the female gaze in the sequence where Paro and Chandramukhi take to the road in their quest for Devdas, one sadly positioned in a palanquin and the other taking pains to brave the rough road. This sequence marks a shift from the women's gaze at Devdas to a moment in which their gazes fall on one another. The scene crystallises their socially defined roles as wife and courtesan, the background score sings of "one in the sun, one in the shadow."

As they pass each other, they gaze at one another, perhaps able to relate to a quest for romantic love even if they do not know each other. The unifying nature of the women's gaze in the shot creates a beautiful cinematic moment: Paro and Chandramukhi's lives revolving around Devdas as they exchange a moment's gaze at life's crossroads. The gaze makes Chandramukhi one with Paro, dissolving all her social stigma.

There is a corresponding scene in the 2002 version where Bhansali goes so far as to make Paro and Chandramukhi meet on the occasion of Durga puja. This is followed by the "Dola Re, Dola Re" song and dance sequence where the female leads' gazes (Paro's and Chandramukhi's) towards each other are active, which crystallises female bonding and affectionate companionship. Their gazes simultaneously celebrate their desire, love, and longing for the male subject (Devdas). Here Devdas is absent and exists only as an image of love and desire in the minds of Paro and Chandramukhi. The female spectator here identifies with the gaze of the heroines and their desire for Devdas.

The presence of Paro's brother-in-law (the male/villain) Kalibabu and the camera's constant cuts to the threatening nature of his look directed at the dancing female duo do not represent any kind of scopophilic pleasure but only anticipate forthcoming complications that will arise from such a situation (Parvati, a *thakurain* dancing with a woman of the *kotha*). The male actor's gaze treats the woman (Chandramukhi) as a representative of decadent femininity, an outcast. To a certain extent, the controlling nature of the look of the villain in the dance sequence quite significantly disrupts the construction of woman as a pleasurable spectacle. The third look is the alternating gaze of the camera: at the dancing duo and at the male spectator (the villain).

In the scene, Chandramukhi's acceptance of Parvati's invitation, her presence in Parvati's household to take part in a religious festival, her marginalised position within the social hierarchy, and her otherness all lead to oppression and conflict. Chandramukhi and Parvati's dance sequence articulates their desire for Devdas. This is an affirmation that the articulation of desire from their point of view is inextricably bound to prevailing modes of subordination and domination in society.

I shall substantiate this claim with reference to the lyrics in the song: the avenues through which desire moves are not free from social hierarchies and class. The lyrics of the song, which alternate between Paro and Chandramukhi, combined with their gazes at each other, make the social distinction clear even though the song celebrates their friendship and bonding:

> Chandramukhi: "Tumne Mujhko Duniya de di,
> Mujhko Apni Khusiya De Di"
> (You have opened the world to me
> You have given me all your happiness)
> Parvati: "Unse kabhi na hona door
> Haan maang mein bhar lena sindoor"
> (Never be far away from your love
> Do wear sindoor on your forehead)
> Chandramukhi: "Unki bahon ka tum ho phool
> Main hoon kadmo ki bus dhool."
> (You are the beautiful flower he holds in his hand
> And me only the dust of his revered feet.) (*Devdas*)

Here Paro asks Chandramukhi to wear *sindoor* on her forehead and subtly suggests that Chandramukhi get married to her love. Chandramukhi's gaze towards Parvati is immediately one of respect, of gratefulness towards

Parvati for being so thoughtful and affectionate. She conveys this to Paro through her meaningful gaze. After the song, Chandramukhi's spirited defiance and sharp retort towards the villain serve to save her esteem as she steers her way out of the conflict, accepting her otherness with dignity. In the course of my essay, I have discussed the female "gaze" in two phases. First, the heroine's gaze at Devdas, and second, their gazes at each other. Now I discuss a third: Chandramukhi's gaze disrupting the male gaze. To explore this gaze, I look at Bhansali's film where Chandramukhi's agency disrupts the male gaze by refusing to be fetishised in a *mujra* sequence held at her *kotha* (brothel).

Chandramukhi has elaborately prepared a *mujra* (courtesan's performance) for Devdas and eagerly awaits his arrival so the *mujra* can begin. Though trained to be seductive and charming as a courtesan, the image of Chandramukhi that dominates the scene is of a woman destined to lead a lonely and tragic life at the margins of power and seclusion. The *mujra* sequence in Bhansali's film invests in elaborate sets, props, decor, and costume. The villain Kalibabu is awaiting a performance by the dancing girl in a hall lit by chandeliers and decorated with candles. Chandramukhi's defiance and spirited manner disrupt any possibility of male viewing pleasure as she strikes a deal with the villain to perform (as her profession demands and therefore out of compulsion) only if Devdas does not arrive. Here Chandramukhi disrupts male viewing pleasure within the scene (the villain's gaze).

As she waits for Devdas's arrival we as viewers share Chandramukhi's point of view and apprehend that Devdas may fail to arrive within the stipulated time. As the candle is about to be consumed by its own flame and Chandramukhi is on the verge of losing the deal, she reaches out for the *ghungru*[5] gifted to her by the villain. The sequence also critiques the immorality and exploitative nature of the institution of the courtesan up to this point.

As she is about to begin her performance we see Devdas's hazy image gradually becoming prominent at a distance. A jubilant Chandramukhi begins to perform, but this time out of her love for Devdas. Throughout the sequence, Devdas's presence is entirely passive. He not only refuses to participate in any viewing pleasure from Chandramukhi's performance but his passivity to the performance reminds one that his presence is out of

---

[5] *Ghungru*, also known as dancing bells, have been used in dance performances in India from ancient times. They are worn tied around the ankles by dancers. They are widely used in Bharatnatyam, Kathak, Kuchipudi, and Odissi performances and are used to maintain the rhythm of the dance steps.

compulsion. He is there only to return the two nights that Chandramukhi had spent nursing him back to life.

The only other male character in this scene is the villain of the film who is now relegated to a marginalised position and is doomed as he fails to connect with Chandramukhi's emotional world. In the scene, the man is not centred. In fact, he occupies a very narrow space on the extreme left. Through her dance rhythms, gestures, postures, and most importantly her gaze, the villain is marginalised and is coerced into taking up the *ghungru*, a potent signifier of the "other" woman's threatened humiliation by the male. In accepting the *ghungru*, he is now made to share the domain of the courtesan and his humiliation is complete.

The sequence shows how the "other" woman succeeds in disrupting the potential fetishistic gaze; her rebuking gaze is now directed towards the villain, further helping her oust the male from the space of the *kotha*. Chandramukhi's position as the iconic *nautch* girl of Indian cinema, who projects female desire, is problematised in this scene. Firstly, there is a conscious effort on her part to refuse objectification as a seductress. Secondly, there is a constant oscillation—in her role as spectator, gazing at Devdas as an object of devotion, and in the director's simultaneous attempt to make her a spectacle.

Two distinct identificatory processes for the audience are in operation. The first involves an active identification with the female gaze, the second, a passive identification with the image of Devdas. The female spectator can easily identify with Chandramukhi and needs no sexual transfiguration. The focus on Devdas's face—his eyes reflect his desire for Paro and his suffering as well as his passivity towards Chandramukhi in the scene—attracts female spectators, conforming with their image of why precisely Devdas is the romantic and sad "hero."

It is this delicate balance of dignity and pathos in his persona that makes Devdas so romantically appealing to the women in his life and to Indian audiences at large. Chandramukhi understands Devdas's suffering for Paro and empathises with Devdas as she realises that her love for him is a similar kind of devotional, impossible longing. She will never have his affectionate companionship for he will remain eternally wedded to Paro. Her devotional gaze at Devdas throughout the film is a reflection of this understanding.

In the final scenes of Roy's and Bhansali's films, Devdas arrives at Parvati's doorstep to breathe his last. Parvati, realising Devdas's evident death, runs wildly to meet him, disregarding her social status as mistress of an influential feudal estate and her familial responsibilities as a wife and mother. Her family had been unaware of her concealed emotional attachment to Devdas; in a climactic, emotionally charged melodramatic sequence, they succeed in locking her within the gates of the huge family estate. Her family prevents the lovers' reunion and forever imprisons Parvati in a life of accepted social respectability. Devdas dies on her doorstep—and this is precisely where romance triumphs. For ages, this tragic ending appealed to the Indian ethos of being torn between one's passion and social norms, only to ultimately deny individual happiness.

The mantle of the traditional Hindu image of virtuous Indian womanhood, or the "woman of eternal sacrifice," and the continuous negotiation of Paro's and Chandramukhi's identity under such a rubric in Roy's and Bhansali's films is openly dismissed in Anurag Kashyap's *Dev D* to reconstruct the existence of an aggressive sexuality in its female characters.

Dev D is a modern take on the classic novel. While watching *Dev D,* we ought to forget pre-decided mutual chastity, perhaps the single-most important factor why Devdas and Paro's romance is immortalised in our consciousness. For the uncoy heroine in *Dev D* represents a highly liberated female sexuality where Paro is not shy about her desires. Paro and Lenny (Chandramukhi) are bold, sensuous, angry, aggressive, and refuse to be stereotyped into the limited definitions of sexual identities.

However, dominant patriarchal structures are not seen dissolving in the film nor is the film a shift from the male gaze. This, again should not take away from the (arguably) empowering nature of certain aspects of the film, most notably sexual agency and its aesthetics enhanced by cinematography and editing. Though the lyrics, character roles, and themes often resonate with dominant patriarchal discourse and its objectification of women, it is the social construction of Lenny's sexuality that is significant.

Ostracised from society after her mobile phone MMS (multimedia messaging service) clips are made public, she decides to be an outsider (opting to be a sex worker) rather than be a conformist. She resists familial pressure to conform and reconfigure her identity. The cultural relocation of *Dev D* partially foregrounds a narrative of feminist resistance to the dominant socio-cultural structures that the film seeks to critique. However, despite sufficient resistance, women's "rebellions" are ultimately submerged within patriarchal definitions of sexuality.

The lead male character only partially suffers from the Devdas syndrome. This is not colonial Bengal of the early twentieth century, but India at the dawn of the twenty-first century, waking up to a world of MMS clips, sex clubs, and ecstasy-coke concoctions. The characters reflect the sensibilities, conflicts, aggression, independence, free thought, exuberance, and recklessness of today's youth. This is a generation caught between Eastern roots and Western sensibilities. In this twenty-first century reinterpretation, characters and relationships gain a completely different dimension as they evolve amidst global consumerist culture.

With *Dev D*, Anurag Kashyap does not concentrate on the story's theme of how love is destroyed by people abiding by centuries-old social customs. Kashyap adapts the original story and looks at the negative shades of Devdas's character. He sees how Devdas has emerged as an "adjective" in modern India (Interview). A man from a wealthy family who enjoys the finer things in life becomes locked in a world of drugs, pornography, and prostitution. The diegesis relates to the anxieties and frustrations of masculinity through Dev's sufferings.

Announcing a bold departure, in its handling of the theme, treatment of sexuality, and revision of the parental role in romance, *Dev D* sets new trends in rewriting the romance genre of Bollywood and heralds a definitive breakthrough. The narrative makes significant alterations to revive the "romance" genre and appropriates the love motif of the iconic Indian love legend to a postmodern setting, articulating the point of view of a displaced youth in a world of globalised youth culture. Tradition here is simultaneously a site of contestation and debate. The emergence of a new media environment, multiplex culture and a new Indian consumer class make their presence felt in this twenty-first century adaptation.

The usual parental role in Bollywood romance stands revised in *Dev D*. Anurag Kashyap says it was a conscious decision to portray the women as he did. "I wanted women who aren't a undimensional paragon of virtue but are interesting." There is no parental opposition; instead, Dev is advised by his father to iron things out with his love, Paro. Similarly Paro coolly tells her own father that if she has to do "anything" with a man, it would be with Dev.

Indian parents, once the favourite "villains" in Bollywood love stories, end up as props in *Dev D*. The film reflects a trend in popular cinema. Bollywood films now essentially do away with external factors such as overbearing parents and differences of caste, community, and economic background. Instead, they focus on relationships. Kashyap says *Dev D* is right for India in 2009. "It is about time people understand that love stories should be dealt with on a one-to-one basis. Love is between two people, not an entire family," he says.

In this essay, I have tried to study popular Bollywood *Devdas* adaptations through close textual reading and by analysing the nature of the gaze in film narratives. Focusing my study on issues relating to the gendering of spectatorship, film stars, and Bollywood's intersections with global culture over the past decade, I have attempted to highlight the significance of understanding *Devdas* adaptations in a broader social and cultural context.

Foregrounding the nature of the female gaze and inviting its audience to share a female point of view in a male-centred narrative, the three *Devdas* adaptations not only negotiate but also reconstruct female identities and problematise social and patriarchal constructions of female sexuality.

Seen simply as another variation of the archetypal story of unfulfilled love, like that of Laila and Majnu, Heer Ranjha, or Sohini Mahiwal,[6] *Devdas* could at most be accorded a mythic status. One of the reasons behind Sarat Chandra's enduring popularity could well be his essential conservatism. Though Sarat Chandra was a rebel, he never destabilised basic middle-class values regarding male–female relationships. In his novels, women achieve salvation only through *seva* (service) and sacrifice, while men retain the right to act arbitrarily or not to act at all. Devdas's self-indulgent path of self-destruction exclusively remains a male prerogative. Parvati could not have chosen such an escape route. Whatever apparent changes might have taken place in the twenty-first century, evidently these male fantasies continue to endure.

Over the several adaptations of the love legend, "the Devdas syndrome" has emerged as a benchmark for the ultimate in Hindi melodrama. What the syndrome signifies, perhaps, is the failure of romantic love in a conservative society. One wonders whether the strength of the changed ending in *Dev D*, as Dev decides to move on with Chandramukhi (here Lenny), almost spells the demise of the Devdas legend. But such a conclusion may not be easily drawn.

Certain characteristics of the syndrome, like identifying with the pain of lost love, will continue to haunt youth psychology as young people derive a cathartic pleasure from the experience. The sheer on-screen magic

---

[6] "Layla and Majnun," also known as "The Madman and Layla," is a classical Arabic story of star-crossed lovers. There is however a parallel version of the legend. In both versions, Majnu goes mad after Layla's father prevents him from marrying her. In India, the story was the basis for *Layla Majnu*, a film made by Harnam Singh Rawail in 1976 starring Rishi Kapoor and Rajneeta Kaur. A popular tragic romance of the Sindh and Punjab, "Sohni Mahiwal" is a medieval poetic love legend. Sohni's parents disapprove her match with her lover and in time both die for the sake of love. It was made into a film in 1984, *Sohni Mahiwal*, starring Sunny Deol and Poonam Dhillon. A popular tragic romance of Punjab, *Heer Ranjha* tells the story of the doomed love of Heer and her lover Ranjha. The epic poem acquired a legendary status and has been made into several feature films.

of Dev and Paro's romance in the Indian film industry has continued to intrigue and baffle critics for ages, just as *Devdas*'s psychological appeal for generations perhaps defies logic.

If *Devdas* to a past generation embodied the romanticised despair of youth, it also celebrated their inaction and defeatism. In our fiercely competitive and globalised world, what we need to explore now is whether passivity or defeatism can still be made to look attractive? And also whether today's viewers still empathise with a hero who wills his own destruction. In Indian society, where honour killing is rampant due to the prevailing notion of dishonouring one's own family because of class-based marriages, the Devdas myth has not lost its relevance and refuses to fade from collective memory.

Works cited

Ahmed, Akbar S. "Bombay Films: The Cinema as Metaphor for Indian Society and Politics." *Modern Asian Studies* 26, no. 2 (1992): 289–319.

Arora, Poonam. "Devdas: India's Emasculated Hero, Sado-Masochism and Colonialism." Accessed 3 June 2009. http://legacy.chass.ncsu.edu/jouvert/v1i1/Devdas/html.

Chatterjee, Sarat Chandra. *Devdas*. Gitanjali, 2002.

De Lauretis, Teresa. *Alice Doesn't: Feminism, Semiotics, Cinema*. Indiana University Press, 1984.

Kashyap, Anurag. *Anurag Kashyap speaks About Dev D.* YouTube, Eros Now Music, 2 February 2009. https://www.youtube.com/watch?v=L5Fch4rLeV8

Krishnaswamy, Subrahmanyam, and Eric Banouw, editors. *Indian Film*. Oxford University Press, 1963.

Mulvey, Laura. 1989. "Visual Pleasure and Narrative Cinema." In *Visual and Other Pleasures*. Macmillan, 1975.

Rajadhyaksha, Ashish, and Paul Willemen. *Encyclopaedia of Indian Cinema*. BFI Publishing, 1994.

Shreshtova, Sangita. "Dancing to an Indian Beat: 'Dola' Goes My Diasporic Heart." *Global Bollywood: Travels of Hindi Song and Dance*, edited by Sangita Gopal and Sujata Moorti. Orient Blackswan, 2010, pp. 243–63.

Vasudevan, Ravi S. "Addressing the Spectator of a Third World National Cinema: The Bombay Social Film of the 1940s and 1950s." *Asian Cinemas: A Reader and Guide*, edited by Dimitris Eleftheriotis and Gravy Needham. Edinburgh University Press, 2006, pp. 295–313.

Works consulted

Joshi, Lalit. "Cinema and Hindi Periodicals in Colonial India (1920–1970)." *Narratives of Indian Cinema*, edited by Manju Jain. Primus Books, 2009, pp. 19–51.

Mukherjee, Madhuja. "New Theatres: New Perspectives. Film Discourse: Revising Cultural Sites." In *Deep Focus*, pp. 101–2.

Rai, Amit S. "Contagious Multiplicities and the Nonlinear Life of the New Media." *Untimely Bollywood, Globalization and India's New Media Assemblage*. Duke University Press, 2010, pp. 55–71.

Sahgal, Nayantara. "Discovering Bimal Roy." *Bimal Roy: The Man Who Spoke in Pictures*, edited by Rinki Roy Bhattacharya. Penguin Viking, 2009, pp. 54–58.

CHAPTER 5

REFLECTIONS ON MASCULINITY AND POPULAR ROMANCE: *JAANE TU YA JAANE NA*

Abbas Tyrewala's *Jaane Tu Ya Jane Na* was released in 2008. In this Bollywood hit, college friends find their way into adulthood and try to keep their friendship going as they leave college. Very popular, this heart-winning romcom explores complexities of citation and the cultural practices of romantic love in the new millennium. Allusions to transnational Hollywood romcoms, Samuel Beckett's *Waiting for Godot*, and Mills & Boon fiction abound in the film. Simple yet self-reflexive in its meta-filmic dimension, the film helps re-examine the issue of how love is arrived at in the world of young adults. The comedy drama is also instrumental in revealing how destiny is structural, giving shape to its narrative and its romance as a whole.

The supporting character of Mala reminds one how intertexts are constructed. When supporting characters Jiggy and his friends interact with Mala at the airport and convince her to listen to Jai and Aditi's unconventional love story in flashback, we discover that the tale contains sophisticated insights into fictional layers of romantic love and its sexual politics. What the film foregrounds to its youth audience is a horizon of expectations about what constitutes or what we essentially understand as "romance." Hence, *Jaane Tu* may be read as a critical commentary on South Asian romantic culture, relationships, and their representation in popular media.

Mala's preconceived notions of romance and the frame-within-a-frame narrative lead to her transformation and help her reconstruct her notions of romance. Initially Mala is not fascinated by the romance genre; however, she ultimately develops a keen desire for romance and introduces herself to Jai and Aditi as "Jiggy's girlfriend" as the framing tale ends. Interestingly, but not quite evident, Mala gradually evolves as a desiring subject. The audience and Mala share a cognitive activity, which relies upon strategies of understanding that the perceiving audience may have learned through experience. The cinematic experience of "romance" to millennial youths in *Jaane Tu* involves intelligent frame-making and frame-breaking.

When the story-within-the-story begins, both Aditi (Genelia D'Souza) and Jai (Imraan Khan), the best of college buddies, firmly believe that they are not in love. As the film proceeds, the spirited, impulsive Aditi attempts to frame masculinity as she nurtures her own notions of masculine behaviour. The peace-loving Jai's restraint shatters Aditi's illusions, making Aditi all the more confident that Jai is not the "man" Aditi craves. Aditi believes she loves macho man Sushant. As Selinger states, "cocky, muscular, older, a Black Belt alpha male, Sushant is exactly the guy Aditi wanted" (58). On the other side, Jai imagines himself to be in love with Meghna. Sushant exists as a foil to Jai, while Meghna is a pleasant counterpoint to Aditi. As Meghna makes multiple uses of fiction, she engages Jai in imaginative verbal games of image-making to distract herself from harsh realities with all her unworldliness and charm.

Consequently, the Jai-Meghna and Aditi-Sushant subplot develops and reaches a satisfactory climax. The Meghna plot cautions viewers not to shut one's eyes to the fictional world of romance to the extent that one can no longer see harsh reality. The Sushant narrative tells us not to blindly believe in the world of romance narratives that romanticise alpha-heroic males. Such a romance/fantasy world may have its own dangerous consequences.

The film gradually shatters Aditi's notions of normative masculinity. Aditi learns that "Sushant is also jealous, manipulative, selfish, and abusive: in every way the opposite of Jai" (Selinger 58). Much of the comedy in the film is derived from the way the film upsets youth culture's assumptions about masculinity or the assumption of their friends that Jai and Aditi are in love with each other. It invalidates such common or easy inferences and ideas such as Mala's assumption in the framing tale that romance or notions like "made for each other" are all "crap." She snaps, it "happens in Mills & Boon, not in real life." Mala's irreverence and resistance to romantic love's predestined outcomes establish an equivalence between romantic love, popular romance fiction, and visual pleasure. The film, though not the first among its genre, is an honest attempt to subvert formulaic notions of conventional romance.

We are amazed by this meta-textual romance's intelligent deployment of visual imagery in its dream sequences. Many viewers remember the recurring dream sequence in which a masked figure on horseback usually chases and then beats a wicked character (reminding us either of Inspector Wagmare, who insults Jai's mother, or Aditi's boyfriend Sushant, who slaps Aditi). Much later, it is revealed to Jai and the audience that the masked character is Jai himself. It is Inspector Wagmare who has been repeatedly criticising the non-violent Jai of real life for his "violent streaks." Therefore, these dream sequences in the film demand deeper probing on the part of Jai and his viewers.

The audience is not easily duped into believing that this meta-filmic world of romance is a world of fiction. That the dream sequences have a deeper significance, that the ride on horseback would turn into reality sooner or later is quite evident. Towards the end of the film, as he unwittingly and unintentionally fulfils all the "conditions of masculinity," Jai realises that it is his past vision in the structure of a dream that has forever haunted him and has now come true. For Jai, the dream is not an arena of subjection, nor of fantasy, but instead denotes his capacity to frame mental representations of events yet to be realised—they take shape as mimetic representations of reality.

Such reduplication of images through dreams, or *mise en abyme*, directed by debutant Tyrewala, are mimetically powerful. They are capable of moving us, like any real act of chivalry, through the activation of our imagination, prompting us to reflect on what we see and anticipate as to how Jai would mirror such an act of bravery/chivalry.

In its comic scenes, *Jaane Tu* metaphorically yet ironically burlesques the recurring "Ranjhore ka Rathore" trope defined in a pompous manner by Jai's late father (Naseeruddin Shah) that happens to be his royal clan's characteristic masculine code—"ride on horseback, thrash someone, and get arrested." These conditions Jai must fulfil someday to be a true Rathore. In the *mise en scènes* here, the portrait of the dead man played by Naseeruddin Shah repeatedly comes to life as he interacts with Jai's mother. Contrary to his mother's belief, Jai's father announces with an amusing grandiloquence that "his" apparently polite son will uphold family tradition by adhering to the "Ranjhore ka Rathore" masculine code and prove himself a true Rajput. However, it is Jai again who unwittingly imitates such a code, which apparently defines Rathore masculinity. In doing so, however, the film affectionately spoofs and ridicules such codes of conduct. In its unique style it meaningfully parodies the absurdity of such comic and absurd exaggerations.

Firstly, Jai had been breaking that mould (though not consciously) by refusing to be "masculine" (to Aditi's disdain). Earlier Jai, using his grey cells rather than his fists, escapes fighting the macho cowboys at a disco. Secondly, a reflexive frame-break occurs when Aditi's expectations that Jai will be the macho male to save her are not met by Jai. Thirdly, much later, when Aditi expects nothing, Jai thrashes Sushant when he gets to know that Sushant has slapped Aditi on the face. Finally, a simple twist in the tale occurs when Jai fulfils all three conditions of Rathore manhood and prevents his love Aditi from leaving for a New York film school at the dramatic airport-set climax sequence. He unknowingly becomes a party to this frame-making process. It culminates in Jai's father's victory speech from the photographic frame. With its coming-of-age tale, Jai and Aditi discover that they actually love each other and are ultimately convinced of their predicament.

Among characters that remain close to our hearts is the tongue-in-cheek social activist Savitri Rathore (Ratna Pathak), Jai's protective mother, who always comes up with cool advice but is never overbearing. The complexities of the sibling bond portrayed in Aditi and Amit's relationship and Meghna helplessly falling in love with Jai despite a troubled childhood both continue to strike a chord among young audiences of all times. Aditi and Jai's wonderful chemistry and spirited performances make us conscious of the spark that went missing in Hindi cinema for almost a decade. Remarkably bouncy too is A. R. Rahman's musical score, with its "Pappu Can't Dance" and "Kabhi Kabhi Aditi" numbers.

Jaane Tu reminds one of other increasingly globalised, sleek, youth-oriented films like *Dil Chahta Hai*, *3 Idiots*, and *Om Shanti Om*—films that affectionately parody conventional romance and popular Hindi film styles through their film-within-a-film song sequences. These films have song sequences that are both citations and parodies of past Bollywood film songs like "Woh Ladki Hai Kahan" (*Dil Chahta Hai*), "Zooby Dooby" (*3 Idiots*), and "Dhoom Taana" (*Om Shanti Om*).

With its refreshing, unconventional take on the romance genre, *Jaane Tu* is a witty celebration of romance and contemporary youth culture. It is an investigation of how the frames of representation, our expectations of the genre, and the intertextual dialogue with romance fiction such as Mills & Boon and other romance narratives unite in creating our experience of the cinematic frame in which its urban, globalised youth rediscover "romance."

Works cited

Dil Chahta Hai. Directed by Farhan Akhtar, performances by Saif Ali Khan, Aamir Khan, Akshaye Khanna, and Preity Zinta. Excel Entertainment, 10 August 2001.

Jaane Tu Ya Jaane Na. Directed by Abbas Tyrewala, performances by Imran Khan and Genelia D'Souza. Aamir Khan Productions, 4 July, 2008.

Om Shanti Om. Directed by Farah Khan, performances by Shah Rukh Khan and Deepika Padukone. Red Chillies Entertainment, 9 November 2007.

Selinger, Eric Murphy. "My Metatextual Romance: Thinking With (and About) *Jaane Tu Ya Janne Na.*" *Mosaic: A Journal for the Interdisciplinary Study of Literature* 47, no. 2 (2014): pp. 51–66.

3 Idiots. Directed by Rajkumar Hirani, performances by Aamir Khan, R. Madhavan, Boman Irani, and Kareena Kapoor. Vinod Chopra Films, 25 December 2009.

CHAPTER 6

IRRFAN KHAN: AN UNDERSTATED GENIUS

While the entire world was battling the lethal Covid-19 pandemic, a versatile actor of Indian cinema was silently battling a rare disease and breathing his last at Kokilaben Dhirubhai Ambani hospital, Mumbai. Detected with a cancerous neuroendocrine tumour, he fought until the last like a warrior and died a warrior's death on 29 April at the age of 53. He left the world when his career was at its peak and had he lived he would have given more gems to cinema. The loss of veteran actor Irrfan Khan has caused irreparable damage to the film industry and the gaping, unbridgeable void he has left us will stay with us in the decades to come.

Irrfan's entire life was a struggle trying to come to terms with his own failures and disappointments in the early stages of his then largely unsuccessful acting career. A graduate of the National School of Drama, he managed to bag a role in 1986 on the small screen. His arrival in the film world was as silent as his departure. Braving all odds, but never succumbing to disillusionment, he struggled relentlessly to give some shape to his initially unrewarding career. His determination and perseverance did not allow space for despair. An acting role in Mira Nair's *Salaam Bombay* (1988) did not bring him much visibility. Nevertheless, he tasted success with his international debut in the British Indian mythical adventure *The Warrior* (2001), the film serving to relaunch his film career.

Interestingly enough his friendship and collaboration with the diasporic film-maker Mira Nair worked to his advantage: Irrfan gradually found an opening and became a familiar face in Hollywood. His journey continued with films such as *Slumdog Millionaire* (2008), *Life of Pi* (2012), *Jurassic World* (2015), and *Inferno* (2016). Abroad, Irrfan had the opportunity to work with veteran actors such as Tom Hanks and directors such as Danny Boyle, Ang Lee, Michael Winterbottom, and Wes Anderson, to name only a few.

His career took a giant leap when he played the quintessential Indian father in Mira Nair's adaptation of Jhumpa Lahiri's *The Namesake*

(2006). Ashima (Tabu) agrees to an arranged marriage with Ashoke (Irrfan), but quite unlike the charming prince from a fairy tale, Ashoke does not sweep Ashima off her feet. Unlike present-day commercial film heroes, who are usually attractive metrosexual male types—handsome, with six-pack abs and chiselled jawlines—Irrfan was different, looking like a real-life person without the looks of a romantic lead.

Yet Irrfan proved that conventional good looks and a star background are not all that it requires to make it big in the industry. The first-generation immigrant father and husband of *The Namesake*—Irrfan as Ashoke Ganguli—by then had captivated hearts at home and around the world, through his moving portrayal of a quiet romance between two kindred souls. Blending modern love with traditional customs, Irrfan and his co-star Tabu took this diasporic film on migrants caught between two worlds to dizzying heights.

Irrfan often played a character in all its ordinariness, a trait unique to him, and he imbibed his ordinariness. He portrayed dismay without making it look dastardly, exhibited credulity without making it look like ignorance. The beginning of his recognition in India came with *Maqbool* (2003), the Mumbai film industry's attempt to culturally relocate Shakespeare's *Macbeth* to gangland Mumbai. Maqbool opened up fresh vistas for a staggering actor who was struggling to make his presence felt in a fiercely competitive film industry. Alongside a Don Corleone-like underworld don, Abbaji, played by Pankaj Kapur, Irrfan shared screen space as Kapur's trusted lieutenant, Maqbool. Together with many senior actors such as Naseeruddin Shah, Om Puri, and Kapur, Irrfan as a budding actor astonishingly displayed the confidence of a veteran. Something raw, something fresh was immediately noted in his performance.

Unafraid of exploring the potential of his craft, Irrfan plays the role of Maqbool in all its villainous, yet tragic, grandeur. His agitating mind, murderous motives, and palpable guilt-stricken persona struck a chord amongst Indian audiences. The critically acclaimed film earned accolades abroad where Irrfan was now well known to a Western audience. It is his acting prowess that made Vishal Bhardwaj's dark tale of violence, love, betrayal, and revenge so compelling. With Maqbool, Irrfan's career took a charismatic turn and he became a household name.

Irrfan blasted the myth that success is only assured to actors when they continuously perform in the genre to which they most conform. If Irrfan could leave his imprint in a gangster flick like *Maqbool*, his talent equally shone in a vast array of other genres: as the investigating cop Ashwin Kumar in the crime thriller *Talvar* (2015); in the biopic of a seven-times athletics champion turned violent Chambal valley rebel in

Paan Singh Tomar (2012), for which Irrfan won the National Award as best actor; or as the unconventional romantic hero in *Life in a ... Metro* (2007), *Piku* (2015), *The Lunchbox* (2013), or *Qarib Qarib Singlle* (2017), in which the poet Yogi (Irrfan) even makes fun of his own appearance.

Often intriguing is the way his rationality and romantic streak wrestle with one another as he seeks to find a fine balance. This came easily to Irrfan as he never ceased to experiment. When Irrfan played Monty in Anurag Basu's *Life in a ... Metro* as early as 2007, the audience knew that here was an actor who could think, act, and play the hero out of the box. Irrfan's portrayal of the not-so-charming yet ever so witty Monty is a sheer delight. A prospective groom to Shruti (Konkona Sen Sharma), he delivers earthy wisdom with ease and a characteristic sense of humour.

In *The Lunchbox*, Irrfan pulls it off with a measured pace and a classical restraint quite unlike in staple romance films. Saajan Fernandes may not be his most challenging role, but it was definitely the unique portrayal of a sturdy character actor. Graceful and dignified in his demeanour, the serious method actor's delicate performance makes this urban fable of hope very emotionally poignant. The idea of two solitary human beings, here a man with a frozen heart played poignantly by Irrfan and a woman, connecting with each other in a modern city yet remaining unknown to each other even as their intimacy grows through letters has a considerable old-world, epistolary charm. Irrfan, an actor par excellence, and Nimrat Kaur, with their quivering pent-up repressed emotions remind us of Celia Johnson and Trevor Howard in David Lean's classic *Brief Encounter*, a heart-wrenching saga of British restraint and repression.

With each film, Irrfan knew how to raise the bar. He was a man constantly creating, dismantling, and then reconfiguring his own benchmarks. Otherwise who else could have portrayed a solitary man's loneliness and grief combined with his languid demeanour with such dexterity in *The Lunchbox?* He could bring out a character's stern, gentle reserve that never truly abandons him with great finesse. He could with great emotional accuracy make visible the excitable poise of a new relationship. With no grand romantic gestures, no out of the way adventures or sentimental misunderstandings, Irrfan spoke volumes through his eyes and gestures. He could make palpable the silent thrills, pains, and tenderness of falling in love.

As the years passed by, there was a tremendous zeal on Irrfan's part to internalise the character he was playing, yet there was also a parallel distancing through which this thoughtful actor scrutinised his given roles to give us its unique Irrfanesque appeal. It was not entirely a director's version of a character. For a man of his calibre, no character was entirely scripted, yet paradoxically all the films that he acted in were written, it seems, with Irrfan in mind. Whether as Lafcadia in *The Warrior* (2001), as Raj Batra in *Hindi Medium* (2017), Rana Chaudhary in *Piku*, or as Rajit Ratha in *The Amazing Spiderman* (2012), his prolific acting skills never failed to impress. All these roles cemented his strengths and consolidated his achievements. Hollywood, however, failed to explore the true Irrfan. Unfortunately, his acting ability remained unexplored and to a certain extent under-utilised in Hollywood at his death.

The world witnessed an actor who would diligently observe, introspect, and then perhaps engage in a kind of dialogue with a "given" role on a philosophical level. The result was sheer magic on screen. His magnanimity shone with a rare brilliance unparalleled in commercial cinema. His acting prowess reminded us of art cinema and yet Irrfan was doing it effortlessly for mainstream commercial films. He brought a nuanced sensibility to "Bollywood" (a name he rightly objected to) with his nonchalant, casual, quintessentially understated acting style that Indian cinema embraced endearingly.

As Rohdaar in *Haider* (2014), Irrfan had told us "main tha, main hoon, aur main hi rahunga." In *The Namesake*, Ashoke's (Irrfan's) words to his toddler son Gogol, "Remember that you and I made this journey, that we went together to a place where there was nowhere else to go," sadly resonate in our hearts and haunt us today.

Confidence, wisdom, integrity, courage, and honour defined Irrfan's star persona, though Irrfan perhaps will be fondly remembered not as a star. Stardom was like an ill-fitted robe for Irrfan. He was not someone distant and afar but someone close to our hearts. He would rather prefer to be remembered as one of the finest actors of Indian cinema.

Works cited

Brief Encounter. Created by David Lean, performances by Celia Johnson and Trevor Howard. Eagle Lion Distributors, 1945.
Khan, Irrfan, performer. *Haider*. VB Pictures, 2014.
—, performer. *Hindi Medium*. Maddock Films, 2017.
—, performer. *Inferno*. Columbia Pictures, 2016.
—, performer. *Jurassic World*. Amblin Entertainment, 2015.
—, performer. *Life in a Metro*. Ishana Movies, 2007.
—, performer. *Life of Pi*. Fox 2000 Pictures, 2012.
—, performer. *Maqbool*. Kalaidoscope Entertainment, 2003–4.
—, performer. *Paan Singh Tomar*. UTV Spotboy, 2012.
—, performer. *Piku*. MSM Motion Pictures, 2015.

—, performer. *Qarib Qarib Singlle*. Zee Studios, 2017.
—, performer. *Salaam Bombay*. Channel Four Films, 1988.
—, performer. *Slumdog Millionaire*. Celador Films, 2008.
—, performer. *Talvar*. VB Pictures, 2015.
—, performer. *The Amazing Spiderman*. Columbia Pictures, 2012.
—, performer. *The Lunchbox*. DAR Motion Pictures, 2013.
—, performer. *The Namesake*. Mirabai Films, 2006–7.
—, performer. *The Warrior*. Film 4, 2001.

Chapter 7

Revisiting Mumbai Gangster Flicks: *Maqbool* in Perspective

Introduction

There have been several interesting cross-cultural film adaptations of *Macbeth* by film-makers from all over the world, yet little or no work had been done to adapt this play as an Indian film to an Indian context. Vishal Bhardwaj's *Maqbool* (2003), the first Bollywood adaptation of *Macbeth*, was an attempt by its director to recontextualise the Shakespearean play in an Indian context. The film foregrounds a local theme, making a specific political statement to its audience. What emerges is a reinvention of a Shakespeare play in the idiom of Indian language, of film culture, of primary traditions, and of the interests of Indian culture.

With *Maqbool*, Shakespeare revisits Bollywood, as the film ventures to appropriate and assimilate Shakespeare to Bollywood's gangster genre in modern-day Mumbai. This essay proposes to consider the film in the context of contemporary urban violence, establishing the critical and social territory within which *Maqbool* was produced and is consumed. I aim to identify how Shakespeare is updated and made relevant in a postcolonial Indian sociocultural milieu, given the contexts of violence and social unrest that pervade both the film and the Shakespearean play.

In the 1990s, with the Shakespeare film revival worldwide, directors like Kenneth Branagh, Franco Zeffirelli, Baz Luhrmann, and John Madden have attempted to popularise the Bard for a contemporary audience. With *Maqbool*, Vishal Bhardwaj admits, "Macbeth, in particular, can be adapted to fit any period or setting. The corporate world, politics, educational system or underworld."[1] This essay looks at *Maqbool* as a

---

[1] Roy, "Shakespeare, Post-modernism, Popular Culture and the Hindi Film: *Agnipath*—A Case Study." See http://www.geocities.com/postmodernism and cinema/shakespeare.html.

critical prototype of the 1990s/2000s gangster film that interestingly preserves the reconfigured parallels and overtones of the Shakespearean text. It concomitantly addresses contemporary discourses of criminality, gang violence, and political connections with the underbelly in contemporary urban India as part of its filmic discourse.

A brief history of Shakespeare films in Bollywood

Maqbool is not the first film to venture to Indianise the Bard. Such a claim is unfair, keeping in mind several earlier Indian films that have used Shakespearean storylines, motifs, and themes and assimilated the Bard to an Indian context. Shakespeare in fact occupies a unique position in the Indian film industry, as the Bard's plays have been a treasure house of ideas for several Bollywood films. For decades, the ingredients/*masala* of popular Bollywood mainstream cinema, as Amitava Roy identifies, have had their sources in the "Shakespearean formula of passion, perversion, sex, violence, melodrama, song, dance, the supernatural, revenge, multiple murders, mistaken identities, the intermingling of the grave and gay, the tragic with the comic" (Roy 2007). Such films include popular blockbusters of the romance genre like *Bobby* (dir. Raj Kapoor, 1973), *Henna* (dir. Randhir Kapoor, 1991), and *Qayamat Se Qayamat Tak* (dir. Mansoor Khan, 1998), all of which were variations of the *Romeo and Juliet* archetype. *Agneepath* (dir. Mukul Anand, 1990) uses "Shakespearean techniques of composition and even Shakespearean sequences."[1] Gulzar's *Angoor* (1982) acknowledges its debts to the Shakespearean original—the film recontextualises *The Comedy of Errors* in a modern Indian setting and was highly popular among its audience. With the dawn of the new millennium, Farhan Akhtar's debut directorial venture, *Dil Chahta Hai* (2001), a great box office hit of the "NRI genre," borrowed from Shakespeare's *Much Ado About Nothing*.

After *Maqbool*, Bhardwaj's venture continued with two more Shakespearean films to form a trilogy—*Omkara* (2006), an Indian appropriation of *Othello*, and *Haider*, an Indian appropriation of *Hamlet*. *Omkara* was followed by Vidhu Vinod Chopra's family drama *Eklavya* (2007), a loose adaptation of *Hamlet*.

Bhardwaj's *Maqbool* transfers Shakespeare to a Mumbai mafiosi *mise en scène* where a politics of lust and passion, combined with a saga of massacre, unfolds. Shakespeare is used as a backdrop and is readily assimilated to a pop cultural Indian context.

History of 1990s Bollywood gangster films

The Bollywood gangster genre of the 1990s may be considered a revitalised genre. As Jyotika Virdi observes in the essay "Deewar/Wall (1975): Fact, Fiction, and the Making of a Superstar," traces of the genre may be located as early as the 1950s in Bollywood classics with Chaplinesque heroes such as *Awaara* (dir. Raj Kapoor, 1951), and *Shri 420* (dir. Raj Kapoor, 1955). *CID* (dir. Raj Khosla, 1956), an experiment in Indian film noir is considered the first and one of the best modern Bollywood crime thrillers. After a temporary descent into criminality, the heroes of these films are shown to overcome their vices and are hopeful of the future. However, that hope gradually turns to disillusionment due to the prevailing social system almost twenty-five years after Independence.[2] The film world saw the rise of the angry man hero of the 1970s in a "benchmark film" like *Deewar* (dir. Yash Chopra, 1975), which perhaps paved the way for the "sophisticated, well-crafted and successful gangster films" of the 1990s, where the anger and despair of the 1970s was replaced by "deep cynicism" (Virdi 225–33).

Stacked with gangsters, Ramesh Sippy's *Sholay* (1975) is "a landmark in Indian cinema, forever changing the production and reception of popular cinema in the past twenty-five years"; it revises the Western gangster genre by including several local cinematic features and conventions (Gopalan 324). Gopalan asserts that Sippy's innovative cinematic style was fully developed a decade later by film-makers like Ram Gopal Verma and others. Verma, along with a host of new directors in the film industry of the 1990s, infused mainstream cinema with their directorial style, newly shaping and reviving the Indian gangster genre.

A spate of Bollywood action films of the 1990s/2000s featuring identifiable patterns in the unfolding of their narratives deploy similar stylistic aspects, *mise en scènes*, motifs, dialogue, thriller aspects, fights, chases, and gun-fuelled action sequences that help in the identification and development of the Bollywood gangster film genre. Bollywood films do not subscribe to genre conventions as mainstream Western films do because Hindi films often tend to blur genre distinctions by incorporating elements of love, romance, horror, song and dance sequences, and melodrama. As Kaushik Bhaumik observes, "According to them [some scholars], the main generic quality that distinguishes Bombay cinema from

---

[2] See Virdi (2009), "Deewar/Wall (1975): Fact, Fiction, and the Making of a Superstar," in *Global Bollywood*, ed. A. P. Kavoori and Aswin Punathambekar, 223–38. Oxford and New York: Oxford University Press.

all other cinemas is its peculiar mix of melodrama and music" (190). For several decades, Bollywood has concentrated on making films with all the required *masala* to cater to popular tastes and the requirements of its audience.

The Mumbai underworld workings of mafia dons and their connections to the Bollywood film industry were the recurrent theme of Ram Gopal Verma's gangster trilogy *Satya* (1997), *Company* (2001), and *Sarkar* (2007). Vishram Sawant's *D: Underworld Badshah* (2005), produced by Ram Gopal Verma, is a sequel to Verma's *Company* and foregrounds similar intentions. Viewed as slick action films, Verma's films are stylistically different from the "experimental" film *Black Friday* (2004) based on an original work titled *Black Friday: The True Story of the Bombay Blasts* by S. Hussain Zaidi and filmed by Anurag Kashyap. *Black Friday* attempts to tell the real story behind the 1993 serial blasts and the narrative of real-life underworld dons like Dawood Ibrahim and Tiger Meman who were responsible for the disaster.

Maqbool: real-life Indian gangsters and contemporary urban violence

The character of Abbaji (Pankaj Kapoor) in *Maqbool*, though suppressed, undoubtedly replicates the life of the underworld Mumbai-based mafia dons Dawood Ibrahim and Abu Salem and their gang, who are infamous as D-Company and are believed to provide ground support to jihadi terrorist groups like Lashkar-e-Taiba. The film stands out as an example of how Shakespeare could be contemporised and made relevant in an era when India was left devastated by the terrorist attack on Mumbai, now termed the 26/11 horror, which unfailingly reminds us of the 9/11 attack on the United States. A journey into the underworld crime world, the viewing experience becomes more meaningful if seen in the light of the terrorist attack in Mumbai. It has even been suspected, as per newspaper reports and crucially observed by Russia, that Dawood Ibrahim probably sponsored the Mumbai terrorist attack.[3] *Maqbool* released just five years

---

[3] "Dawood's Network Involved in Mumbai Attacks: Russia," *Economic Times* 18 December 2008, 19 December 2008, 5+. As this article reports: "Russia believes that underworld don Dawood Ibrahim was directly involved in the Mumbai terror attacks and his network was used by the terrorists to carry out the multiple attacks. Moscow, which has been sharing intelligence with New Delhi, further believes that Dawood's drug network, which runs through Afghanistan, was used to finance the terror attack."

prior to the Mumbai attack is a pointer in this direction. One may go back and watch the film in the light of the terrorist attack and delve deeper into its real significance.

Maqbool (Irrfan Khan) reminds us of Dawood Ibrahim's principal lieutenants in Mumbai, Mohammed Ali and Chhota Shakeel. Just as the Dawood racket thrives and the cops turn a blind eye in present-day India, so in *Maqbool*, where the don (Abbaji) and his lieutenant (Maqbool) rule and bathe in crime, the cops remain indifferent. The mafia clans are infamous for their notorious connection to the Bollywood film industry. This claim is later elaborated in the essay with reference to other films of the decade.

The two cops in *Maqbool* are almost treated as slaves by the mafia gang; sufficiently bribed, they consciously participate and support the criminal activities of the mafia family. The simple reason for this is that the cops enjoy their status as the caretakers of their nation and at the same time wish to consolidate their positions by maintaining their bond with the mafia power block. Abbaji and the mafia family remind us of other real-life mafia dons in India like Tiger Meman, Babloo Srivastava, Ejaz Lakdawala, and Mumbai gangster-turned-politician Arun Gawli (the inspiration for the character of Manoj Bajpai in *Satya*). Situating *Maqbool* in such a context, Bhardwaj quite rightly claims that "My film is not meant for Shakespeare scholars. . . . My interpretation is not text-bookish, . . . I have tried to be true to the play's spirit [rather] than to the original text" (Bhardwaj, Rediff Interview). Interestingly, there were even several Western films in the second half of the twentieth century, like William Reilly's *Men of Respect* (1990) and Ken Hughes's *Joe Macbeth* (1955), that were gangland ruminations on *Macbeth*.

Filmic representation of Bollywood's link with the Mumbai underworld

The trend of portraying real-life Indian gangsters and underworld dons through films perhaps begins with *Deewar*, in which the powerful Mumbai-based don Haaji Mastaan's life is paralleled in the narrative of the film and the life of the lead male character, Vijay. As Mohamed notes, Vijay's change from a working-class background to an underworld don is inspired by Haaji Mastaan's life. In later gangster films like *Parinda* (dir. Vidhu Vinod Chopra, 1989) and *Satya,* the film world witnessed the rise of stars like Nana Patekar and Manoj Bajpai. The real-life don Haaji Mastaan again features in late 1990s films and beyond as the old don: for example, he is shown to be physically challenged yet still in control but politely defied by his sons in *D: Underworld Badshah*. Mastaan is gradually replaced by younger-generation figures like Mallik (Dawood Ibrahim) and Chandu (Chota Rajan) in the critically acclaimed box office hit *Company* (2002). In the film, the actor Mohanlal plays the role of D. Sivanandan, the man who many believe was responsible for the downfall of Dawood in Mumbai.

The gang members in *Company* address the mafia operatives as *bhai* (brother); *bhai* is a term of endearment that strengthens the bond among gang members. The 1990s/2000 gangster films cited here along with *Vaastav* (dir. Mahesh Manjrekar, 1999),[4] which are believed to have been inspired by the life of Chota Rajan, may be seen as generic predecessors of *Maqbool*. Films immediately succeeding *Maqbool* include *Sarkar* along with Raj Kumar Santoshi's *Family* (2005). Ram Gopal Verma and Anurag Kashyap may also have influenced the Oscar-winning Danny Boyle film *Slumdog Millionnaire* (2009). Though not a film of the gangster genre, Boyle's film depicts the grim and horrifying realities of the Mumbai underworld.

Maqbool and a range of other generic films subtly comment on the multi-layered concealed interlinking of the Indian film industry with Dawood Ibrahim, the kingpin of crime and violence. In these films, there are explicit references to Bollywood's link to the transnationally connected underworld. In *Black Friday*, Tiger Memon and Dawood Ibrahim are shown to be working and operating from Dubai. As chief suspects in the Bombay blast of 1993, they escape to Dubai to avert arrest. In *Company*, the entire gang of Aslam Bhai escapes to Hong Kong. I shall analyse a single scene each from *Company* and *Sarkar* now to substantiate the fact that such films make it a point to highlight Bollywood's connection with the transnational Mumbai mafia.

A scene in *Company* shows Chandu (Vivek Oberoi) saving Mallik (Ajay Devgan), whose life is endangered by the sudden attack of a rival gang whose leader is Soorti. Here it should be noted that both Mallik and Chandu are working for the mafia don Aslam Bhai/Haaji Mastaan. Mallik and Chandu go to watch a film shoot sponsored by their "company." The scene showing the attack on Mallik in the actual film is followed by other shootings that result in the media highlighting Bollywood's links with the underworld; this points to how art is wedded to violence. The meta-language of such gangster films encompasses the subtle rendition of relations that allegedly exist between gangland

---

[4] *Vaastav* (1999), starring Sanjay Dutt, along with *Maqbool* draw inspiration from Ram Gopal Verma's *Satya*, for which Bhardwaj directed the soundtrack.

bosses—who are seen as clandestine sponsors of the Bollywood film industry—and the film-makers who make art. Thus, these films effectively portray the meta-narrative that binds the post-70s rise of gangland films with their post-90s reincarnation: the palpable and threatening presence of a violent underworld that is out to control Bollywood with an iron fist.

In *Sarkar*, while the title character (Amitabh Bachchan) is not an underworld don, the film does comment on the workings of the underworld. Sarkar's elder son, Vishnu (Kay Kay Menon), is shown producing a Bollywood film; he later forms ties with the underworld and kills the hero of his own film in a fit of rage. In the two films, the frame-within-a-frame and film-within-a-film structure highlight and bring to focus the director's jab, though tongue in cheek, at Bollywood's connection with the Mumbai mafiosi.

In a scene in *Maqbool*, the gang members of Jahangir Khan/Abbaji (Pankaj Kapur) discuss the choice of directors and producers for a film. One of them asks Nimmi/Lady Macbeth (Tabu) rather casually who she would prefer to have as director in the film. Subsequently Abbaji makes Maqbool/Macbeth the supervisor of the Bollywood film industry, as predicted earlier by one of the cops who is obsessed with astrology. In the Mumbai mafia community, the supervision of the film industry is considered a great honour and a recognition of one's services. (This is just one of a number of instances in which *Maqbool* engages with *Macbeth*—Macbeth becomes the Thane of Cawdor before he actually becomes the king). Within the terms of its appropriation, *Maqbool* finds innovative ways of reframing the concerns of the source text, becoming in the process a recontextualisation of Shakespeare.

Right after the 1993 Bombay Blast, the successful real-life actor Sanjay Dutt's connection with the underworld was suspected by the Bombay police, and the actor was arrested (and later released on bail) on charges of hiding weapons in his Mumbai residence. The horrifying murder of Gulshan Kumar, owner of the T-Series brand of audio and video cassettes, was believed to be the consequence of his supposed connection with the underworld. In 1993, the death of actress Divya Bharti, famous for *Deewana*, was related to her link with the Mumbai mafia. However, the last two instances circulated as rumours for which there is no substantial documentary evidence.

The Godfather remakes in Bollywood

The mafia don Abbaji/Jahangir Khan in *Maqbool* is drawn partially from Marlon Brando's Don Corleone character from the film's inspiration, *The*

Godfather. Indeed, both *Maqbool* and Verma's *Sarkar* may be seen to be indebted to *The Godfather* (dir. Francis Ford Coppola, 1972) and a range of other Hollywood and Western films. Ram Gopal Verma acknowledges his debt to Francis Ford Coppola, who inspired both the technical style and the story of *Sarkar* (Verma, Interview). Earlier in an interview, Verma confessed that he knew every shot in *Sholay* and *The Godfather*.[5] *Sarkar*'s gritty narrative fuses politics with the Mumbai underbelly. Sarkar, inspired by Coppola's Vito Corleone, is a powerful extra constitutional authority and almost exists as a parallel government. Sarkar's younger son, Shankar Nagre, is based on the character of Michael Corleone. His radical elder brother, Vishnu, who betrays his father and family, reminds us of Santino Corleone and Fredo Corleone. Yet, at the same time, Verma clarifies firmly that *Sarkar* is not an imitation. Its story and screenplay are located in an Indian milieu, particularly in the context of Mumbai's power superstructure. Verma states:

> this is my extremely personal and original take on the Mario Puzo novel. . . . Finally, I would state that *Satya* and *Company* were just preparatory blue prints for the film *Sarkar*. With this film [*Sarkar*], I hope that my trilogy on crime and punishment, within the reality of our country, our city and our neighbourhood, has come a full circle. (Ram Gopal Verma, Interview)

Research shows that Bollywood has a significant history of remaking Hollywood films and that it imitates foreign films. This unfortunate fact can in no way be overlooked.[6] There is also a similarity between *Maqbool* and Mike Newell's film *Donnie Brasco* (1997) in the situation where Lefty (Al Pacino) sees a young protégé in Donnie (Johnny Depp), which is mirrored with Abbaji in *Maqbool*. Abbaji finds Maqbool promising and nurtures him accordingly. Under Abbaji's tutelage, he is accepted in the Mafia family and it is decided that he will succeed Abbaji in taking charge of the thriving Bollywood film industry.

As a Bollywood film, *Maqbool* may be seen to resist Hollywood's imperialistic system. In such a context, the relation between *Macbeth* and *Maqbool* may be looked upon as a cultural translation, an exchange, not based on any hierarchical order. One may cite Walter Benjamin's

---

[5] Interview with Naseeruddin Shah, *Filmfare*, May 1998.
[6] With the release of the much-hyped Aamir Khan vehicle *Ghajini* (2008), which is rightly believed to be a copy of Christopher Nolan's *Memento*, and the Shah Rukh Khan vehicle *Rab Ne Bana Di Jodi* (2008), a copy of *Irma La Douce*, Bollywood to date cannot be freed from the charges of plagiarism frequently levelled against it.

statement that translation does not aim to recapture what is embedded in the original, but frees it to be symbolised in another language (53). In the Indianised appropriation, much of Shakespeare's text is disguised for the purpose of localisation.

Maqbool and cultural relocation

This section of the essay argues that the film narrative of *Maqbool* reminds a discerning audience of its literary original. One would hardly fail to overlook the continuous and consistent parallels with Shakespeare's play in the film. I shall therefore first cite Poonam Trivedi's observation in *Literature Film Quarterly* (2007) that *Maqbool*, surprisingly, retains all the major relationships and events of Macbeth (or distinct overtones from *Macbeth*): Duncan's/Abbuji's trust in Macbeth/Maqbool; the prophesying witches/cops who plant the seed of ambition; the seduction of Maqbool into treachery by his beloved wife/here Abbuji's mistress, Nimmi; the drunken guard; the killing of Abbuji in his sleep; the ensuing suspicion and fear; the poisoning of the bond with fellow captain/henchman, Banquo/Kaka, and his subsequent slaughter by Maqbool; the escape of his son Fleance/Guddu who survives to be the inheritor; the setting in of guilt and retribution; the hallucinating Lady Macbeth; the beguiled Macbeth; the avenger Macduff/Boti; and the tragic end (unusual for Bollywood).

However, a direct conflict within its diegesis results in quibbles which neither the film nor any of its characters are able to resolve. We wonder what the logic is behind implanting so much guilt and self-recrimination into Maqbool, who is used to such ruthlessness. What is interesting in the film is the shared body of the storyline and ideas with the Shakespearean text upon which the creative variation has been attempted. On the subject of Shakespeare appropriations, Julie Sanders observes that as spectators we must be able to participate in the play of similarity and difference between the source and appropriated film text (Sanders 46).

Among the numerous inversions of Shakespeare's text in *Maqbool*, one particularly significant one is the cops taking on the role of the witches and also providing comic relief like the porter in *Macbeth*. They also have traits of the Shakespearean wise fool. Interestingly enough, Shakespearean images are embedded in the film narrative of *Maqbool* at several significant points, acting as an explanatory comment of meaning.

Macbeth's concern with prophecy has parallels with the *kundali* (horoscope) designs in *Maqbool*. These designs further act as a signifier of forthcoming violence. Bhardwaj's use of visuals and patterns, especially in regard to Pundit's horoscope design, highlights the use of graphics in the film—the horoscope design smeared with blood predicting violence and death. The fate of Maqbool oscillates with the movement of the planets. In the opening shot, Mumbai's horoscope dissolves in a close-up shot of Maqbool's face, which is our first glimpse of him. In the film, the horoscope designs function metaphorically for the ways in which the human and natural worlds, the known and the unknown, interact to destroy the overreaching Maqbool.

The scene where Maqbool sits for a relaxed chat with the friendly cops/witches, and one of them, Pundit, intensely concentrates on the horoscope design may be interpreted as a scene of forthcoming violence in all its symbolic overtones. Some kind of arbiter of faith, the horoscope design in Bhardwaj's appropriation predicts both success and failure for Maqbool—that he will rule the underworld by dethroning Jahangir, but that one day Kaka's son, Guddu/Fleance, will inherit the dominion. Purohit/Second Witch warns, "Don't laugh. His tongue foretells evil." This foretelling has undercurrents of violence and is accompanied by insights of wisdom for the future course of events, as in Pundit's recurring comment—"Aag ke liye paani ka darr bane rehna chahiye" ("It's critical to maintain the balance of power in this world. Fire must fear water").

The recognisable motifs and signifiers in *Maqbool* are those of violence and the parallels with the source text—*Macbeth*—continue to persist. Let us take the scene where Nimmi and Maqbool are on their way to the mosque to offer prayers. She cunningly gets rid of Abbaji to plant the seeds of treachery in Maqbool's mind. As Nimmi talks to Maqbool, a loud raucous chatter of crows is heard, reminding us of Lady Macbeth's comment, "the raven himself is hoarse,/ that croaks the fatal entrance of Duncan/ Under my battlements" (*Macbeth* 1.5). Shakespeare's text remains a barely visible (but nonetheless significant) backdrop (Fischlin and Fortier 53). The scene culminates in a mosque and Shakespeare is wedded to the conventions and etiquettes of Islam. Nimmi exercises her sexual allure to seduce Maqbool and cultivates in him a sense of jealousy and disgust. Her hints that Guddu/Fleance is the next heir to Jahangir's chair ("Beta nahi hota to damaad hi waaris hota hai" ["In the absence of the son, the son-in-law is the heir"]) are manifestations of her psychosexual dominance over Maqbool.

Ben Jonson's famous observation that "Shakespeare was not of an age but for all time" is an indication that Shakespeare remains available to subsequent ages to adapt the Bard as they wish. "His cultural value lies in his availability" (Sanders 2007, 48). As Marsden notes, "each new generation attempts to redefine Shakespeare's genius in contemporary terms, projecting its desires and anxieties onto his work" (1).

The narrative of *Maqbool* has all the necessary *masala* to please its popular mass-market cinema audience. Also, "matching Bollywood's generic requirements, the director includes several song and dance numbers, which enforce the Hindu priorities of virginity, marriage and polarized gender roles" (Jess-Cooke 178). These are not only "Hindu priorities," but priorities that stem from a distinct Indian culture. Yet what makes *Maqbool* outstanding is the metaphoric and graphic depiction of violence. The horoscope design smeared in blood on the glass planes acts as a visual reminder of forthcoming violence—the murder of Abbaji, the images of blood, Nimmi's suffering at the sight of blood and the subsequent horror of her mind.

Maqbool portrays emotional exhaustion through visual clues acting as signifiers to the turmoil in Maqbool's mind. His rebuke of Ahmed for not cleaning the blood from animal slaughter and his subsequent hallucination at the sight of blood unfailingly recall the dagger soliloquy in *Macbeth* to an audience familiar with Shakespeare.

In the course of the narrative, Maqbool becomes "in blood/ Stepp'd in so far" (*Macbeth* 3.4) so that there is no turning back. The film's quest for images and parallels with its literary predecessor continues. The killing of Kaka/Banquo in the Kali temple is a gruesome act of violence by Maqbool's hired killers that is followed by the escape of Guddu/Fleance. The act of inflicting violence on Kaka and his failed attempt to kill Guddu only drowns Maqbool deeper in crime. The agonising scream of Sameera (a character without a Shakespearean parallel) at the sight of Maqbool is a moment where Maqbool has been converted into a tyrant in Sameera's subconscious mind. It serves to unleash a renewed sense of horror. As calamities and misfortune multiply for Maqbool, a quick succession of scenes follow that project the gradual downfall of Maqbool's domain. These scenes lead to a scene that shows the image of Maqbool's newborn baby fighting for life in an incubator.

Visual clues like the conscious selection of light remain unmistakable in Nimmi's moments of hallucination, in the intense scenes of her conscience being ripped apart. Again, such scenes are a re-creation of Lady Macbeth's sleepwalking scene. Towards the end of the film there is a close-up shot of Maqbool and Nimmi; the light used in this shot is a significant blue shade. The scene is captivating for its interplay of light and darkness. It depicts a world of guilt-stricken individuals desperately trying to make sense of their existence in a world of unpardonable sin they have delved into.

The haunting background score is riveting as it establishes the dark, film noirish mood of the film. The music is also a rich source to convey the trauma of tormented souls. Throughout the film, the background score recurs and deepens the mood of impending doom. The visuals and non-linguistic sounds evoke an aesthetic response to the depiction of violence. In the process they surpass the use of language for such a depiction. These techniques perhaps influenced Verma's *Sarkar*, in which sound is used to similar effect, and help convey meaning, as silence pervades much of the diegetic space.

Towards the end of *Maqbool*, the newborn child is lovingly cradled by Sameera and Guddu: the sight of the innocent newborn arouses Maqbool's emotions and makes him reach out in a gesture of self-surrender. The sight of the newborn almost kills his lust for power, revenge, and blood. Innocence succeeds in overpowering violence and the rejection of "horrid deed in every eye/ that tears shall drown the wind" (*Macbeth* 1.7) is here given its creative transposition. Tears stain the glass door through which Maqbool was stealing a glance at the newborn babe; perhaps, here Maqbool comes to the ultimate realisation of the futility of violence and bloodshed. The film ends with a close-up shot of Maqbool as Boti/Macduff shoots him, leaving the promise of redemption shattered. The sequence that ends with the death of Maqbool is the most sublime shot in the film—inflicting and projecting violence, this time on the killer, in all its sublimity.

Conclusion

In *Maqbool*, Shakespeare is wedded to an Islamic/Urdu tradition to announce the end of a world of violence. *Maqbool* embraces and depicts an intense attachment to Islam, the characters drawing heavily on the Urdu vocabulary. The gangsters are shown to be committed to and have full faith in Islam in their dress codes (head caps) language, codes, behaviour, and offerings of prayers while on a pilgrimage to the mosque. The scene in which Maqbool kneels on the ground and offers prayer to God a few days after the killing reveals his faith in Islam, which exists as a normative belief system in the film. The characters' adherence to the conventions of Islamic etiquette is made quite apparent.

In stark contrast to this Islamic discourse lies the Hindu discourse of the two cops who are fascinated with astrology, which is akin to witchcraft. Another Bollywood underworld film with such Islamic overtones is *Gangster* (dir. Anurag Basu, 2006), believed to be based on the mafia don Abu Salem (Shiney Ahuja) and his lover Monica Bedi (Kangana Ranaut). The film reminds one of *Maqbool* in its politics of violence, power, and passion and for its tragic undertones. *Gangster* is also akin to *Maqbool* in being a dark tale of violence, love, betrayal, and revenge.

Maqbool and the gangster films of the 1990s/2000 emerge as suspenseful tales of intrigue and shifting power relations, with conspiracies and deception all around. Yet *Maqbool* is stylistically and aesthetically different from other Bollywood gangster films of recent decades. A critical overview of films studied in this article proves that representational politics manifest a propensity to glamorise violence. Violence in human nature is instigated by greed for power, profit, and money. As a natural and effortless choice to avenge wrongs or as a betrayal of trust, violence in gangster films acts as a tool that is deployed by both criminal heroes and criminal villains. Screenplays and dialogue in such films tend to manipulate audience responses to which killings are justified and which are not, between deserved and undeserved acts of murder.

In its venture in the field of appropriation, *Maqbool* transports and absorbs Shakespeare within the cultural imaginary of a nation and clearly declares itself to be the "new Shakespeare" (Cartmell 2008). Its dark and disturbing critical commentary on *Macbeth* is achieved by transposing the theme of violence of the Shakespearean play—whether state authorised or personal—to a postcolonial, Indian, sociocultural milieu and the discourse that emerges, definitely critiques the politics of urban violence in India. In evoking an aesthetic response to representations of graphic and visual violence combined with its use of non-linguistic registers as metaphors for violence, within a moral framework, *Maqbool* redefines the periphery of the gangster genre and stretches the generic boundaries of globalised Bollywood's gangster films.

Works cited

Bamber, Martin. "Macbeth." sensesofcinema.com/2008/cteq/macbeth. Accessed 9 November 2008.

Benjamin, Walter. "The Task of the Translator." Translated by Harry Zohn. In *Illuminations*, edited by Hannah Arendt. Routledge, 1968, 69–82.

Bhardwaj, Vishal. The Rediff Interview, 2003. in.rediff.com/movies2003/nov/06vishal.html. Accessed 3 December 2008.

Bhaumik, Kaushik. "Consuming 'Bollywood' in the Global Age: The Strange Case of an 'Unfine' World Cinema." In *Remapping World Cinema: Identity, Culture and Politics in Film*, edited by S. Dennison and S. H. Lim. Wallflower Press, 2006, 188–98.

Cartmell, Deborah. "Film as the New Shakespeare and Film on Shakespeare: Reversing the Shakespeare/Film Trajectory." *Literature Compass* 3, no. 5 (2006), 3 March 2008. www.blacwell-compass.com/subject/literature/article_viewarticle_id=lico_articles_bpl375. Accessed 6 December 2008.

Fischlin, Daniel, and Fortier, Mark, eds. *Adaptations of Shakespeare: A Critical Anthology of Plays from the Seventeenth Century to the Present.* Routledge, 2000.

Gopalan, Lalitha. "'Hum Aapke Hain Kaun.'" *Asian Cinemas: A Reader and Guide,* edited by Dimitris Eleftheriotis and Gary Needham. Edinburgh University Press, 2008, 56–89.

Jess-Cooke, Carolyn. "Screening the McShakespeare." *Screening Shakespeare in the Twenty-First Century*, edited by Mark Thornton Burnett and Ramona Wray. Edinburgh University Press, 2006, 127–46.

Jorgens, J. J. *Shakespeare on Film.* Indiana University Press, 1977.

Kennedy, Dennis, ed. Introduction to *Foreign Shakespeare*: *Contemporary Performance.* Cambridge University Press, 1992, 2.

Marsden, Jean, ed. *The Appropriation of Shakespeare.* Harvester Wheatsheaf, 1991.

Muir, Kenneth, ed. *Macbeth.* Arden Shakespeare, 1997.

Rothwell, Kenneth S. (2000). *A History of Shakespeare on Screen: A Century of Film and Television.* Cambridge: Cambridge University Press.

Roy, Amitava. 2007. "Shakespeare, Post-modernism, Popular Culture and the Hindi Film: *Agnipath*—A Case Study." http://www.geocities.com/postmoderniosm and cinema/shakespeare.html. Accessed 25 September 2008.

Sanders, Julie. *Adaptation and Appropriation.* Routledge, 2007.

Trivedi, Poonam. "'Filmi Shakespeare.'" *Literature Film Quarterly*, 2007. www.findarticles.com/p/articles/mi_qa3768/is200704/ain19432570/pg 9html.

Verma, Ram Gopal. "We Didn't make the Film, It Made Itself." Interview by Sankhayan Ghosh. July 03, 2019.

Virdi, Jyotika. "Deewar/Wall (1975): Fact, Fiction, and the Making of a Superstar." *Global Bollywood*, edited by A. P. Kavoori and Aswin Punathambekar. Oxford University Press, 223–38.

Filmography

Agnipath. Directed by Mukul Anand, performances by Amitabh Bachchan, Mithun Chakraborty, and Danny Denzongpa. Dharma Productions, 16 February 1990.

Angoor. Directed by Gulzar, performances by Sanjeev Kapoor, Deven Verma, and Mousumi Chatterjee. A. R. Movies, 5 March 1982.

Black Friday. Directed by Anurag Kashyap, performances by Kay Kay Menon, Pavan Malhotra, and Aditya Shrivastava. Mid Day Multimedia, 13 August 2004.

Bobby. Directed by Raj Kapoor, performances by Rishi Kapoor and Dimple Kapadia. R. K. Films, 28 September 1973.

Company. Directed by Ram Gopal Verma, performances by Ajay Devgun, Manisha Koirala, and Vivek Oberoi. Varma Corporation & Vayjayanthi Movies, 12 April 2002.

D: Underworld Badshah. Directed by Vishram Sawant, performances by Randeep Hooda, Chunky Pandey, and Isha Koppikar. K Sera Sera & RGV Films, 3 June 2005.

Dil Chahta Hai. Directed by Farhan Akhtar, performances by Saif Ali Khan, Akshaye Khanna, and Aamir Khan. Excel Entertainment, 10 August 2001.

Donnie Brasco. Directed by Mike Newell, performances by Al Pacino, Johnny Depp, and Michael Madsen. Mandalay Pictures, TriStar Pictures, & Mark Johnson Productions, 28 February 1997.

Eklavya. Directed by Vidhu Vinod Chopra, performances by Amitabh Bachchan, Sharmila Tagore, and Saif Ali Khan. Vinod Chopra Productions, 16 February 2007.

Family. Directed by Raj Kumar Santoshi, performances by Amitabh Bachchan, Akshay Kumar, and Nawazuddin Siddiqui. Amitabh Bachchan Corporation ,13 January 2006.

Gangster. Directed by Anurag Basu, performances by Emraan Hashmi, Kangana Ranaut, and Shiney Ahuja. Vishesh Films, 28 April 2006.

Henna. Directed by Randhir Kapoor, performances by Rishi Kapoor, Zeba Bakhtiar, and Ashwini Bhave. R. K. Films Ltd., 28 June 1991.

Joe Macbeth. Directed by Ken Hughes, performances by Paul Douglas, Ruth Roman, and Bonar Colleano. Columbia Pictures, 18 October 1955.

Maqbool. Directed by Vishal Bhadwaj, performances by Irrfan Khan, Tabu, and Pankaj Kapur. Kaleidoscope Entertainment and NH Studioz, 30 January 2004.

Men of Respect. Directed by William Reilly, performances by John Turturro, Katherine Borowitz, and Peter Boyle. Columbia Pictures, 18 Jan. 1991.

Omkara. Directed by Vishal Bhardwaj, performances by Ajay Devgun, Saif Ali Khan, and Vivek Oberoi. Shemaroo Entertainment Ltd., 28 July 2006.

Parinda. Directed by Vidhu Vinod Chopra, performances by Anil Kapoor, Jackie Shroff, and Nana Patekar. Vinod Chopra Films, 3 November 1989.

Sarkar. Directed by Ram Gopal Verma, performances by Amitabh Bachchan, Abhishek Bachchan, and Kay Kay Menon. Ram Gopal Verma Films and Alumbra Entertainment and Lotus Film, 1 July 2005.

Satya. Directed by Ram Gopal Verma, performances by J. D. Chakravarthy, Urmila Matondkar, and Manoj Bajpayee. Ram Gopal Verma Films, 3 July 1998.

Sholay. Directed by Ramesh Sippy, performances by Dharmendra, Sanjeev Kumar, Hema Malini, Amitabh Bachchan, Jaya Bhaduri, and Amjad Khan. United Producers and Sippy Films, 15 August 1975.

The Godfather. Directed by Francis Ford Coppola, performances by Marlon Brando, Al Pacino, and Robert Duval. Paramount Pictures and Alfran Productions, 14 March 1972.

Qayamat Se Qayamat Tak. Directed by Mansoor Khan, performances by Aamir Khan and Juhi Chawla. Nasir Hussain Films, 1 March 1988.

Vaastav. Directed by Mahesh Manjrekar, performances by Sanjay Dutt, Paresh Rawal, and Namrata Shirodkar. Adishakti Films, 7 October 1999.

CHAPTER 8

NEGOTIATING INDIAN TRADITION AND MODERNITY: GLOBALISATION AND HINDI CINEMA

Hindi cinema is the most popular cultural discourse of modern India. This essay traces the specific historical conjuncture of India's entry into the transnational economy over the past twenty years, the centrality of NRIs to India traversing this deterritorialised space/identity, and the representation of the diaspora in the cultural imagery of Hindi films in an era of economic liberalisation and corporatisation. The essay discusses the Indian film industry's challenges operating in a deregulated global electronic mediascape since the era of globalisation swept India by storm in the 1990s.

The globalisation of Indian cinema is not an alien concept. It is not entirely new nor does it belong altogether to the 1990s and beyond. We are aware of the history of Indian cinema's flow worldwide. Indian cinema in the past has been characteristically influenced by world cinema, particularly European and Hollywood cinema.

In 1927, *Dil Farosh*, an adaptation of Shakespeare's *The Merchant of Venice* was released. Shakespeare films since then have operated dialectically, in their approach to the global/local question. Indian adaptations of Shakespeare were largely influenced by Parsi theatre. Today, Shakespeare's cultural capital has made him a remarkable asset to the market and has contributed to the global economy.

In the 1920s, the Indian film-maker and owner of Bombay Talkies Himanshu Rai made Indo-German collaborative films. In his films, "educated Hindu women" were represented by Eurasian actresses underlying the problem of representation. His film *Karma* (1933) was a collaborative venture with I. B. B. of England. *Achyut Kanya* (1936) was directed by a German director, Frank Osten. Foreign technicians were working for Indian cinema at times.

Hindi cinema gained an international presence when Chetan Anand's *Neecha Nagar* was recognised at the Cannes Film Festival in

1946. *Dharti Ke Lal* (1946), centred on the Bengal Famine, was an IPTA production; it was Indian cinema's first social-realist film and witnessed widespread distribution in the Soviet Union. In this way, Indian film gradually acquired a foothold in overseas markets. Socialist films like Bimal Roy's *Do Bigha Zameen* (1953) were sent to international film festivals.

Actors like Raj Kapoor and Nargis were popular beyond India with films like *Awaara* (1951) and *Mother India* (1957). They were popular in South Asia, the Soviet Union, Africa, Fiji, and the Middle East. It should be noted that the internationalisation of Bollywood occurred initially through non-Western worlds.

In Bengal, Satyajit Ray was drawn to independent film-making from the parallel cinema in Bengal. Ray met French film-maker Jean Renoir and was considerably influenced by Vittorio De Sica's Italian neorealist film *Bicycle Thieves* (1948). The Japanese director Akira Kurosawa and the Polish film-maker Andrzej Wajda also considerably influenced Ray. One must not overlook these historically significant periods, processes, and cultural exchanges in the history of Indian cinema's globalisation.

Pather Panchali (1955) was awarded the International Human Document award at the Cannes Film Festival in 1956. *Aparajito* was awarded the Golden Lion at the Venice Film Festival in 1956. Indian Cinema received recognition from the West. Ray's cinema was included in the category of world cinema, as a form of art cinema in contrast to the commercial and popular cinema associated with Hindi cinema's or Bollywood's formula films. This may not be the early phase of globalisation or what we understand as globalisation in the modern era but this was Indian cinema going global before the institutionalising of the overseas diasporic box-office.

The mainstream Bollywood film *Sholay* (1975), one of the most successful in the history of the Hindi film industry, borrowed from Sergio Leone, Akira Kurosawa, John Ford, and Sam Peckinpah.

During the era of Satyajit Ray, the film-maker faced constant financial constraints. If we refocus on history, we will see that studios in India, post-independence, were weakened by poor sales and rising fixed costs after the devastation of the Second World War. After the cataclysmic event of Partition in India, the studios were outnumbered by the new production companies. In a market of cut-throat competition, these companies outshone the old Indian studios; however, even the companies struggled for film finance. The struggle continued for five decades.

These small production companies did not enjoy a cordial relation with financiers, unlike the studios. Gradually, production companies came up with film formulas that endearingly came to be known as the "masala films" or formula films of Bollywood. These masala films were a spicy mix of romance, drama, comedy, action, and song and dance sequences. Miraculously, this new Bollywood formula with music and dance numbers, melodrama, lavish productions, emphasis on stars, iconic stars, and spectacle appealed to the majority of Indians across regional, social, cultural, and religious divides. This formula proved its market value by being commercially viable and was therefore pursued by generations with slight variations and refinement.

Gradually, with economic liberalisation in 1991, globalisation affected Mumbai's culture industry and cinema in a completely new dimension. The economic tidal wave of globalisation almost took the world by storm. Globalisation resulted in further cultural diversity and hybridised identities. India witnessed the advent of cable television and the phenomenal growth of satellite television in the 1990s. It started rapidly changing viewer's world views. Foreign images, dubbed American films, new images from the advertising industries, and MTV "Most Wanted" shows were now part of Indians' daily viewing experience. A key dimension of globalisation is connectivity and a flourishing global network. Globalisation made way for the creation of a global mass market for mainstream films. The gradual shift from video to satellite television, DVD, the internet, and the downloading of films allowed producers of even niche films to reach audiences around the world.

Mumbai's Hindi-film culture industry, since globalisation, entered a new economic, social, and cultural arena where its representations included a larger community. Indian film now had new overseas audiences in the United Kingdom, United States, West Asia, and other countries. This shared cultural space that Hindi cinema provides keep all communities connected to a shared cultural past—not only Indians, Bangladeshis, Pakistanis, or Hindus, Muslims, and Sikhs, but also for instance the vast heterogeneous South Asian communities in the United Kingdom. This has also accounted for the emergence and rise of Bollywood as a culture industry. Indian films like Sanjay Leela Bhansali's *Devdas*, Ashutosh Gowariker's *Lagaan*, and Karan Johar's *Kuch Kuch Hota Hai* were more popular in the United Kingdom than in India. Karan Johar's *Kabhi Alvida Na Kehna* (2006) was more popular in the United States than in India. All these films had a considerable impact on the vast South Asian diasporic community.

Since the 1990s, in the international market, Bollywood saw a sudden growth in export earnings from Indian immigrants settled abroad in North America, the United Kingdom, and a range of Arab countries. Soon after, markets in East Asia and in countries such as Singapore and Australia began to rise. The diasporic community started making large investments in Bollywood and new immigrants gave rise to a profitable export market because their capital was much higher than those of Indian home consumers or old Indian diasporas.

In 2001, the size of the old and new Indian diasporas combined was estimated to be twenty million people globally. Now, South Asian diasporic settlers scattered all over the globe who were in a position to invest started to directly participate in Bollywood, not just as consumers but as investors in productions and infrastructure, leading to what we understand as consumer co-creation. Affluent members of the South Asian diaspora in the United Kingdom, United States, and Australia now made significant contributions to the growing market of Indian films. Diasporic businessmen craving a connection to their homeland channelled their emotions by investing in Bollywood film productions. This investment gave them a sense of responsibility, of belonging to India and re-establishing severed cultural relations.

Production finance came from business entrepreneurs attracted by the glamour of the entertainment industries. NRIs (people of Indian origin domiciled abroad) were actively courted by the Indian government with attractive investment schemes. Such NRI investment combined with the construction of multiplexes all over India only helped strengthen Bollywood's external and internal economies.

International markets played a key role in revamping globalised Mumbai's Hindi-film culture industry. The rising demand of the diaspora for Bollywood films made it viable to invest in distribution and exhibition abroad. Bollywood was earning revenue from distribution in overseas markets. This led to the consolidation of new international markets for the Indian film industry, especially in the West. When a film is declared a hit at the box office, it leads to substantial profit for producers, production companies, distributors, and private investors.

Since the 1990s there has been a paradigm shift in film narratives as well as film-related industrial practices in India. Despite its hundred-year-plus history, Indian cinema was granted official industry status by the Indian government only in 2001. Earlier, in the 1980s, the large-scale presence and size of mass audiences in single-screen cinema halls determined the commercial success of films. Abruptly, such day-to-day practices became irrelevant to the emerging new Bollywood cinema. At the time of writing, in a Covid-19 world, single-screen cinema halls in metropolitan cities are suffering the most. However, multiple windows of distribution that are now available are altering the industries' distribution practices: worldwide releases, telecast rights, DVD releases, product-placement deals, music sales even before the film is released, merchandising spin-offs, and so on. All these are sources of free-flowing revenue.

Independent distribution companies like Eros, Shemaroo, and Reliance Entertainment were also investing rapidly in the Indian film industry. Bollywood's external and internal economies were being strengthened by tremendous investments from Mumbai's booming telecom, software, and media conglomerates. In the past, Steven Spielberg entered into a partnership with Anil Ambani (then financially solvent) and their professed aim was to cater to a global audience.

A rapidly growing middle class, which was also a fast-growing consumer class in India, was rapidly expanding the market. With new economic reforms introduced by the Narsimha Rao government, with Manmohan Singh as finance minister, there was a remarkable shift in the government's policy.

By the end of the 1990s, Indian state governments had begun cutting entertainment taxes. The formal liberalisation of cinema since the late 1990s has allowed it to benefit from actual rewards in the form of lower production charges, tax benefits, and film-makers accumulating production finance from banks and other corporate financial institutions, thereby according it a legitimate economic and symbolic status. Indian film production companies have urged the Indian government to seek to formalise co-production treaties with other countries. Gradually India has entered co-production agreements with other countries, which has helped the countries involved to borrow technically qualified workers at a multitude of shooting locations. For instance, Film France, a French government initiative co-produces quality films with India and other South Asian countries. *Dheepan* (2015), a recent film about Sri Lankan Tamil refugees in Paris by Jacques Audiard, gained acclaim at the Cannes Film Festival.

Production houses solely from India have their own preferences. In productions by Sooraj Barjatya, emphasis is on the centrality of the family. Barjatya's blockbuster hits like *Hum Aapke Hai Koun . . !* (1994) and *Hum Saath Saath Hai* (1999) are epic family dramas foregrounding family conflict. Family drama was again back with Aditya Chopra's *Dilwale Dulhaniya Le Jayenge* (1995) and Karan Johar's *K3G* (2001). In the family dramas of the mid 1990s, the focus was on anxieties surrounding achieving romantic couplings or couples struggling to attain a desired partner.

After the onset of globalisation, the dominant narrative featured in most of the films centres on an upper-middle-class or NRI family. Directors like Yash Chopra, Aditya Chopra, and Subhash Ghai made films with NRI Indians in mind. Such films with particular filmic codes and styles not only appealed to NRIs abroad but also to non-Indians or South Asian communities who had been displaced from their homelands.

Films like *Dilwale Dulhaniya Le Jayenge*, *Kal Ho Na Ho*, and *Kabhie Khushi Kabhi Gham* all predominantly featured NRI (non-resident Indian) characters. *Dilwale Dulhania Le Jayenge* (1995) is perhaps the foundational text for modern diasporic films. *DDLJ* narrates the diasporic experience of a family that has relocated to the United Kingdom. The film is a clear departure from monolithic classifications of NRIs as either longing for their homeland or morally depraved. Shah Rukh Khan as Raj represents an NRI figure who has, to a degree, negotiated being both Indian and English.

Raj, the NRI hero of the film, remains "Indian at heart" and Western in wealth to render his precarious location in relation to the nation state and global capitalism. In this film, Indianness is now determined by geopolitical location or wealth, and also by performance (maintenance) of religio-cultural and "traditional Indian values" and morality that encapsulate the "real India." Raj in *DDLJ* remains morally "Indian" and, in doing so, immediately changes the story from an innocent love story to a love story infused with the traditional values of the homeland. In making his choice to respect tradition, he is the unconventional new hero-figure, the NRI who not only found prosperity in the diaspora but has maintained the essence of India within him abroad. It is a radical film for its time, because it treats the diaspora as a new cultural space where Indian values can be transported and negotiated by a willing, extrovert NRI. But a lack of autonomy and agency is distinctly noted in the female character, Simran.

In *DDLJ*, home is produced not only as a territory, community, nation-state, and place (rural Punjab as a metonym of India), but also as a structure of feeling associated with a particular time for the older non-cosmopolitan generation represented by Simran's father Baldev. Feeding the pigeons in the United Kingdom and back home in Punjab is a metaphor for diaspora, movement, and mobility. The lush green, gold-speckled fields of rural Punjab stand in for the nation and national culture. Punjab is embodied by feminine figures adorned in colourful costumes, with scarves swaying in the fields calling home the *pardesis* (those overseas) through dance and song. Here India and the United Kingdom are distinct. India is represented by a modern yet traditional village community, vibrant and colourful, contrasting sharply with the United Kingdom, which is seen in terms of the alienating, cold, urban cityscape of London. This opposition and distance is deconstructed only towards the end.

Baldev wants a groom for his daughter who is a born-and-bred Punjabi, not someone like Raj, who has been raised in the United Kingdom and has inherited, as he believes, certain "Western vices." Baldev's daughter apparently, therefore, is faithful to Indian codes of womanhood; however, such faithfulness is also successfully problematised in the film.

Bollywood reinforces the notion that Indian men's cultural authenticity remains predicated on their ability to control their women. Baldev's control (his disciplinary and controlling gaze directed at his two daughters) is central to his mission to keep Hindustan alive in London, which has manifested in his ability to control his daughters.

Raj, the cosmopolitan, NRI hero, who wears a leather jacket, rides a motorbike, and easily tricks Baldev by stealing a bottle of beer from his shop, must convince Baldev of his cultural Indian background in order to win Simran's hand. This is how a homeland–hostland binary is played out in *DDLJ* and the film gestures to how such binaries are erased as Raj (who is highly cosmopolitan and Westernised) is after all the "real" Indian.

When *Don* was released in India and in export markets in 2006, it was an immediate blockbuster. A remake of an iconic Amitabh Bachchan popular hit, it was dubbed into six Indian languages. It topped the list with its huge overseas marketing budget of USD 1.9 million and in return it earned USD 2.2 million overseas. For such films, a stronger distribution network is now visible that is used for aggressive marketing. Marketing infrastructure is being developed to target diaspora audiences and pave the way for Bollywood's glorious presence at international film festivals. Mainstream European and US TV channels and international film festivals are now beginning to purchase Bollywood films. One should not forget Karan Johar's export success with his films like *Kabhi Khushi Kabhi Gham* (2001), *Kabhi Alvida Na Kehna* (2006), or *Kuch Kuch Hota Hai* (1998).

Bollywood not only is nationally popular and globally successful but also is one of the most important cinemas of the world. It is a global cinema that consciously positions itself against the hegemony of Hollywood. It has been and continues to be an international cinema familiar to viewers from the Middle East to Russia and to parts of Africa. More recently, with the transnational migration of South Asians as part of globalisation,

Bollywood too has been reterritorialised with an increasing presence in North America and Europe. Bollywood has proved itself successful for translocal, cosmopolitan, and diasporic viewers. Expectations are high for the diasporic and crossover appeal of Bollywood and diasporic cinema and attendant productions for cosmopolitan and Western audiences.

It is therefore not surprising to see the increasing commercial success of Indian films in Britain and North America. Films like *Kuch Kuch Hota Hai, Hum Aapke Hain Koun . . !, DDLJ, Devdas,* and *Taal* have consistently appeared in the annual list of top twenty most popular foreign language films in Britain during the turn of the millennium. For instance, *Kuch Kuch Hota Hai* was the top grossing foreign language film in 1998, earning almost 1.5 million pounds. In 2002, the BFI (British Film Institute) launched "Imagine Asia," its programme of South Asian and diasporic films. This programme was designed to boost the visibility and presence of and recognise the significance of South Asian cinemas. One is reminded of Bollymadrid, a festival in Spain that celebrates Bollywood and mainstream Hindi cinema in Spain.

Subhash Ghai's *Pardes* (1997) chronicles the journey of an Indian to America. Since globalisation, Indian cinema has often featured corrupt Indian American characters on screen who are notable for their irreverence towards "Indian traditional values" once they have settled abroad. At the same time, these films as cultural texts are the bearers of a message that Indian cultural values and morality are assets that the Indian diaspora may carry with them while they are trying to relocate to foreign countries or adapting to a foreign culture.

The female protagonist in *Pardes*, aptly named Ganga, arrives in the United States as an immigrant bride. She is represented as a repository of cultural integrity while she is temporarily uprooted from her homeland. In *Kabhi Khushi Kabhi Gham* (2001) and *Kal Ho Na Ho* (2003), Indian diasporic women carry their "Indianness," or carry Indian tradition, with them to foreign shores. Their dress, customs, adherence to rituals, and religion are signifiers of their strong connection to India.

Issues faced by Indian American families are often central to these films. In *Dostana* (2008), two immigrant men pretend to be a gay couple to flout immigration laws. *My Name Is Khan* (2010) and *New York* (2009) (set from 1999 to 2008) dramatise the discrimination and violence South Asian Americans experienced after the 9/11 attacks and their aftermath.

The large-scale popularity of Karan Johar's films and *Kal Ho Na Ho* (2003) influenced the views of South Asian American youths on fashion, family, religion, and race. These films are now important cultural texts for second-generation immigrants.

The trope of NRIs reaching out to India is no longer the territory of upper-class, wealthy Indians, nor is it restricted to returning home from the West to parts of northern India. The South Indian film industry regularly makes films on middle-class Keraleans returning from Gulf countries. The phenomenon is similar in Tamil cinema, where Tamils are shown returning from host countries abroad. The lifestyle of an Indian who has settled abroad was the subject of films like *Kaho Naa . . . Pyaar Hai*, *Taal*, *Kites*, *Murder*, *Don*, and so on. Now, mobile Indian-origin NRIs are spread all over the globe. Initially visible in the United Kingdom, Fiji, and North America, NRIs may now be found in large numbers in Australia, New Zealand, South Africa, the Czech Republic, Egypt, and Morocco, as well as in transnational areas of Southeast Asia.

In an era of globalisation, images of consumer culture are increasingly used to negotiate between modernity and tradition. Glamour is commoditised and sold as a dream to aspiring youths. In Madhur Bhandarkar's *Fashion* (2008), Meghna Mathur (Priyanka Chopra) is new to the world of modelling. The phenomenal success of a small town girl perpetuates the notion that such dreams of glamour are within the consumer's grasp. The film reiterates the idea that photography and electronic and print media surrounding the fashion/film industry continue to perpetuate the voyeuristic gaze of consumer culture.

Alongside the new issues of travel, tourism, and consumerism, the focus in *Dil Chahta Hai* (2001), however, was on male bonding. The film gave rise to a number of friendship films or "buddy movies" that followed suit like *Dostana*, *Zindagi Na Milegi Dobara*, *Cocktail*, *Yeh Jawani Hai Deewani*, and so on. These friendship films, of which *Dil Chahta Hai* was the trendsetter, present Mumbai's urban culture as hybrid and complex, merging cultural specificities with larger youth subcultures. *Dil Chahta Hai* is a film about the Indian diaspora in Australia. The film is a witty celebration of contemporary urban youth culture at the turn of the millennium. The film found eager young audiences in India but also in the diasporic community of affluent NRIs around the world. The film is a template for an increasingly globalised, sleek, stylised, youth-oriented contemporary Bollywood cinema. Anurag Kashyap's post-global Bollywood *Devdas* adaptation, *Dev D* (2009), also represents such urban youth subcultures.

Music played a leading role in making the pioneering global Hindi film *Dil Chahta Hai* a watershed in Hindi cinema, with its refreshing take on romance and the parental role in romance. The Hindi film songs in

Farhan Akhtar's debut combined music styles from across the globe, such as Australian Aboriginal didgeridoo music, rock, light jazz, pop, and hip hop in the "Jaane Kyu Log Pyar Karte Hai" song sequence, particularly during the helicopter crane shot above Sydney Opera House. Films such as this are all shot in iconic diasporic locations like New York, London, Dubai, or Sydney. Such wild mixing of musical styles is a new phenomenon in Hindi film songs. Again, *Dil Chahta Hai* may be read as a loose adaptation of Shakespeare's *Much Ado About Nothing*.

Bollywood song and dance sequences have always been the key to the production and consumption of such films. In the song sequence "Jaane Kyu Log Pyar Karte Hai," the imaginary does not disrupt the narrative, nor is it a space where the characters act out a fantasy. Rather the sequence discusses the advantages and disadvantages of falling in love, the pitfalls involved in romance. The lyrics form a logical argument and take recourse in counter logic and persuasion as the potential lovers treat this song sequence as a space for negotiation.

Recent Hindi film music is now more open to foreign musical aesthetics, increasing musical blending and fusion from composers of the past and present from India and abroad. Often this sonic resemblance to a Western sound and tune is explicitly quoted, representing and simultaneously acknowledging a cross-cultural recognition that music comes from the heart, that music can effortlessly transcend artificial borders and boundaries. The overwhelming effect of love and its universal appeal is summed up in Elizabeth's love for Bhuvan in *Lagaan* as she sings "I am in love."

With the advent of globalisation, its quick spread, and the cross-border movement of NRIs between Europe, the United States, Canada, and India, the contrast between the "Indianness" of popular Hindi film music and its foreign counterparts is gradually being erased. Yet the presence of such elaborate song and dance sequences is a means of cultural assertion, in order to hold on to something that Bollywood may claim as its own. Asserting "Indianness" is also Bollywood's way of countering Hollywood's global domination of the film industry. This is how the Indian film industry tries to counter the challenges of globalisation, re-emphasising the idea that globalisation does not necessarily entail a Westernisation of culture.

Zoya Akhtar's *Zindagi Na Milegi Dobara* (2011), a friendship film effortlessly foregrounding travel, tourism, and consumer culture, is distinctively Indian, but with styles and narratives resembling Hollywood, like another Hindi film, *Don* (2006). Such films appeal to Western and Indian audiences alike. Moving away from the "masala" films or "formula movies" that Bollywood produced in the 1970s and 80s, global Bollywood since the turn of the new millennium is more hi-tech using special effects and Western-style cinematography, and blending Western and neo-ethnic Indian cultures effortlessly, both in India and on foreign shores.

Engagement with rural subjects and their subjectivities (except for *Lagaan*, 2001, in mainstream cinema) or documentary dramas like Anusha Rizwi's *Peepli Live* (2010), a film on farmer suicides, are gradually being relegated to the background. Mainstream Bollywood now focuses more on stories of yearning for upward global mobility.

In the 1970s and 80s the dominant form of cinematic masculinity was the image of the "angry young man." Amitabh Bachchan was the star of Hindi cinema. His was a carefully constructed screen persona of the angry young man. The masala films in which Amitabh played the hero usually had the following components: big city underworld crime, martial arts, exaggerated fight scenes with hitting noises, car stunts, alluring cabarets, dance sequences with dozens of extras, comedy, romance, and family melodrama.

Films in which "Big B" featured as heroes gave voice to anti-establishment frustration and anger felt by the subaltern classes, while simultaneously denoting a cultural style and subjectivity acceptable to middle-class audiences. His masala films popular with the urban working class, like *Deewar* (1975) and *Muqaddar Ka Sikander* (1978), were about the inefficiency and corruption of Indian life and the hero's subsequent disillusionment. The angry young man hero thematised social and economic conflicts, which characterised the postcolonial Indian state; his screen persona asserted a political vision for the state to uphold.

Since then, Amitabh Bachchan has acted as a leading player in the global expansion of Hindi cinema, not only as a star or popular icon but in his leading role in real life in the corporatisation of the industry (Amitabh Bachchan Corporation Ltd.), thereby securing a transnational presence for the Indian film industry.

Yash Raj Films is another of the most successful companies, which has had a huge turnover and acted as a business model. With such professionalism and professional marketing practices, Indian cinema has gained a wider transnational visibility. In the last fifteen years, Hindi cinema has found an unexpected niche in European markets. In Germany, annual Bollywood festivals began in 2008, pointing to the growing popularity of Hindi films abroad. In London, they have had "Kuch Kuch Bollywood" nights in nightclubs after Karan Johar's *Kuch Kuch Hota Hai* found crossover appeal in the United Kingdom.

Women film-makers have provided fresh perspectives on the Indian film industry. The films of diasporic women film-makers like Deepa Mehta, Mira Nair, and Gurinder Chadha are some instances. Their films largely appeal to a global audience, with films such as *Monsoon Wedding*, *Bend It Like Beckham*, *Bride and Prejudice*, *Salaam Bombay*, *Fire*, *Water*, and *Earth* gaining popularity as well as critical acclaim. These directors are all diasporic and reside abroad. Their success made way for co-productions with leading Bollywood companies, with films like *Bollywood/Hollywood* (2002), *The Namesake* (2006), and *The Reluctant Fundamentalist* (2012).

The recent Indian Shakespeare adaptations—films such as *Maqbool* (2003), *Omkara* (2006), and *Haider* (2014)—are markers of a new global cinema rather than the destruction of local cultures. These films may be viewed in relation to Shakespearean play texts as well as in relation to popular culture, indigenous culture, and media technologies, examining the ways Shakespeare has been manufactured in the present day.

Omkara is an appropriation of *Othello* and uses gangland Uttar Pradesh as its setting. The appropriation indulges in gender issues, caste and communal politics, clan rivalries, and gang culture to explore universal human emotions. *Haider*, an adaptation of *Hamlet*, interestingly recontextualises the setting to 1990s conflict-driven Kashmir.

Shakespeare adaptations in post-2000 India have shown the creation of a global cinema rather than the destruction of indigenous cultures. Indian Shakespeare adaptations in the new millennium have shown the hybridity of contemporary film-making practices. They have alerted us to the intersections of the local and the global. Loose adaptations of *Romeo and Juliet* like *Ishaqzaade*, *Issaq*, and *Ram-Leela* are films that surpass regional concerns, attempting to preserve the local in the language of the global. Shakespeare has become global because of the ability of his works to be adapted to thousands of varied locations, including Asia. Therein lies Shakespeare's universality, marketability, and global cinematic appeal.

With globalisation what has emerged is a kind of Hindi global cinema that has successfully reached out to the diasporas, the Indian home market, and Western audiences. This kind of cinema is competing with Hollywood big-budget blockbusters and Western-style products in the multiplex, not only in India but overseas.

When Aamir Khan's *Dangal* (2016) was released it was the most successful non-Hollywood release ever in China. Though Aamir Khan was popular in China for films like *3 Idiots* (2009) and *PK* (2014), the runaway success of *Dangal* in China prompted Chinese production companies to turn their gaze from the West to the East. Given China's huge market potential, it is indeed to Bollywood's advantage that Chinese companies have now expressed eagerness in engaging in partnership and distribution rights with Bollywood. In India, there is concern about China's economic impact on India, growing military power, and relationship with Pakistan, and over Chinese and Indian territorial disputes. Despite these concerns, Bollywood has made a place of its own in the huge Chinese market.

The challenge for the Indian film industry in an era of globalisation lies in preserving a sense of uniqueness that we may identify as home culture, preserving its Indianness while still being open to a globalised system. At a time when Indian cinema is far more diverse than it has ever been in the past, Bollywood is attempting to hold on to the idea of an essence of Indian cinema. Indian cinema's marketability is becoming a matter of Indianness. No wonder that Bollywood keeps alive a sense of continuity amidst change.

Works consulted

Bouka, Eleni, Merkouri, Maria-Marina, and Theodore Metaxas. "Identifying Bollywood as a Crucial Factor of India's Economic Development: A Review Analysis." *MPRA Working Paper Series*, University Library of Munich, 2015.

Lorenzen, Mark. "Go West: The Growth of Bollywood." *Creative Encounters* 26. Copenhagen Business School, 2009.

Majid, Sabita. *Manufacturing Global Indianness: Bollywood Images, 1995–2005*. Simon Fraser University Archive, 2008.

Miller, Jonathan R. "The World and Bollywood: An Examination of the Globalization Paradigm." *Anthós* 7, no. 1, article 5, 2015.

Pillania, Rajesh K. "The Globalization of Indian Hindi Movie Industry." *Management* 3, no. 2 (2008): 115–23. University of Primorska, Faculty of Management Koper.

Poduval, Satish. "Introduction: Globalisation, the National-Popular, and Contemporary Indian Cinema." *Zeitschrift für Anglistik und Amerikanistik: A Quarterly of Language, Literature and Culture* 57, no. 1, 15 March 2014.

Part 2

At the Crossroads of Adaptations

CHAPTER 9

CLASSIC SHAKESPEARE CINEMA AND AUTEUR DIRECTORS

1

Shakespeare on film has had an impressive international profile and a strong global reach for over a century. The Anglo-American version of the Shakespeare film was shaped by auteur directors like Laurence Olivier, Orson Welles, and Kenneth Branagh. The other three international film-makers who have most shaped Shakespeare to the traditions of their own cultures are the Japanese film-maker Akira Kurosawa, the Soviet film-maker Grigori Kozintsev, the Italian film-maker Franco Zeffirelli, and the Indian film-maker Vishal Bhardwaj. Among several major directors who contributed to the Shakespeare on screen debate after the silent era but prior to globalisation were Joseph Mankiewicz, Roman Polanski, and Peter Brook. *King Lear* adaptations are not discussed in this article because they will be discussed in chapter 10, "King Lear on Redemption or Apocalypse Road: Kozintsev, Kurosawa, Brook, and Levring."

Laurence Olivier's *Hamlet* (1948) has been seen as the most "Freudian" and psychological interpretation of the play. It blends theatre with film in such a fashion that the two can hardly be distinguished. The incest between mother and brother-in-law is actually a reflection of Hamlet's repressed desire to kill his father and marry his mother. It perhaps remains the most influential Shakespeare film ever made. Olivier had played Hamlet on stage, in both England and Denmark, some ten years before the film. The entire film makes use of fog and deep shadows. Olivier's Castle Elsinore is maze-like, stony, and cold because of the brooding *mise en scène* and baroque style. The visual style of Olivier's film owes much to the film noir genre. Full of gothic ambience, the castle has huge rooms, winding staircases, dark corridors, and long vistas through receding archways.

Its ethos works in Olivier's film to highlight the corruption of the Danish court and, at the same time, to contribute to the atmosphere of mystery, intrigue, and surveillance in the play. Olivier makes drastic cuts to the play's text to transform it into a screenplay. Olivier erases Rosencrantz and Guildenstern, Fortinbras, Francisco, Reynaldo, and the second gravedigger. The voice-overs reveal Hamlet's innermost thoughts. But he does not confide much to the audience who are eavesdropping, overhearing his thoughts and feelings. Olivier's final leap down onto the king from a fifteen-foot height before killing him had an appeal of its own, reminding one of Olivier's 1937 stage production that was even more gymnastic. The boundaries of theatrical and filmic space are very deftly handled.

In India, Olivier's *Hamlet* deeply inspired Kishore Sahu's *Hamlet* (1954). The dark interiors, misty battlements, framing arches, and stair imagery are taken straight from Olivier's film. Mala Sinha plays the role of Ophelia. Sahu was an actor, writer, director, and producer. He scripted, directed, and starred in several films based on classic European sources (Rajadhyaksha and Willemen 203). Nargis plays the all-time favourite Shakespeare character, Juliet, in Akhtar Hussain's 1947 film *Romeo and Juliet*. *Cleopatra* (1950) features Bina Rai as Cleopatra. Both these films were box-office failures.

Laurence Olivier's *Hamlet* was perhaps influenced by Hitchcock's camera movements in *Rebecca* (1940) and Orson Welles's *Citizen Kane* (1941) for the mysterious chiaroscuro or play of light and shadow. Olivier adapted Welles's revolutionary use of deep-focus photography. Welles's mode of direct address to the camera was followed in Olivier's *Richard III* and later again taken up by Ian McKellen in *Richard III* (1995).

Olivier's portrayal of Richard III in his film of the same name in 1955 had traits of Hitler and Walt Disney's version of the Big Bad Wolf. The actor and director plays the role of Richard as a villainous Machiavel. Richard's mode of direct address to the camera was considered a brilliant innovation on the part of Olivier, receiving much critical acclaim. Speaking directly to the camera during his soliloquies has the effect of inviting the film audience to be co-conspirators. This device was later taken up by Richard Loncraine in his film of *Richard III*. In the *Richard III* films of Olivier (1955) and Loncraine (1995), both directors use direct eye contact with the camera to draw us into their world and give us glimpses into Richard's thoughts and motives that none of the other characters in the drama have or could have.

Orson Welles, the great embodiment of the auteur, as film director, actor, and screenwriter at the same time, directed three Shakespearean films, *Macbeth*, *Othello*, and *Chimes at Midnight*. In *Macbeth* (1948), Welles shortened the play by two-thirds, cut entire scenes, and rearranged his source material. A low-budget production, the world of *Macbeth* it presents is deglamourised. The film originated in Welles's voodoo production in Harlem (1936) and the play was also staged in 1947 at the Utah Centennial festival. Welles himself describes the play as a "violently sketched charcoal drawing of a great play" (qtd. in Manvell 59). The director emphasises the brutalism and primitivism of the source text. Physically Welles's *Macbeth* "is a film of dark interiors, of a cramped and rain-swept world of crags and man-made stone labyrinths" (Higham 139).

Lady Macbeth played by Jeanette Nolan is frightening for she resembles the wicked Queen in Disney's *Snow White and the Seven Dwarfs* (1937) (Cartmell 19). Welles makes women the evil-doers. Orson Welles's overwhelming presence as Macbeth almost drowns out the other characters. His long-take and deep-focus style heighten the theatrical impact. Rothwell notes how the stylisation, surreal effects, and chiaroscuro lighting of German expressionism and Eisenstein's *Alexander Nevsky* contributed to Welles's filmic grammar (77). Many low-angle and deep-focus shots are derived from his experience of filming *Citizen Kane* (1941).

Orson Welles's *Othello* (1952) is perhaps his masterpiece. It has orchestrated shots, very symbolic of the narrative. *Othello* was filmed in Italy, Morocco, and different locations at different times in high-contrast black and white. The director drastically cuts and edits Shakespeare's text eliminating most of Iago's soliloquies. Kathy Howlett observes how the art of the Venetian Quattrocentro painter Vittore Carpaccio influenced Welles's *Othello* visually. Anderegg mentions that the visual style of Othello has affinities to the European art cinema tradition. In every possible way, the film is a powerful, poetic rendition of Shakespeare's play.

Much of Shakespeare's language is sacrificed in Welles's *Othello* and the narrative is replaced by visual relationships that require participation on the part of the viewer in creating a structural whole from the fragmented perspectives of the camera or the deep focus often deployed. The constant use of point of view shots emphasises the viewer's sense of fragmentation. In the death scene, Welles makes the camera's and the character's gazes operate in an interesting way. The camera's gaze alternates between Othello's erotic gaze at Desdemona for he "kills Desdemona adoring her" (qtd. in Howlett 56) and Desdemona's objectification, which reveals her perspective on Othello. His strangling of Desdemona is almost a grim parody of sexual desire.

The frequent images of bars and fences represent the world of deceit and cunning that Iago inflicts on his duped subjects. Images of cages, dungeons, labyrinths, crosses, and bars reflect the web of lies in which Othello is trapped. The camera work combined with the editing suggests discontinuity and disruption. As already stated, Welles's film is inspired by Venetian art and manifests skilled use of visual imagery.

The opening scene, the most impressive, lasting over three minutes, contains thirty-eight shots without dialogue or diegetic music. The action of the scene conveys the bodies of Othello and Desdemona being taken for burial; meanwhile, the treacherous Iago is imprisoned in a cage that is slung high above the funeral procession and crowd. The film noir tone and the use of chiaroscuro in the scene set the mood of the film.

The funeral procession of Othello and Desdemona and their slow progress toward the harbour is shot in silhouette against the horizon. This scene appears before the credits and is not found in Shakespeare's text. *Othello* is akin to a crime drama with a black-and-white visual style that has roots in German expressionism. Welles's use of perspective and deep focus expertly creates a visual texture. Combined with the right kind of music, it adds to the beauty, suspense, and surreal nature of the film.

The large Christian cross that is carried in front of Desdemona's body contrasts with the bars of Iago's cage. It helps confirm his villainy: his paganism in contrast to the two dead characters, who are implied to be morally upright and Christian. In the murder scene, the handling of the *mise en scène* is significant. The treatment of architecture and shadows, in terms of exterior–interior juxtaposition portrays how Iago infiltrates Othello's psyche.

Sergei Yutkevich's *Othello* (1955) is the "product of a cultural moment when the Soviets, partially freed from the shadow of Stalin, were in the process of redefining their relationship to culture in general and to the West in particular" (Anderegg 163). Yutkevich's scholarly work *Shakespeare On Film* includes a detailed study of work by Olivier, Welles, and Kozintsev.

Vishal Bhardwaj's *Omkara* (2006), an Indian *Othello* appropriation, indulges in caste politics, clan and communal politics, and gang culture to explore universal human emotions. The film's locale is the interiors of Uttar Pradesh. It narrates the tale of Om Kara or Omi Shukla (Ajay Devgan). Omi (the Othello figure) is a gifted, fearless chieftain who heads a gang of outlaws that includes the crafty Langda Tyagi (Saif Ali Khan/Iago figure) and the dynamic Kesu (Vivek Oberoi/Cassio) among his lieutenants. Billo (Bipasha Basu) a singer/dancer is Kesu's love interest and performs the rocking song and dance number.

The story takes interesting twists when Omi appoints Kesu not Tyagi as his chief lieutenant. Tyagi's pride is humiliated and engulfed in envy as he conspires to falsely implicate Omi's beautiful, fair lover Dolly

(Kareena Kapoor/Desdemona) in a love affair with Kesu. With the unwitting aid of Indu (Konkona Sen Sharma), Tyagi's wife, accompanied by the willing submission of Raju, a fellow grouch who is head-over-heels in love with Dolly, Tyagi's vicious plan materialises. The common motif of sexual jealousy, sexual anxiety, and domestic violence is derived from *Othello* and works well in *Omkara* to foreground communities with their specific local ethos. Focusing mostly on clan rivalries, local rivalries, and the power dynamics involved in such conflicts, *Omkara* projects the contemporary postcolonial milieu of India. However, Tyagi's malevolence is motivated, unlike that of Iago. The crime is here related to class warfare, lawlessness, and violence against women. Gradually the plot gives rise to a bloody tale of deceit, betrayal, and murder. With both *Maqbool* and *Omkara*, Shakespeare appropriations in India reached a global audience for the first time. Both these films project complex female desires.

Joseph L. Mankiewicz's *Julius Caesar* (1953) features method actor Marlon Brando as Mark Antony. Brando's splendid physique combined with his great acting skill means that it remains one of the most remarkable film performances to date. Unlike Mankiewicz's film, Renato Castellani's *Romeo and Juliet* (1954) is believed to have failed due to its poor casting.

2

Akira Kurosawa's *Throne of Blood* (1957) is a Japanese appropriation of *Macbeth*. There is rich cultural intertextuality at work, with Kurosawa finding cultural analogues in Japanese history. In the film, Washizu (Macbeth) and Miki (Banquo) meet a single ghost-like figure instead of the three witches of Shakespeare's play. The ghost-like figure or evil spirit is spinning a wheel, which not only is the wheel of fortune but also, critics have considered, a metaphor for the film projector, a glance at Kurosawa's own act of creation. As Donaldson suggests, there are other metacinematic references in the scene too: the flickering light source, the insubstantiality of the spirit and her hut, and the screening effect the film-maker deploys. The film has been treated as a "metacinematic allegory" (Donaldson 58).

Donaldson notes that Kurosawa uses fog as an editing aesthetic in the sequence where Washizu and Miki, the two warriors are lost in the forest (36). The warriors try to find their way to open fields but the landscape is shrouded in fog. The two warriors mounted on horseback impulsively follow one way after another until Kurosawa consciously uses fog as an editing aesthetic. In this scene there is no dialogue, the soundscape is dominated by the sound of the horses and their hooves.

Throne of Blood and *Ran* (discussed in the next chapter) forcefully raise questions about the ways in which fidelity is viewed. These films transpose *Macbeth* and *King Lear* into the conventions of *jidai-geki* (Japanese period film). Rather than labour to replicate the language, medium, or cultural context of their Shakespearean sources, they make noteworthy changes in plot and characterisation; nevertheless, they are regularly included as part of the Shakespeare film canon for their faithfulness to the Shakespearean "spirit."

3

Film-maker Grigori Kozintsev's Russian-language version of *Hamlet* (1964) was the first major Shakespeare film of the 1960s. It has achieved cult status as an artistic triumph. As a critique of Stalinist power politics, Kozintsev gives us a political reading of the play. His Hamlet is so virile and decisive that his conflict with Claudius and Polonius has been allegorised by Bernice W. Climan as an "Aesopian attack on Stalin" (quoted in Rothwell 183). Comparisons are obvious between Claudius and Stalin's dictatorships.

Inspired by Akira Kurosawa's *Throne of Blood*, which uses the symbolism of fog, rain, and forest, Kozintsev's *Hamlet* depicts images of sea, stone, iron, and fire. They act as recurring tropes among the black-and-white sets of this existential film. Cosmic images of fire, water, and stone engulf the human characters within the confinement of the castle. Terrifying images of entrapment prevail and Denmark is visualised as a prison. Whereas Laurence Olivier's inspiration was unmistakable, unlike Olivier, Kozintsev reinstates Rosencrantz and Guildenstern and young Fortinbras. Ophelia is portrayed as an innocent and pathetic victim.

Polish director Roman Polanski transforms the tragedy of *Macbeth* (1971) into a cruel and absurd nightmare that perpetually repeats itself. The film was condemned for its brutality of vision. Violent films were in vogue in the 1960s and 70s, such as Alfred Hitchcock's *Psycho* (1960), Stanley Kubrick's *A Clockwork Orange* (1971), and Polanski's own *Rosemary's Baby* (1968).

In Polanski's world of violence and murder, the central metaphor is that of blood. In Polanski's *Macbeth*, the imaginary dagger becomes a real dagger. The film is noted for its unconventional editing and point-of-view shots. The film takes as its text Macbeth's "I am in blood/ Stepped in so far, that should I wade no more/ Returning were as tedious as go o'er" (3.4.142–44). Polanski's Scotland, whether under the rule of Duncan or the usurper, is as brutal as it is beautiful. The young actors Jon Finch and Francesca Annis play the roles of Macbeth and Lady Macbeth.

Polanski makes extensive use of close-ups, internal monologues, and voice-overs—a strategy pioneered by Laurence Olivier in *Henry V* and *Hamlet*. In Polanski's *Macbeth*, we are included in the conspiracy, we remain witnesses to a character's self-imposed psychological journey into emotional isolation and self-imprisonment. Polanski deftly borrows images from past directors like Sergei Yutkevich and Orson Welles, especially their use of reflections. The director was displaced by the Nazis as a child. He spent years in Polish exile. His wife Sharon Tate was brutally murdered by the Manson gang. Not surprisingly, his filmic rendition reminds us of Elizabethan and Jacobean revenge tragedies, combined with the Senecan motif of blood and murder. Both Kurosawa and Polanski give us a world of hallucination and surreal vision in their own unique ways.

4

Zeffirelli's *Romeo and Juliet* (1968) is diffused in popular culture and was directed at the contemporary youth market. The *mise en scène* sports the rich, lush colourful look of a Renaissance world and showcases Botticelli-inspired costumes. Set in the bright world of Verona, the film manifests borrowings from new wave and neorealist cinema. The director also draws on his expertise in opera for style and emotional resonance. The street scenes create a plausibly tense atmosphere rife with the threat of potential and actual violence, with the tribal livery of the rival youth displaying clashing colours.

The director's visual style in the film might be called heightened realism. The settings are realistic, and the costumes and locations are all historically authentic and believable. Zeffirelli's *Romeo and Juliet* may be less reflective and philosophical than Shakespeare's, but it nonetheless became very popular with young film audiences in 1968, becoming a big commercial success. Youth, energy, and passion characterise Zeffirelli's *Romeo and Juliet*, while the film has an Italian Renaissance setting.

The film's teenage stars, Olivia Hussey's large-eyed, compelling presence as Juliet and Leonard Whiting's young though dull Romeo, appealed to younger audiences, which led to enormous popular success. The same approach was continued in Baz Luhrmann's *William Shakespeare's Romeo + Juliet*. Like Shakespeare's play, the primary concern of Zeffirelli's film is the perfect blending of innocence and experience, of youthful energy and sexual passion. Zeffirelli set the relationship of Romeo and Juliet against the backdrop of an authoritarian, aloof older generation and a culture of violence. References to the anti-war movement and the sexual revolution abound. Shakespeare here almost serves as a voice of the counter-culture. Today the film, like Olivier's *Hamlet*, has become a cult classic and of historical interest.

In terms of European film-making, Zeffirelli's *Hamlet* (1990) was substantially different from earlier stage and film versions of the play, showing greater indebtedness to popular American film and Hollywood conventions. Hamlet here is played by the popular Hollywood star Mel Gibson and Gertrude by Glenn Close. Laurence Olivier's film of *Hamlet* was a source of inspiration, as Zeffirelli himself admitted: Olivier, he said, was "my hero since I was a boy," and in adult life became his personal friend and collaborator on film and theatre productions (quoted in Howlett 24).

Zeffirelli's film shares a similar setting with Olivier's version. Both films feature cold, dark stone castles and are film noirish in style. The Freudian subtext of incest between mother and son in Olivier's film is treated as the primary focus in the Zeffirelli's adaptation. The encounter between Hamlet and Gertrude is infused with passion and violence. The film received much attention for the terrifying mock rape of Gertrude by Hamlet. As he thrusts her and both are in passionate conflict, Hamlet terrifies her: "Nay but to live/ In the rank sweat of an enseamed bed/ Stewed in corruption, honeying and making love/ Over the nasty sty!" (3.4.82–84). Crowl comments, "Zefferelli helped to bring the Shakespeare film from the art house to the modern cineplex, where the genre discovered it could compete with conventional Hollywood films" (Crowl, *Cineplex* 95). Though unacknowledged by critics, actor Helena Bonham Carter as Ophelia is particularly impressive in the mad scenes of *Hamlet*.

5

In the United States, Kenneth Branagh's British film version of *Henry V* made in 1989 generated a revival of interest in Shakespeare as a potential source of material for commercial and artistic success following the stagnation in this area possibly caused by the failure of Polanski's *Macbeth* at the box-office. Russel Jackson states:

> The success of Kenneth Branagh's modestly financed *Henry V* ($5m negative cost) in 1989 appears to have inaugurated a new wave of confidence in Shakespearean projects, enhanced by the same director's *Much Ado About Nothing* (1994), which cost only $18m to make and grossed over $22m in the USA on its initial theatrical release. (Quoted in Rasmus 40)

Samuel Crowl also observes that Branagh's *Henry V* "helped to create the most intense explosion of English language Shakespeare films in the century" ("Flamboyant Realist" 226). Crowl further states that Branagh may be treated as being single-handedly responsible for the revival of the Shakespeare film genre in the 1990s. What Branagh's film did for the revival of Shakespeare on screen is only comparable to Olivier's success with his *Henry V*, which led to a huge number of Shakespeare films. Branagh's war film *Henry V* reflects post-Vietnam and post-Falklands disillusionment with military conflict and so is generally ambivalent about its depiction of Henry himself. Branagh presents an introspective, self-interrogatory Henry who is acutely aware of his soldiers' suffering. Furthermore, Branagh in his introduction to the published screenplay expresses the hope that whatever "liberties" there are in his film are "Shakespearean in spirit" (Branagh 12). The film therefore suffers from a dilemma between the desire to reinvent and the impulse to faithfully reproduce the Shakespearean original.

Franco Zeffirelli's *Hamlet* (1990) and Branagh's *Henry V* (1989) incorporated elements of the action blockbuster to produce Shakespearean cinema for a mainstream audience. In Kenneth Branagh's *Henry V*, the film's battle of Agincourt is one of the most dramatic battle scenes found in Shakespeare films. For the same reason, King Henry's character is so compelling to film audiences. For its use of slow motion and eye-level shots, the film is indebted to Orson Welles's *Chimes at Midnight*. Film audiences found Branagh's Saint Crispin's Day speech and the wooing of Princess Katharine of France effective. As Branagh aids in developing the viewers' iconographical code, the stylistic patterning of the film also seems natural.

The chief respect in which Branagh distinguishes his Henry from Laurence Olivier's is that his is not Machiavellian. His Henry has no hint of duplicity in his character. Unlike Olivier, who presents a Henry whose "personality is already complete at the start" (Donaldson 68), Branagh's Henry is a young boy seeking an appropriate voice and direction. Al Pacino, the Hollywood actor/director remarks: "Branagh opened it all up with *Henry V*. Now you say Shakespeare on Film in Hollywood and people listen" (qtd. in Rosenthal 215). Branagh's method of focusing on a young boy struggling to make sense of a world of cruelty and violence is later seen in Taymor's *Titus Andronicus* adaptation *Titus* (1999), in her projection of the character of Young Lucius. Branagh's film is intertextually rich in recalling Vietnam War films such as *Apocalypse Now* (1979), *Platoon* (1986), and *Good Morning, Vietnam* (1987), all of which were popular in the 1980s.

Branagh's four-hour, "full-text" *Hamlet* is believed to be the most obsessive and perfectionist of all Shakespeare films, for it preserves intact every line of the original play and, thus, delivers a 242-minute epic version of Shakespeare's play. Branagh's *Hamlet* is also, perhaps, the most political of the film versions. Thoroughly cinematic, with its 70mm sweep and numerous flashbacks, the film is interesting for its special effects and extensive use of mood music. Yet in preserving the full text and given its running length, in many ways it shows the influence of theatre. In the "To be or not to be" soliloquy, the Prince is not only looking at himself in a full-length mirror but also, like Macbeth contemplating the killing of Duncan, thinking of the king who is watching behind a two-way mirror.

The romantic screwball comedy genre manifests itself in Branagh's commercially successful *Much Ado About Nothing* (1993). Here Branagh is not simply a Hollywood populariser but makes every effort to successfully merge Shakespeare and Hollywood; nevertheless, the film has been criticised for its broad comedy and populist approach. While *Much Ado* borrows images and ideas from films as diverse as *The Magnificent Seven*, *Singin' in the Rain*, and *Some Like It Hot*, Branagh's greatest achievement lies in his treatment of the Shakespeare text, which is combined with intertextual glances at the witty Hollywood comedies of the 1930s known as "screwball" (Crowl, *Cineplex* 27). With Beatrice's empowerment, the film succeeded in bringing Shakespeare to a youth audience in a way that had only been achieved before by Zeffirelli's *Romeo and Juliet* (1968). Again, for the visual impact of *Much Ado*, Branagh is indebted to Zeffirelli's *The Taming of the Shrew* (1966). The film's final sequence returns to Balthasar's song as Beatrice, Benedick, Hero, Claudio, and the community sing and dance their way through the villa's courtyard and garden, which are captured by a dazzlingly ambitious uncut steadicam shot that lasts over four minutes and saturates the *mise en scène* with festive celebration.

Written, directed, and produced by Kenneth Branagh, *In the Bleak Midwinter* (also known as *A Midwinter's Tale*) (1995) highlights an actor's dynamic involvement with Shakespeare's dramatic art. The film focuses on the rehearsals for a stage production of *Hamlet*, and is structured around a play within a film. *Hamlet* is only a starting point for the prolonged rehearsals depicted. It is interesting to study how the film generates meaning through its framing practices (Howlett 178). Among Branagh's other Shakespeare films is a musical rendition of *Love's Labour's Lost* (2000) and an Oriental romance, *As You Like It* (2006). Branagh's film adaptations reignited the debate about the relationship between Shakespeare and popular culture. Like Olivier and Welles,

Branagh is a major film auteur who developed his own unique style of translating Shakespeare for the screen.

Among other interesting Shakespeare appropriations of the decade, *West Side Story* (1961) deserves mention. *West Side Story* is Shakespeare's tragic melodrama *Romeo and Juliet,* exquisitely realised in song and dance by rival teenage gangs on the streets of Manhattan's Upper West Side. The parental figures virtually disappear. Other musicals of this period are doubly derivative, as they draw inspiration from theatrical events rather than Shakespeare as their primary source. They include *The Boys from Syracuse* (1940), *Kiss Me Kate* (1953), and *Catch My Soul (Santa Fe Satan)* (1974), which are appropriations of *The Comedy of Errors*, *The Taming of the Shrew*, and *Othello*, respectively.

If *Much Ado* by Kenneth Branagh preferred sun, flesh, and festivity, then, Trevor Nunn, the director of *Twelfth Night* (1996), created a darker, more complex treatment of festivity by highlighting *Twelfth Night*'s issues relating to gender, cross-dressing, and androgyny. Nunn conceives of Feste as the film's voice, its narrator. Nunn's screenplay radically revises Shakespeare's text as it repositions and highlights Feste's songs. The melancholy madness that Nunn creates is gradually replaced by Feste's alternative version of life. Feste's sad final song thrusts the viewer back to the melancholy atmosphere of the entire film. Viola/Cesario is the major focus of the film. Though the film casts skilled performers like Imogen Stubbs (Viola) and Helena Bonham Carter (Olivia), the film suffers because of its "naturalistic" and "realistic" approach to Shakespeare film-making. Michael Hoffman's *A Midsummer Night's Dream* (1999), though more visually striking than Nunn's *Twelfth Night*, lacks energy and dynamism. The director turns his attention to Bottom, played by Kevin Kline, who is here turned into a handsome dandy. The Victorian-style fairies are a bit oddly juxtaposed with Ovidian satyrs. Adrian Noble's imaginative adaptation of *A Midsummer Night's Dream* (1996) relies on minimal visual concepts and is highly imaginative in giving us a cinematic rendering of the play. The film is noted for its elegant simplicity.

No wonder the "Shakespeare on film" discipline for decades has generated challenging academic discussions, debates on performance strategies, and meaningful cultural dialogue. The genre has made its strong and vibrant presence felt through a large spectrum of generic guises. If we trace its trajectory from the late nineteenth century into the first decade of the twenty-first, the corpus of Shakespeare on screen has manifested itself through multiple forms: adaptations, musical comedies, romcoms, art cinema, gangster and crime films, erotic thrillers, teen films, and several others. We are left awestruck by the Bard's generic adaptability and flexibility. With the advancement of digital technology and multiple virtual platforms gaining ground during the Covid-19 pandemic, Zoom Shakespeare productions have become a recent phenomenon. We hope that the playwright and the appeal of his art will continue to be transformed into new genres and identities that we cannot yet predict. Shakespeare's art will reach out to its global audience in myriad ways that we cannot yet foresee.

Works consulted

Anderegg, Michael. "Welles/Shakespeare/Film: An Overview." In *Orson Welles, Shakespeare, and Popular Culture*. Columbia University Press, 1999, pp. 154–71.
Branagh, Kenneth. *Hamlet: Screenplay and Introduction*. W. W. Norton, 1996.
Buhler, Stephen M. *Shakespeare in the Cinema: Ocular Proof.* State University of New York Press, 2002.
Cartmell, Deborah. *Interpreting Shakespeare on Screen*. St. Martin's, 2000.
Crowl, Samuel. *Shakespeare and Film: A Norton Guide*. W. W. Norton, 2008.
—. *Shakespeare at the Cineplex*. Ohio: Ohio University Press, 2003.
—. "Flamboyant Realist: Kenneth Branagh." In *The Cambridge Companion to Shakespeare on Film*, edited by Russell Jackson. Cambridge University Press, 2000.
Davies, Anthony. *Filming Shakespeare's Plays: The Adaptations of Laurence Olivier, Orson Welles, Peter Brook, Akira Kurosawa.* Cambridge University Press, 1988.
Davies, Anthony, and Stanley Wells, editors. *Shakespeare and the Moving Image*. Cambridge University Press, 1988.
Desmet, Christy, and Robert Sawyer, eds. *Shakespeare and Appropriation*. Routledge, 1999.
Donaldson, Peter S. *Shakespearean Films/Shakespearean Directors.* Unwin Hyman, 1990.
Henderson, Diana E., ed. *A Concise Companion to Shakespeare on Screen*. Blackwell, 2007.
Higham, Charles. *The Films of Orson Welles*. University of California Press, 1970.
Hindle, Maurice. *Studying Shakespeare on Film*. Palgrave Macmillan, 2007.

Howlett, Kathy M. *Framing Shakespeare on Film.* Ohio University Press, 2000.
Jorgens, J. J. *Shakespeare on Film.* Indiana University Press, 1977.
Kott, Jan. *Shakespeare Our Contemporary.* Anchor, 1966, 348–49.
Lanier, Douglas. *Shakespeare and Modern Popular Culture.* Oxford University Press, 2002.
Legatt, Alexander. *Shakespeare in Performance*: *King Lear.* 2nd edition. Manchester University Press, 2004.
Manvell, Roger. *Shakespeare and the Film.* Applause Theatre, 1991.
Olivier, Laurence. *Henry V, Produced and Directed by Laurence Olivier.* Lorrimer, 1984.
Rajadhyaksha Ashish and Paul Willemen, ed. *Encyclopaedia of Indian Cinema.* New Delhi: OUP, 2002.
Rasmus, Agnieszka. *Filming Shakespeare from Metatheatre to Metacinema.* Peter Lang, 2008.
Richard III. Directed by Laurence Olivier, performances by Laurence Olivier, John Gielgud, and Cedric Hardwicke. 1955.
Richard III. Directed by Richard Loncraine, performances by Ian McKellen and Annette Bening. United Artists, 1995.
Rothwell, Kenneth S. *A History of Shakespeare on Screen: A Century of Film and Television.* Cambridge University Press, 2000.
—. "Representing *King Lear* on Screen: From Metatheatre to 'Meta-Cinema.'" *Shakespeare and the Moving Image*, edited by Anthony Davies et al. Cambridge University Press, 1988, 211–33.
Sanders, Julie. *Adaptation and Appropriation.* Routledge, 2007.

CHAPTER 10

KING LEAR ON REDEMPTION OR APOCALYPSE ROAD: KOZINTSEV, KUROSAWA, BROOK, AND LEVRING

1

King Lear is considered one of Shakespeare's greatest and darkest tragedies. The play has had multiple filmic transcreations over the years. Grigori Kozintsev's *Korol Lir*, a Russian adaptation of the Shakespearean play, was shot from 1967 to 1969 and released in 1970. The film foregrounds a bleak landscape inhabited by "poor naked wretches" of whom Shakespeare's Lear laments he has taken "too little care."

By showing the poor and homeless on the roads, *Korol Lir* opens out the space of the play. The crowd represented by Kozintsev in the opening scene and in the storm scene may be a group of farm workers now in a destitute condition. In Shakespeare's play we never see them, they are just an idea in the playwright's imagination. This Russian transcreation effectively reduces Lear (played by Yuri Yarvet) to a poor peasant or even a beggar. Lear cannot be distinguished, say, from a mass of refugees or a crowd of homeless people.

Yuri Yarvet with his aged countenance, fragile frame, and withered look actually suited the role of Lear, as Kozintsev never wanted to project a majestic-looking king. Rather he wanted an unimposing actor/king who would gradually mingle with the common folk and effortlessly become one amongst them as he utters: "Poor naked wretches, whereso'er you are,/ That bide the pelting of this pitiless storm,/ How shall your houseless heads and unfed sides,/ Your loop'd and window'd raggedness, defend you/ From seasons such as these? O! I have ta'en/ Too little care of this . . ." (3.4.28–32). No space is allocated to the poor in Shakespeare's play, in Shakespeare's representation of Lear's kingdom. In Kozintsev's film, they are a powerful presence.

In Kozintsev's film, Lear falls in with a group of poor peasants just as Edgar disguised as the bedlam beggar joins the procession of beggars. Indeed, the most significant element of the Kozintsev film is its landscape design: a desolate, arid landscape through which the beggars carve their way out into the wilderness.

Like Shakespeare's Lear, Yuri Yarvet as Lear in the Kozintsev version expresses his grief to Gloucester and the disguised Edgar: "they told me I am everything. 'Tis a lie, I am not ague-proof" (4.6.104–5). In his capacity for tragic suffering, Lear empathises with his fellow creatures, the poor and the homeless beggars. In his suffering, he attains majestic grandeur.

In the opening scene of *Korol Lir*, peasants and beggars climb uphill to stand outside the castle where Lear will engage in the "division of the kingdom." When Cordelia in her "faulty admixture of pride" and Kent with his "saucy roughness" displeases the King, he expels them not only from his affection but from the body politic. Once he divides Cordelia's share between Goneril and Regan, Lear, in the film, vigorously marches off.

A complicated tracking shot follows him through the palace, into the stables, his retinue at his heels, past magnificent horses, elegant hounds, setters, ferocious greyhounds, and falcons. As Lear ascends the stairs, he stands at the edge of a precipice, God-like, for the inevitable denouement. The peasants and beggars, people without rights, kneel in low angle as the mighty Lear assumes a commanding position on the parapet. From his position on the castle wall—the unreal *mise en scène* awe-inspiring and magniloquent with fire and smoking pots—he proclaims his banishing of Cordelia.

In a quick cut, Kozintsev reinforces the severing of the filial bond between father and daughter by showing Cordelia and the Prince of France being blessed by a priest as Cordelia sets off for France.

In the storm-scenes of the Kozintsev adaptation there is a wild quartet of madness—Lear, Edgar as Poor Tom, the Fool, and the "poor naked wretches" are packed together into a shabby hovel where they have taken shelter to protect themselves from the pitiless storm. It is not the thunder and lightning of the Shakespearean play text, but Lear in a dark hovel with the homeless beggars that marks the climax of *Korol Lir*.

2

Filial ingratitude is the theme of Akira Kurosawa's *Ran* (1985), a Japanese period piece, costume drama, and appropriation of *King Lear* set in the world of the medieval samurai. In *Ran* (1985), Kurosawa redefines tragedy into visual terms. *Ran* is almost a war film, with Hidetora as the Lear figure. The film-maker turns Shakespeare's daughters into sons, partly in response to Japan's samurai tradition; to make an even more daring gender reversal, he collapses Cornwall and Edmund into a single female character, Lady Kaede, the wife of Hidetora's eldest son.

The spatial arrangement in *Ran*, particularly in the confined spaces of samurai culture, is confrontational. The static world of interior spaces provides the site of the rebellion of Lady Kaede (first Taro's, then Jiro's wife) and also emerges as the site of her subordination. For women, in Kurosawa's *Ran*, space becomes a place of systematisation and hierarchisation. In the assigned domestic space that has powerfully reshaped her identity, Lady Kaede appropriates the forms of Samurai power and authority. Gender distinctions are blurred in Lady Kaede's vindictive and predatory sexuality and it significantly contributes to the sexual politics of Kurosawa's filmic rendition of a Shakespeare play.

Lady Kaede resists stereotypical definitions of herself as a widow or nun and reclaims her position in the Ichimonji family by threatening to expose Jiro's murder of his brother and then by seducing the frightened Jiro. Her revenge extends well beyond the Ichimonji family to the entire Ichimonji clan and society, which have shaped her silent, rebellious desires.

The basic themes of old age, family tension, and inheritance issues cut across cultural divides and make *Ran* relevant for all times and all cultures. However, Kurosawa's adaptation, unlike Kozintsev's film, shows nothing of the life of the homeless. "The poor naked wretches" are conspicuous by their absence.

A film on warlords and warriors, *Ran* operates in a military context using war, not the Shakespearean storm, to depict chaos. The destructive powers reach out to embrace an apocalyptic vision of the world. Hidetora (Lear) is haunted by guilt and remorse for men he has brutally slain. When taking shelter from the storm, he retorts, "Because of me, my loyal men died a useless death."

Ran, a cross-cultural adaptation, is based on the legend of Mōri Motonari (1495–1571). The patriarchal bias of Japanese society in *Ran* dictates that Hidetora (Lear) divide the kingdom among his three sons, Taro, Jiro, and Saburo (Cordelia), rather than to three daughters, and suffer the consequences.

Lady Kaede is the victim of this patriarchal power. The film is largely about the emergence of politically powerful women, the stone-faced Lady Kaede, with her exquisite talent for the cold-blooded manipulation of men.

The movement towards a radical turn in culture with the emergence of a powerful female figure is manifested particularly in the storm scene in *Ran*. Subsequently Hidetora's rage is guided by the battle between Taro and Jiro. Hidetora wanders through the carnage of the battle. Kurosawa gives his unique vision of Lear's call for the "all-shaking thunder" to "strike flat the thick rotundity of the world" (3.2.7–9).

3

In Kozintsev's *King Lear*, the storm scene is marked by nature's fury amidst man-made violence and the young Fool seems almost to stand for sanity. Unlike *Ran*, *Korol Lir* uses the storm with its spectacular thunder and lightning as the key image of chaos. Oleg Dal's intuitive fool in *Korol Lir*, like Shakespeare's fool, stands for worldly common sense and his is the voice of reason.

The fool's masked social criticism is shrewd and replete with cynical paradoxes. He can never forgive Lear's treatment of Cordelia. He begins to pine away after Cordelia's banishment and his bitter jokes continually remind the King of the injustice he has meted out to Cordelia. The "all licens'd fool" plays his wistful pipe—presented as a clarinet solo in Shostakovich's score—that opens and tragically ends Kozintsev's adaptation. It reminds one of the plaintive noh flute played by Sue's brother Tsurumaru (Gloucester) that haunts Lear (Hidetora) in Kurosawa's *Ran*.

Often, in the Fool's derision, the Shakespearean Fool's sanity is an irreverent thrust at Lear's dignity and a subversion of his authority. The Fool in Kurosawa's *Ran*, the loyal, effeminate Kyoami (Fool), with his rhymes and songs, forms a kind of choric counterpoint to the main themes of the Shakespearean play. He tells Hidetora he was indeed a fool to give away his house and land. The inconsequentiality of the Fool's talk in *King Lear* disguises its profundity:

> FOOL: . . . I can tell why a snail has a house.
> LEAR: Why?
> FOOL: Why, to put's head in; not to give it away to his daughters, and leave his horns without a case.
> . . .
> FOOL: Yes indeed: thou woulds't make a good Fool. . . . If thou wert my Fool, Nuncle, I'd have thee beaten for being old before thy time.
> LEAR: How's that?

FOOL: Thou should'st not have been old till thou hadst been wise.
LEAR: O! Let me not be mad, not mad, sweet heaven; Keep me in temper;
    I would not be mad! (1.5.27–44)

The cynical realism of the Fool's comment, with its dense complexity of imagistic relationships, is vividly projected in the Kozintsev adaptation and we realise that the fool's pessimism (reinforced by the sound of the flute) is deep-rooted.

Oleg Dal's insane fool anticipates Lear's madness. He is present even after the third act and reappears to comment on Lear's folly. In Kozintsev's last scene, the lonely fool plays the flute again as he is heard weeping amongst ashes. Yuri Yarvet (Lear) earlier had thus taken up the Fool's thought that all men are fools: "When we are born we cry that we are come/ to this great stage of Fools" (4.6.180–81). When Lear has to sign the blood contract in *Ran* accepting that he no longer heads the house of Ichmonji, Kyoami cries out, "Man is born crying. When he has cried enough, he dies."

In *Korol Lir*, Edgar (the legitimate son of Gloucester) is disguised as Poor Tom and joins a procession of beggars. Edgar strips off his clothing, smearing his naked arms and face with dirt. We even have Kozintsev's underplayed rendition of the storm scene—underplayed because the director was more concerned with the man-made nature of violence, not cosmic violence. Poor Tom's proverbs in the storm scene are the "voice of the kingdom," the "embodiment of peasant wisdom."

The final scene in Kozintsev's film shows peasants trying to rebuild their village. In its stoic acceptance of death and in Lear's journey from "hideous rashness" to defiance, vulnerability, and wisdom, the film powerfully depicts the profundity of tragic suffering. Lear's suffering is represented with such grand pathos that the death of Cordelia provokes frenzied trauma. Lear's "Never, never, never, never, never" echoes and reverberates in Kozintsev's *mise en scène* in all its tragic intensity.

In Kozintsev's film, Lear's psychological journey is a solo journey of redemption into spiritual oblivion. In *Ran*, the journey to a world being turned upside down and into chaos is an allegory of the hopeless condition of humanity.

4

Contrastingly Peter Brook's *King Lear* (1971) owes as much to the French new wave as to Orson Welles, Bertolt Brecht, and Jan Kott. His bleak, savage and existential rendition of *King Lear* was filmed in North Jutland and Denmark. The cold was intense and the film depicts a winter world of ironic despair. Fur and fire are everywhere in the scenes but there are no ornaments. Fire has a destructive role and is the image of war. The film breaks single scenes into short episodes, redistributes them, and creates a structure of its own.

Brook employs deliberate Godardian techniques of alienation. Distancing techniques such as awkward camera angles, zooms, subtitles, and rapid acceleration, constantly break the film's narrative flow in what becomes an essay on how to translate metatheatre into metacinema. The use of title cards, minimalist lighting, and the consistent use of handheld cameras includes a variety of Brechtian alienation devices.

As Kenneth S. Rothwell observes, "Like a 'New Wave' director, Brook employs discontinuities: zoom fades, accelerated motion rapid editing, complex reverse-angle and over-the-shoulder shots, montage, jump cuts, overhead shots, silent screen titles, eyes-only close-ups and hand-held cameras" (Rothwell, "Representing *King Lear* On Screen" 219).

Kristin Levring's use of jump cuts, flashbacks, and extreme close-ups in his film *The King Is Alive* (2000) recall Peter Brooks's 1971 absurdist, avant-garde adaptation. In Levring's film, the setting is the barren, arid landscape of an abandoned mining town in the Namibian desert. In every possible way, it reminds us of Brook's *King Lear* shot in a desolate landscape in the freezing North Danish wastelands of Jutland.

Levring's film is a product of the Danish Dogme 95 movement, which emerged in the mid-nineties countering Hollywood's global domination of the film industry. Its stark, bleak presentation of an absurdist universe is like Brook's absurdist *Lear*. Its adherence to a strict set of rules does not allow artifice and expensive technologies. Such factors clearly foreground its anarchic intent. Jack Jorgens rightly contrasts the Lears of Kozintsev and Brook by describing Kozintsev's as "a Christian-Marxist story of redemption and social renewal," while Brook's is a "bleak existential tale of meaningless violence in a cold, empty universe" (Jorgens 236).

Levring's film, a modern take on the Lear narrative, is not a direct adaptation but rather an inspired appropriation of *King Lear*. It is one of the few films that tries to negotiate the cultural, psychological, and social uses of a Shakespearean text.

The cinematic style of *The King Is Alive* places it well outside the mainstream of conventional film production. Without attempting to appropriate the narrative of *King Lear* in its entirety, *The King Is Alive* borrows mostly from Shakespeare's *King Lear* and partly uses *Hamlet* as a source of inspiration. However, undeniable connections are established between characters in Shakespeare's Lear and Levring's film soon enough: familial and patriarchal failure, sexual inadequacies, and identity crises.

Levering focuses on the exploration of the psyche and the relationships of its protagonists in real time. Even the nullity and existential angst is echoed in a character named Liz whose comment to her husband, "You don't have to worry. Nobody falls in love. And everybody dies in the end" becomes significant. Such existential crises constantly reminds one of other *King Lear* adaptations like those of Akira Kurosawa and Jean-Luc Godard (*King Lear*, 1987), along with Peter Brook.

The King Is Alive is about a man who attempts to stage a play that has been stripped of all theatrical devices: props, costumes, technological tools, even the text itself. The film presents us with a fragmentary take on the Lear narrative, employing low-budget strategies that stand in sharp contrast to the high production values of other major Shakespeare film adaptations.

The King Is Alive is about a group of Western travellers stranded in the Namibian desert. As they await rescue, they resort to putting on a play (*King Lear*) to maintain morale. One of them is Henry, an aging English actor-turned-Hollywood scriptwriter, who bridges the cultural division within this multifarious group of people. As a means of survival, Henry decides to preoccupy himself by staging an adaptation of *King Lear*, and transcribes those parts of the play he has in his memory.

The characters in the film perform roles from Lear without understanding them but are gradually able to relate to those roles with their evolving subject positions. The Lear text is meticulously interwoven as an intertext as the Shakespearean text begins to make its presence potently felt through the characters in the film.

In Levring's film, performance enables the group to probe deeper and vent repressed emotional issues. The Shakespearean language as recollected through Henry's (the ultimate Lear figure's) memory along with the characters in the film, playing the roles of the Shakespearean text, establish the film's intertextual engagement with *King Lear*. Each of the film's characters reassesses or re-enacts the play from their own point of view, suggesting the prioritisation of the reader or performer over both the text and the author.

Works consulted

Andrew, Dudley. "Adaptation." In *Film Adaptation*, edited by James Naremore. Rutgers University Press, 2000, 28–37.

Berlin, Normand. "Peter Brook's Interpretation of *King Lear*: 'Nothing Will Come of Nothing.'" *Literature/Film Quarterly* 5, no. 4: 299–303.

Davies, Anthony. *Filming Shakespeare's Plays: The Adaptations of Laurence Olivier, Orson Welles, Peter Brook, Akira Kurosawa.* Cambridge University Press, 1988.

Donaldson, Peter S. *Shakespearean Films/Shakespearean Directors.* Unwin Hyman, 1990.

Griggs, Yvonne. *Screen Adaptations: Shakespeare's King Lear: The Relationship between Text and Film.* Methuen Drama, 2009.

Henderson, Diana E., ed. *A Concise Companion to Shakespeare on Screen.* Blackwell Publishing, 2007.

Higham, Charles. *The Films of Orson Welles.* University of California Press, 1970.

Hindle, Maurice. *Studying Shakespeare on Film.* Palgrave Macmillan, 2007.

Jackson, Russell, ed. *The Cambridge Companion to Shakespeare on Film.* Cambridge University Press, 2000.

Jorgens, J. J. *Shakespeare on Film.* Indiana University Press, 1977.

Kott, Jan. *Shakespeare Our Contemporary.* Anchor, 1966, 348–49.

Kozintsev, Grigori. *Shakespeare: The Space of Tragedy.* Translated by Mary Mackintosh. Toronto and Buffalo, 1977.

Lanier, Douglas. *Shakespeare and Modern Popular Culture.* Oxford University Press, 2002.

Legatt, Alexander. *Shakespeare in Performance*: *King Lear.* 2nd ed. Manchester University Press. 2004.

Muir, Kenneth, ed. *The Arden Shakespeare. King Lear.* Routledge, 1972.

Rothwell, Kenneth S. "Representing *King Lear* on Screen: From Metatheatre to Meta-Cinema." In *Shakespeare and the Moving Image: The Plays on Film and Television*, edited by Anthony Davies and Stanley Wells. Cambridge University Press, 211–33.

Sinyard, Neil. *Filming Literature: The Art of Screen Adaptation.* Croom Helm, 1986.

Chapter 11

A Metafictional Detour: Appropriating John Fowles's *The French Lieutenant's Woman* on Screen

When John Fowles's *The French Lieutenant's Woman* was published in 1969 it was immediately identified as several kinds of novel in one. This brilliantly innovative novel was immediately hailed as metafiction, as an existential novel and as a postmodern parody. This structurally complex work was considered as historical fiction as well as a great work of popular fiction. It was an instant bestseller; perhaps because the surface story of a passionate Victorian love affair could be readily enjoyed without having to engage too deeply with its philosophical underpinnings.

As Fowles is a novelist of outstanding merit and imaginative power, critics have considered him a modern-day Thomas Hardy, especially as a chronicler of his beloved Dorset. As a highly self-conscious artist, Fowles fully registers the artifice inherent in the act of writing by foregrounding the fictiveness of fiction itself. With its vivid pastiche of Victorian fiction and famous device of "alternative endings," *The French Lieutenant's Woman* remains his best-known novel.

The title of the novel is sufficiently indicative that the heroine is more important than the hero; indeed, Sarah Woodruff is the "hero" of the novel. However, there is a remarkable reversal of roles whereby a socially deviant Victorian woman assumes control in a romantic relationship. Victorian gender politics firmly forbade such a configuration. Fowles breaks this mould as well as the gender codes of the Victorians by introducing Sarah, who is mysterious, unpredictable, and unfathomable. She is allowed an independent discourse and an existential will, remaining consistently an unresolved mystery.

The novel is set largely in Lyme Regis in the 1860s and recreates a Victorian romance. It reminds us of the world of George Eliot and Thomas Hardy. In Fowles's Victorian story, a wealthy amateur palaeontologist,

Charles Smithson, falls in love with Sarah Woodruff, a passionate governess who people believe has been deserted by a French naval lieutenant. The affair has ostracised Sarah from society. However, like her creator, the novelist, Sarah turns out to be an arch manipulator herself, whose story is an almost complete fabrication. Throughout the novel, Sarah flaunts her "supposed" sexual immorality, thereby freeing herself from all the demands of Victorianism; that is, once she chooses to blatantly defy society, she no longer has to concern herself with its approval. Sarah's scandalous choice in favour of freedom gives her the opportunity to pursue a do-your-own-thing lifestyle. This lifestyle, however, forces Sarah to undertake a journey of isolation and seclusion from Victorian society. Fowles's primary existential concern—freedom—is personified in the character of Sarah. Right from the beginning, she emerges as an epitome of "freedom."

Fowles moves between past and present, adding footnotes, quotations from Darwin, Marx, and the great Victorian poets, and comments on Victorian politics and customs. The book is both homage and critique; we may read it as a Victorian tale of unfolding laws of progress and emancipation, and as a story of repression with layers of sexual and social hypocrisy. Fowles's strong story and varied attacks on Victorian values are carefully amalgamated with literary discussion and the experimentation of the novel. Fowles's interest is not only in criticising the manners and society of the last century, but, concomitantly, in examining and attempting to supersede the more defined, rigid parameters of the novel. Consequently, Fowles's fable goes on to trace historical change: the break-up of the Victorian world picture and the departure from mid-Victorian respectabilities to the aesthetic decadence of the Pre-Raphaelites and early moderns.

The French Lieutenant's Woman blurs the boundary between literature and popular fiction: it uses epigraphs, an extensive vocabulary, and engages with philosophy and literary theory; nevertheless, it relies on popular conventions, such as dealing with separate plots in alternating chapters to increase suspense or even the gradual augmenting of erotic tension. Like a postmodern novel, it pretends to have made a radical break with the past: postmodern critics have focused particularly on Fowles's playful acknowledgement of its literary and historical sources. Yet in his retrospective twentieth-century examination of the Victorian novel, the novelist adopts several techniques to illustrate this parody of historical fiction.

Critics have described Fowles's work as historiographic metafiction that is intensely aware of its own fictionality and forces its readers to notice this phenomenon while experiencing the narrative itself. One of its consistent features is its ironic self-referentiality. Fowles's novel is at once traditional and postmodernist. It is traditional because it is modelled on Victorian novels; the plot is intelligently stereotyped in Victorian fashion—romance, intrigue, misunderstandings, deceit, forbidden love, carnal desire, betrayal, and a classic love triangle between two women attracted to the same gentleman. There are villains, rogues, and lower-class observers to comment and create mischief. Yet concomitantly Fowles makes us believe that his novel is postmodernist because it is self-conscious, uses an intrusive narrator, and has multiple endings, anachronistic references, and epigraphs at the beginning of every chapter.

The trick that Fowles plays with his readers is achieved through the narrator. He personifies many of the novel's contradictions. He usually comments on the action from outside, but twice enters the story. The author employs a playful and probing narrative technique when he addresses the reader directly. He appears in a number of guises: as the narrator-novelist; as the overdressed impresario who enters the train carriage with his hero and turns back his watch (and thus narrative time) to permit the dual ending; and as the disembodied narrator who observes this going on. It is interesting to observe the way Fowles toys with the concepts of authorship and readership and their respective roles in the formation of the narrative.

With its multiple endings, *The French Lieutenant's Woman* remains "a novel of forking paths." It was rather difficult and perplexing when Harold Pinter and Karel Reisz decided to film the novel. The question was, how should one go about it? The fact that this fiction was written from both a mid-Victorian and modern viewpoint further complicated matters. Traditionally film has supplied narratorial commentary by using a voice-over; in this case, however, Karel Reisz and Harold Pinter achieve a similar effect by using more cinematic devices in their 1981 film adaptation. They recast the double ending of Fowles's novel as a film within the film, locating the unhappy ending (the hero loses the heroine for good) at the level of the film's "real world" and the happy ending (hero and heroine reconciled) at the level of the film within the film.

Such a metafilmic rendition of a novel on screen is almost exemplary of the "fidelity of transformation." The most spectacular achievement of the film is the fact that using purely cinematic techniques like the framing modern story and intertwining them with the Victorian romance, Reisz and Pinter managed to recreate the distance between the audience and the Victorian story that Fowles achieved by using the intrusive narrator in his book within the book. If, in the novel, the reader is at once removed from the story because it is a pastiche and a self-conscious novel, then, in Reisz's adaptation, the audience is placed in a similar position by being constantly reminded that this is a film acted out by a cast of people. Thus, we are made aware of a wonderful instance of "fidelity of transition," where a film adaptation considerably alters the source text in order to retain its "spirit."

We as viewers must be aware of what film cannot do that literature can, about differences in the structure and effects of the two media. Thus, in assessing this adaptation, we are never really comparing Fowles's book with Reisz's film, but an interpretation with an interpretation. For just as we are readers, so implicitly is the film-maker, through his work offering us his perceptions, his vision, his particular insight into his source material (the novel). Hence, Pinter's screenplay and Reisz's adaptation of the novel are interpretations.

In the novel, Fowles's refusal to enter Sarah's mind has been a matter of debate. Some feminist critics suggest that Sarah is a feminist heroine because she is pictured as evolving to feminist consciousness and she evolves into a "New Woman" by the end of the novel. Others maintain that it is anti-feminist because Fowles's refusal to enter her mind makes her an object of male desire, rather than a fully rounded, intelligent female character. The film adaptation visualises Sarah (Meryl Streep) in the Victorian tale as an outsider, an outcast, a *femme fatale* because of her seductive power over the hero. Sarah has willed herself to be a fallen woman: she has willed her own destruction. As in Fowles's fiction, Meryl Streep's Sarah is given a far greater and more modern independence than the confining age would normally allow. Thus in a "novel of forking paths" characterised by multiple endings, the novel and its film adaptation leave Sarah indeterminate, free to "emerge" as she wishes from the end of the story/film. As Fowles observes in his *Notes on an Unfinished Novel*, silence from her was better than any line she might have said.

1. *The French Lieutenant's Woman* on screen

In *Postmodernist Fiction*, Brian McHale considers *The French Lieutenant's Woman* "a novel of forking paths." He raises the question of how, if one decided to film this novel, one should go about it. He suggests that one might choose to preserve the self-contradictory structure of the original, with its violation of the law of excluded middle, producing something like Alain Resnais's and Alain Robbe-Grillet's *L'Année dernière à Marienbad* (*Last Year at Marienbad*) (1961)—a film of forking paths. Or one might choose to do what Harold Pinter or Karel Reisz actually did when they made their film of *The French Lieutenant's Woman*, that is, to transform one type of ontological structure into a different but related type with greater chance of being grasped by the average filmgoer.

John Fowles acknowledged, "Another major problem with *The French Lieutenant's Woman* was what one critic called its stereoscopic vision, the fact that it is written from both a mid-Victorian and a modern viewpoint. None of the directors who worked on it ever wanted to dodge that 'diachronic' dilemma, though they came up with many different solutions; nor, incidentally, any of the producers" (Fowles, *Filming* 42). Traditionally, film has supplied narrative commentary by using a voice-over; in this case, however, Karel Reisz and Harold Pinter achieve a similar effect by using more cinematic devices.

The central problem facing the adaptation of *The French Lieutenant's Woman* was not how to render the novel's plot details. The challenge was to capture the narrator's commentary, which is not only elaborate but also modern in its slant. Therefore, instead of turning the twentieth-century narrator into a character, the film introduces the modern framing story that functions as a metaphor for the original.

The love affair between Mike and Anna (Jeremy Irons and Meryl Streep, who play Charles and Sarah) is not a replay of the Victorian, it is more of a dramatisation of the commentary in its juxtaposition of the two stories—the contrasts between Victorian and modern attitudes to love.

The film makes us believe that Victorian love has as much to tell us about modern love as vice versa. The story of Charles and Sarah is juxtaposed with the modern failed romance of Mike and Anna. This is done to preserve the intrusive narrator's commentary on form, an impossible convention in film without resorting to a documentary style. Reisz and Pinter achieve and preserve the novelist's postmodern intentions through the film's questioning of its own medium and form.

Just as Fowles forces the novel's very structure on the reader, the film forces the viewer to realise the very construction of the medium through showing the actors themselves engaged in their own roles, both as characters in the Victorian story and as character actors. The film plays with the viewer's conventional responses to art, insisting on a greater awareness of the film as a cinematic text, not merely as an opportunity to suspend disbelief and live vicariously through characters in a fictional existence.

Seymour Chatman, in his detailed analysis of the film, explains how Reisz achieves this effect by using the technique of "crosscutting":

separate but interspersed assemblage of shots back and forth between two strands of a story that ultimately are tied together. Intercutting in *The French Lieutenant's Woman* is unusual because the modern story is not just one component or strand of the total story (www.britcoun.org). The interrelations between the two are much more complex.

On one level, the modern story serves as a surrogate discourse of the Victorian story, a dramatised alternative to more directly vocal narration. On another level, the modern story is autonomous; it goes beyond framing and even commenting on the Victorian story to present, in its own right and with seemingly "irrelevant" details, a certain modern state of affairs.

This autonomy is hard to recognise in the early part of the film, where the focus remains persistently on the Victorian tale and the modern sequences are brief and elliptical, each usually consisting of a single shot. It takes us a while to understand why we should be concerned about the actors playing the Victorian characters. Only towards the end of the film does their drama begin to approximate and even outweigh that of the Victorians, the outcome of which becomes fairly predictable once Charles learns Sarah's whereabouts.

Throughout the film the modern story intersects thematically and formally with the Victorian story and ultimately it displaces it as the focus of dramatic attention. Pinter's screenplay acts as a bridge from page to screen.

This is how the first scene of the screenplay by Harold Pinter begins.

1. Exterior. The Cobb. Lyme Regis. Dawn. 1867.

A clapperboard. On it is written: The French Lieutenant's Woman scene 1. Take 3.
It shuts and withdraws, leaving a close shot of Anna, the actress who plays Sarah. She is holding her hair in place against the wind.

> VOICE (OFF SCREEN)
> All right. Let's go.

The actress nods, releases her hair. The wind catches it.

> VOICE (OFF SCREEN)
> Action.

Sarah starts to walk along the Cobb, a stone pier in the Harbour of Lyme. It is dawn. Windy. Deserted. She is dressed in black. She reaches the end of the Cobb and stands still, staring out to sea. (Pinter 1)

As Carrière observes, "a screenplay is always the dream of a film. But when it is time to shoot, which is the first moment of truth, 'you almost always have to make do with what is at hand. The compromises begin'" (154). For example, there is not enough money to shoot a particular scene in a particular country or location, or various other factors intervene; above all, there is the pressure of time.

The film begins a bit differently from the screenplay with Anna on the Cobb, in costume. The title page of the screenplay declares that inevitably a number of scenes were cut and some structural changes were made during the course of production. In the first shot of the film, Anna is checking her appearance in a hand-mirror held by a make-up lady. The scene is a film set replicating the Victorian era, with contemporary members of the film crew mixing with the costumed characters; a car can be seen parked in front of nineteenth-century sailing ships. Someone hurries across the frame holding a megaphone, a voice out of shot asks "Are you ready Anna?" (Pinter 1). She nods; the film crew leave the set, the car drives out of the frame, a clapperboard and the off-screen command "Action!" signal the beginning of the Victorian narrative. As she walks up the Cobb (which is now divested of any reminders of the twentieth century), the introductory credits appear on the screen, haunting music plays, and Anna becomes her character: the French Lieutenant's woman.

Gradually the immediacy of the film medium draws the viewer into the alternative narrative. Reisz goes on to introduce the other Victorian characters. Charles is seen looking at his fossils and then, impulsively (as it is very early in the morning and clearly no one is expecting him), going to visit Ernestina at her Aunt's house. Charles asks Ernestina to marry him, to the delighted amusement of the servants, Sam and Mary, who are watching from the kitchen window. The screenplay reads thus:

26. Interior. Conservatory.
Charles under an overhanging branch.

CHARLES
This is not mistletoe, but it will do.

ERNESTINA
Oh Charles . . .

They kiss chastely.

27. Hotel room. Early morning. Present. 1979.

Dim light. A man and a woman in bed asleep. It is at once clear that they are the man and woman playing Charles and Sarah, but we do not immediately appreciate that the time is the present.

A telephone rings.
Mike turns, lifts receiver.

> MIKE
> Yes? (Pause) Who is it? (Pause) Yes, it is. (Pause.) I'll tell her.

Mike puts the phone down, turns on light, wakes Anna.

> MIKE
> Anna.

> ANNA
> Mmmm?

> MIKE
> You're late. They're waiting for you.

> ANNA
> Oh God.

She sits up.
What happened to the wake-up call?

> MIKE
> I don't know.

> ANNA (yawning)
> Who called?

> MIKE
> Jack.

She looks at him.

> ANNA
> Did you answer the phone?

> MIKE
> Yes.
>
> ANNA
> But then—they'll know you're in my room, they'll all know.
>
> MIKE
> In your bed.
>
> He kisses her.
>
> I want them to know.
>
> ANNA
> Christ, look at the time.
>
> He holds her.
>
> ANNA
> They'll fire me for immorality.
>
> He embraces her.
>
> They'll think I'm a whore.
>
> MIKE
> You are.
>
> (Pinter 8–9)

As Carrière observes, a good screenplay is one that gives birth to a good film. Once the film exists, the screenplay is no more. It is probably the least visible component of the finished work. It is the first incarnation of a film and appears to be a self-contained whole. But it is fated to undergo metamorphosis, to disappear, to melt into another form, the final form (Carrière 148).

In the film, the transition from the Victorian to the modern is done through a cut. The sound of a telephone ringing signals the return to the present. At this point, the viewer has seen enough of the Victorian story to be totally immersed in it. The return to the present is a jolt—a cinematic equivalent of the narrator's reminders to the reader of the fictional nature of the text.

The sudden return to the present also makes clear the difference in sexual sophistication between the lovers in the different ages. The Victorian Charles kisses Ernestina, probably for the first time, clumsily and shyly: he bangs her head against his chest in his eagerness to embrace her. The cut to the present has Anna and Mike who, implicitly, have only just met, waking up in bed together.

The juxtaposition of the two scenes, one Victorian and the other modern, illustrate the change in sexual behaviour from the repression of the Victorian age to the easy promiscuity of Mike and Anna. However, although men and women are infinitely more equal than in Victorian times, the sexual double standard lingers on. Anna is embarrassed to be discovered in bed with Mike who on the other hand has no need to worry about his reputation.

Fowles recognised the difficulties that Harold Pinter faced. Robert Bolt, who had been approached early on as a possible screenwriter, had almost persuaded him that "as it stood [. . .] the book was and would always remain unfilmable" (Fowles, *Filming* 37). Fowles realised the need for much more than a faithful rendition; what was needed was "a demon barber—in politer terms, someone sufficiently skilled and independent to be able to rethink and recast the thing from the bottom up. Once again, we had no argument as to the best man for that difficult task. It was Harold Pinter" (*Filming* 39). Pinter and Reisz did just this and came up with what Fowles has called "a brilliant metaphor" for his book (*Filming* 40–43).

The film-within-a-film structure also contrasts the rigid nineteenth-century class system with the present. In the novel, Fowles uses certain characters to symbolise the Marxist winds of change. Ernestina's father is an example of the new wealthy merchant class: his own father was a draper and he has made his money through hard work and good business sense. He is contrasted with Charles, who is rather disdainful about having to get involved "in trade" and who sees his own inherited wealth as his birthright.

Charles's servant Sam also represents a break from the past. He is no longer content to be a servant and wants to improve himself: he epitomises Marx's maker of history, the man in pursuit of his own ends. He, like Sarah, wants to break out of his rigidly defined role and make his own place in life. By showing the characters in their roles in the past and then as actors in the present, the film illustrates how social barriers have diminished. For example, at Mike's lunch party the actor who plays Sam is seen playing classical piano accompanied by the actress who plays Ernestina, a scene unthinkable between their Victorian characters.

Mrs Poulteney chats to Anna about Mike's wife and his lovely children. She knows Mike and Anna have had an affair and still represents a moral guardian but in a much less repressive way than her nineteenth-century alter ego.

Pinter dramatises this argument through the parallel development of the "fictional story" of Charles and Sarah and the "real" story of Mike and Anna. The focus, in each relationship, is on the male half of the couple, the female remaining mysterious. As they play out both their love story and the story of Charles and Sarah, Mike begins to identify Anna with the character she is playing. He is really more in love with Sarah than with Anna as can be seen when he calls out "Sarah!" as Anna drives away at the end.

Anna realises, like Sarah, that she cannot be the fantasy woman that Mike is looking for, she has to be true to herself. The film's theme is the plight of an actor who gets a taste of a better, older way of loving and hence living. Unfortunately for him the world that made this kind of loving possible no longer exists. The character and the actor thus provide reverse images: just as Charles longs for a woman of the future, Mike longs for a woman of the past. It is in this way that the film reflects some of the novel's commentary not only on Victorian morality but also on the present.

Fowles uses the character of Sarah to symbolise a kind of Darwinian progression towards self-actualisation. Sarah does not fit into the patriarchal Victorian era, there is no role that can fulfil her there. She deliberately alienates herself in order to pursue her difficult quest for self-fulfilment.

Charles is Fowles's representation of a dominant species that has reached its end: it is necessary for Charles to adapt in order to survive. Sarah is the instrument of Charles's metamorphosis. She seduces him and then deserts him with the result that he breaks off his engagement to Ernestina and becomes a social outcast. This frees him from the conventions of his society but he finds his freedom painful and frightening.

Except for Sarah, who consistently invents the pattern of her life and who remains, nonetheless, a figment of fiction, each of Pinter's characters, Victorian or modern, obeys the restrictions of some extrinsic artifice. Although the dynamic between Pinter's diachronic plots retrieves and enriches many of the novel's techniques and concerns, its foremost achievement lies in its approximation of Fowles's alternative endings.

Both Fowles and Pinter, by means of similar pretexts, imply that perfect endings are the stuff of fiction. When Fowles withdraws his "narrator" and when Pinter withdraws his "script," the stories conclude otherwise, accentuating the artifices of fiction and imposed definition. Through this device of contradictory endings, both writers extend the condition of inconclusiveness beyond the internal action of the story, referring the problem of closure, in all its dialectical complexity, to the reader or spectator. Thus, when Mike, detained by social obligations, searches for Anna he duplicates Charles's route to Sarah in the final scene of the fiction. Upon reaching her dressing room, however, he finds only her wig; Anna has changed from her Victorian costume and left.

The final shot of the screenplay shows him at the window of his room in which their fictional reunion had transpired, watching her car disappear. His imperative shout, "Sarah!" reverberates as a demand that life imitates art and as a lament over the impossibility of this prospect.

The narrator in the book reports the historical facts of life for a woman in Sarah's position. In the film, it happens in a different way. Anna, whilst researching her part, discovers and relates to Mike that one in every sixty houses in Victorian London was a brothel and that many of the prostitutes had no other way open to them to make a living. She also tells him that with a total male population of one and a quarter million, prostitutes were receiving clients at a rate of two million a week. She comprehends the truth of her character in Sarah's words: "If I went to London I know what I should become. I should become what some already call me in Lyme" (Pinter 19).

Anna comments, "See what I mean? You offend your boss; you lose your job. That's it! You're on the streets. I mean, it's real" (Pinter 19).

Fowles's two endings to the novel echo this existentialist theme. The reader is free to choose the ending they think fit; the narrator even refuses to make the choice of which ending should be the last and therefore more "powerful." As a character in the text, watching Charles sleep on a train, he tosses a coin to determine his fate.

The narrative structure of the film encompasses the two endings quite neatly, having the Victorian couple row off into the calm waters of Lake Windermere in the happy ending and the contemporary couple's affair end unhappily when Anna leaves Mike without any explanation or goodbye. The last scene of the screenplay reads thus:

241. Interior. New House.
Mike runs into the hall and up the stairs on which he first saw "Mrs. Roughwood." [Sarah]

242. Anna's dressing room. Empty.
Mike rushes in. The room is empty. Sarah's long red wig hangs from a block.
He quickly opens another door, which leads into the white room.

243. Interior. The White room.
Moonlight falls across the room. Sounds of the party from below. Suddenly the sound of a car starting up. Mike runs to the window, looks out.
244. Exterior. House.
Anna's white car driving towards the gate.

245. Exterior. House. Window.
Mike at window. He calls out:

>   MIKE
>   Sarah!

(Pinter 104)

2

It has been suggested that Pinter's screenplay, "for all it's virtues [. . .] ultimately fails to do justice to Fowles's work," because the manipulation of reader response, which is so essential to Fowles's narrative purpose, is not matched by the film (Lorsch 151).

Lorsch suggests this could have been done within the structure of the film narrative, for example, using the part in chapter twelve of the novel where Sarah is standing at her window watched by the unseen narrator, who refuses to enlighten the reader as to what she is thinking. A scene could have been included of the film-makers watching the rushes of Sarah at the window and arguing over what she may be thinking, making suggestions such as suicide, fate, and rebellion but never definitively attributing motivation. This would have the same effect as the narrator's obfuscation.

Fowles's "false ending" as early as chapter forty-four, describing Charles's dreary future life with Ernestina, which turns out to be a daydream he is having as he travels to Exeter, marks another key moment of choice in the novel. Charles decides to stop at Exeter and go to see Sarah, who then seduces him. Lorsch suggests this false ending could have been played out in the film as if it were fact, before revealing it as Charles's imaginings. This would again undermine the viewer's confidence in the authoritativeness of the Victorian story and in conventional narrative reliability.

Finally, both the alternative endings could have been acted out by Mike and Anna playing Charles and Sarah, and the director and cast could be seen at the cast party, arguing over which ending to use in the film: "Such a refusal to select a single definitive ending would have driven home Fowles's points about freedom and authority, humanity and God, audience and art" (Lorsch 155).

Since the film was released in 1981, it has polarised critical opinion. Such diversity of opinion can perhaps be accounted for by the book's complexity, by the abstraction of the ideas it brings before the reader. There is an epigraph at the beginning of each chapter of Fowles's novel. This could not be reproduced in the film as the medium of film does not allow this kind of reduplication. As a result, certain depths of Fowles's text are lost in the film. However, one must not forget the constraints of the film medium.

The film's narrative structure undoubtedly succeeds in many areas, keeping much of the spirit of Fowles's novel while altering its form. As Georg Gaston states: "if Fowles's narrator is capable of offering us his judgement, the film's double structure teases us into asking questions. Questions about the nature of love, ego, fictional art, sexual mystery and definitions of progress and evolution" (56).

As Beata Piatek observes, in the film adaptation of *The French Lieutenant's Woman* we are dealing with a peculiar form of "fidelity of transformation." However, the most spectacular achievement of the film is the fact that using purely cinematic techniques like the framing modern story, and in particular by intertwining it with the Victorian story, the director managed to recreate the distance between the audience and the Victorian story that Fowles achieved by using the intrusive narrator in the novel.

The reader of the novel is removed from the story because it is a pastiche and a self-conscious novel; the audience in the cinema is placed in the same position by being constantly reminded that this is a fiction film acted out by a cast of people. Thus we are dealing with a peculiar instance of "fidelity of transition" where the film adaptation considerably alters the source text in order to retain its "spirit."

Fowles said that *The French Lieutenant's Woman* was written at a time when he was beginning to develop strong and perhaps idiosyncratic views on the proper domains of the cinema and the novel. But Fowles immediately asserts:

> This business of proper domains is one of the reasons I am no longer in the least interested in scripting my own fiction. To assemble a book with a considerable and deliberate number of elements that you know cannot be filmed, and then to disassemble and reconstruct it out of the elements that can, is surely an occupation best left to masochists or narcissists. (*Filming* 41)

Another quotation from Fowles at this juncture is relevant:

> The actual process of making a narrative film, however few the characters and simple the locations, is hideously complicated, and expensive; and the greatest gift a good screenwriter can give a director is not so much a version "faithful" to the book as a version faithful to the very different production capability (and relation with audience) of the cinema. (*Filming* 43)

Works cited

Boyum, Joy Gould. *Double Exposure: Fiction into Film*. New American Library, 1985.

Carrière, Jean-Claude. *The Secret Language of Film*. Translated by Jeremy Leggatt. Faber and Faber, 1995.

Chatman, Seymour. *Coming to Terms: The Rhetoric of Narrative in Fiction and Film*. Cornell University Press, 1990.

Fowles, John. "The Filming of *The French Lieutenant's Woman*." 1981. In *John Fowles; Wormholes: Essays and Occasional Writings,* edited by Jan Relf. Vintage, 1999, 38–47.

—. *The French Lieutenant's Woman.* Vintage Classics, 2004.

Gaston, Georg. "*The French Lieutenant's Woman* by Karel Reisz." *Film Quarterly* 35, no. 2 (1981): 51–56.

Lorsch, Susan E. "Pinter Fails Fowles." *Literature and Film Quarterly* (1988): 151–55.

McHale, Brian. *Postmodernist Fiction.* Routledge, 1987.

Pinter, Harold. *The French Lieutenant's Woman and Other Screenplays.* Methuen, 1982.

Piatek, Beata. "British Cinema Pasts: Films Adaptations of Novels." *British Studies Web Pages.* 20 June 2003, elt.britcounc.org.pl/forum/filmrev.html.

CHAPTER 12

DIALECTICS OF EXCHANGE IN WILLIAM WYLER'S AND LUIS BUÑUEL'S ADAPTATIONS OF *WUTHERING HEIGHTS*

Hailed as an unforgettable classic of destructive passion and immortal love, Emily Brontë's *Wuthering Heights* is one of the most psychologically complex, self-reflexive, and indeterminate of Victorian novels. The nuanced exploration of class conflict, power, and patriarchy in this prized 1847 romance significantly undermines conventional notions of gender, class, and propriety. Not surprisingly, therefore, since the 1920s, Brontë's complex, ambivalent gothic romance of love and revenge has remained a treasure house of ideas for an overwhelming number of intriguing film adaptations.

Established directors from inside and outside Hollywood have experimented, trying to appropriate and transcreate Brontë's fascinating yet unfilmable classic. As a literary text, it poses the daunting challenge of narratives embedded within narratives and the use of multiple narrators with multiple points of view. It makes this psychologically complex gothic tale all the more difficult to translate to the screen.

The results have been both amazing and disappointing for lovers of literature and film-going audiences. Directors like William Wyler, Luis Buñuel, Robert Fuest, Peter Kosminsky, and recently Andrea Arnold have been quite successful in working out a nuanced dialectic in their intertextual and performative readings. Arnold's take on the Brontë classic foregrounds elements of race, where a black actor plays the role of Heathcliff. The interesting cultural afterlife of Brontë's one and only classic has witnessed Heathcliff being played by actors such as Laurence Olivier, Richard Todd, Timothy Dalton, Ralph Fiennes, Robert Cavanah, Tom Hardy, James Howson and others, all attempting in their own way to do justice to Brontë's sinister, ominous, and overpowering Heathcliff.

However, the two adaptations that specifically stand out and that I choose to discuss here are William Wyler's 1939 adaptation and the 1954 Mexican adaptation by Luis Buñuel. These adaptations in their intermingled transactions of literature and film work out a subtle dialectic between two houses, Wuthering Heights and Thrushcross Grange, and two families, the Earnshaws and the Lintons.

William Wyler's British film *Wuthering Heights* (1939), starring Laurence Olivier as Heathcliff and Merle Oberon as Catherine Earnshaw, begins with a storm raging outside. The director gives us a long shot of the storm and Lockwood's struggle to combat it. Stunning visuals of a storm are accompanied by fluid camera movements that make it evident a storm rages indoors too, within the mind of the owner of Wuthering Heights, Heathcliff. As we get a sneak peek into the interiors of the dark "Heights" we meet the other characters in the room—Isabella, Ellen Dean, and Joseph—who are all full of apathy and seem to be completely controlled by Heathcliff.

Later, with Lockwood's nightmare, we are made to feel the presence of a ghost, followed by mournful music. A howling snowstorm conveys a sense of the gothic and the spiritual. Throughout, a desolate, storm-tossed Yorkshire moor accompanied by billowing wind remains the dominant motif. The Wyler film is perhaps the most pictorial of Brontë adaptations. The story is recounted through Nelly's flashback, and in Wyler's adaptation Nelly is a more authoritative narrator than in the novel. In the novel "the very mode of narration makes the truth seem as elusive as events in the distant past and are difficult to recall" (Wheeler 71).

Keeping in view Brontë's novel, Terry Eagleton notes: "as a waif and orphan, Heathcliff is inserted into the close-knit family structure as an alien" (103). Hindley considers him a threat. The obscurity of Heathcliff's origins also frees him of any exact social role, as Nelly muses, he might equally be a prince (Eagleton 102). In the film, Wyler remains loyal to Brontë's obscure description of Heathcliff's origins.

In Wyler's adaptation, the childhood scenes take place outside, in bright sunshine, to symbolise a sense of freedom that both Cathy and Heathcliff enjoy in the lush green setting of the moors. The scenes are noted for the children's untamed love of each other and of nature. As Ellen (Nelly) recollects, the grown-up Cathy, is soon drawn towards the life of Thrushcross Grange, a life of comfortable material wealth and security: "That's what I want," she tells Heathcliff, "dancing and singing in a pretty world."

Heathcliff, in turn, after Catherine's return from the Grange as "a lady," warns her that she is turning into a "vain, weak, greedy fool." That she is "torn" between the two lives (in the words of Nelly's voice-over) is apparent in the way she tears off her new dress and runs off to Penistone

Crag with Heathcliff once more, begging Heathcliff's forgiveness and asking him to "fill my arms with heather."

From this point Catherine oscillates wildly between the two worlds, the polite sophistication that Edgar Linton offers and the genuine, untamed passion she feels for Heathcliff that accounts for her escape to Penistone Crag with him.

Wyler's commercially successful *Wuthering Heights* achieved a considerable romanticisation of Heathcliff (Laurence Olivier). For earlier literary critics, Heathcliff may have appeared to be an incarnation of evil qualities: implacable hate, ingratitude, cruelty, falsehood, selfishness, and revenge. However, Brontë was "reluctant to condemn Heathcliff" (Winnifrith and Chitham 113) and gradually through the nineteenth century, attitudes towards Heathcliff mellowed and readers have come to see Heathcliff as the "prototypical hero of Gothic romance" (Winnifrith and Chitham 114). Wyler's film treats Brontë's novel as a novel of romance and ends with Cathy's death and Heathcliff's cry of despair pleading Cathy to haunt him.

Wyler's creative rendition even allows Nelly to play a part in infusing a romantic significance to the ending, as Wright observes: "It is 'not a ghost' that lures Heathcliff to his death, she insists to Lockwood, 'but Cathy's love, stronger than time itself.' He is 'not dead but with her. . . . They've only just begun to live'" (Brontë 173).

Outside Hollywood's established canon, Luis Buñuel's Mexican adaptation *Abismos de Pasión*, treats the canonical literary text differently. In Buñuel's film Catherine/Catalina, like Emily Brontë herself, has a man's intellectual strength, boldness, and utter refusal to conform and a woman's tenderness and sensitivity. Catalina, despite her great love for the fiery tempered Alejandro/Heathcliff, is prevented by pride from marrying her boorish lover.

Buñuel's version recalls Brontë's novel: "It would degrade me to marry Heathcliff now; so he shall never know how I love him; and that, not because he's more mine than I am" (Brontë). Buñuel shows tempestuous storms metaphorically referring to characters at the heights of passion. Storm and weather imagery in the film's visual register are a pointer to the characters' inner turmoil. Despite having a similar nature to Alejandro, Catalina rejects him for the elegance, poise, and refinement of Eduardo's (Edgar Linton) world. Her choice, dictated by pride, is responsible for destroying all that is good in Alejandro. Alejandro disappears; Catalina marries Eduardo/Edgar; Ricardo/Hindley remains in possession of Wuthering Heights.

Buñuel's *Abismos de Pasión* opens at Thrushcross Grange with Catalina teasing Isabel, firing shots, killing buzzards, caging birds, and playfully commenting on Isabel's docile behaviour toward her (Catalina's) husband Eduardo. The opening scene of Eduardo's household in its "normal" state is soon undercut by Catalina's defiance and rebellious nature. Gradually we get to know that her despair stems from having broken with her childhood love, Alejandro; her almost childish wailing expresses a longing to return to the time when she was able to be at one with her passion. Commenting on the novel, Wheeler states, "The tragic consequences of her (Catherine's) marriage are reminiscent of the lives and works of Romantic writers such as Byron and Shelley—over-reachers in a world whose narrowness they despise" (71).

Catalina tells Isabel "I am a good wife. I'll give him (Eduardo) a child. What more does he want?" Though it speaks of Catalina's preference for a life of wealth, prosperity, and social security with Eduardo, it is also evident in her remark that disharmony exists in the family and there is contradiction in Catalina's mind over whether she is violating the order of the existing household. The scene shows that Catherine is unhappy in her "unnatural" union/marriage with Eduardo, the child of calm. Her attachment has always been to Alejandro's all-consuming love. Her nature aligns with Alejandro's. Though his rage and destructive energy is merciless, she is unable to tear herself away from his relentless passion. In marrying Eduardo, she had not only wrenched herself from the Heights but also from Alejandro.

Since Catalina and Alejandro's naturally forged union has been broken by Catalina's marriage, now they must struggle for possession of one another. Buñuel makes it evident in the character of Catalina that even though she married Eduardo, Alejandro is within her; therefore, nothing has been able to dislodge him. With Alejandro, she was driven by passion—fierce even violent passion—but invariably social conventions created barriers between the lovers. Catalina is intertwined with Alejandro by a complex admixture of dependence, resentment, and passion.

Alejandro as a symbol of the oppressed does not hold much ground in Buñuel's film despite Catalina's verbal attempts to establish him thus. In his years of absence, Alejandro, we realise, has acquired the manners and means of a gentleman, and thereafter returns to act as an oppressor. Ricardo's torture of the child Alejandro is only recounted in short dialogues, but never recollected through flashback. Hence, in Buñuel's film there is not much of an attempt to project the ominous Heathcliff figure as a representative of the proletariat as he begins the film and ends his life as a typical capitalist owning one house and renting another. Rather it is Ricardo's neglected child, Jorgito (Hareton), who gradually evolves as a symbol of the downtrodden and destitute.

If we again revisit the opening of Buñuel's film, we know that it opens some years later with an extraneous element, Alejandro, who comes back to the Catalina-Eduardo household (Catherine/Edgar Linton) household, mysteriously wealthy and outwardly more polished and sure of himself. Maria's (Nelly's) exchange with Alejandro here makes it evident that Alejandro has always been perceived as a source of discord, inevitably disrupting the working of the natural order. His return is considered a threat by Maria, for his presence would disrupt the peace of Eduardo's apparently happy domestic household.

In her brief exchange with Alejandro, Maria recalls that Alejandro's trouble-making propensities are inherent to his character; however, she does not recall the atmosphere of conflict in which he had to grow up. Unlike the polished Heathcliff of Laurence Olivier in William Wyler's Hollywood version, Alejandro is more true to Brontë's sinister Heathcliff who seems to carry hell within him. "In *Abismos de pasión*, Buñuel upholds Brontë's equation of passionate love to the torments and anguish of hell" (Fragola 52).

On his return to the Grange, Maria rebukes Alejandro, now a rich gentleman, for being "incurable." What Maria attempts in this scene is to link fiendishness, or devilishness, with a lack of trust on Alejandro's part. Throughout the film, he is forced to remain both devilish and incurable. Maria shuts the door in his face but Alejandro breaks open a window to steal into Eduardo's house. Alejandro's objective is to gain complete control over the destinies of all those who, in some way, are linked to the tragedy of his life.

Maria, in Buñuel's version, judges others by applying standards of normativity that are further based on preconceived ideas of right and wrong, heaven and hell, salvation and damnation, and which are radically challenged by the very nature of the love between Catalina and Alejandro. The old Joseph too links fiendishness or devilishness with Alejandro as he uses a cross and smoke all over the interiors of Wuthering Heights to cast away the spell of the "devil" from the house. The scene is suggestive of Alejandro being labelled as an "imp of Satan" because of his cunning.

The strength of Alejandro and Catalina's attachment is not only shown by the elder Catalina and Alejandro revisiting the places of their childhood (deliberately excluding Isabel from their company) but also expressed by dramatic exchanges of dialogue. Much of the dialogue of the screenplay is taken from the novel. The film features oblique presentations of the lovers' outbursts, with the focus on the love–hate relationship of the protagonists. Often there is a direct request for sympathy on the part of Catalina as she repeatedly maintains fasts in fits of rage. She often locks herself up after her altercations with Eduardo.

The closed bedroom door at Eduardo's household (Thrushcross Grange) becomes a prison in which she willingly confines herself. Her sense of being stifled by conflict sets her within a world that is impossibly out of contact with the domesticated world in which she now must live as Eduardo's wife. Her escapism, her longing, and her aggressive spirit are startlingly vivid in the Buñuel adaptation. No other film adaptation conveys the non-conformist energy of the Brontë text so intensely.

Catalina's desire for Alejandro, the wish for romantic escapism is also a wish for death and the death wish becomes integrally integrated with her love for Alejandro. She is proud of this wish to escape into death, into the glorious world of her imagination. Her death is the means by which she can satisfy her love for Alejandro. In Buñuel's film, therefore, Catalina's love is a longing for an impossible freedom from emotional conflict and her own excessive emotional needs.

Let me recount the scene in which Catalina, Alejandro, and Isabel scamper on the desolate moor. Catalina enjoys Isabel's discomfort when she informs Alejandro that Isabel has fallen in love with him. A violent scuffle ensues as Isabel attempts to break free from the clutches of Catalina. She fails to match Catalina's strength, bites Catalina on the arm, and runs free. Isabel's madness results in a wild flight across the moors. Alejandro chases Isabel and gets hold of her; as he passionately kisses her, Buñuel's camera captures Catalina's tolerant gaze from above and her mocking smile at the pair of newly formed lovers (Alejandro and Isabel). The shot does enough to undercut the male desire that Alejandro projects: that he is apparently reciprocating Isabel's love.

That Alejandro has miserably failed to provoke Catalina's jealousy is captured by her proud female gaze dismissing the very idea of imagining Alejandro and Isabel as potential lovers. However, it points to the fact that Catalina and Alejandro have destroyed the possibility of continuing such a natural and easy expression of their love as projected in Isabel's passion for Alejandro; the strength of their emotion may now only turn into a romantic death-ridden passion.

Under the power of a love–hate relationship, Catalina and Alejandro torture each other. Ordinarily "love is thought to redeem destructive impulses, but in Alejandro's case it is his love for Catalina which motivates his cruelty" (Apter 69). Wagner's *Tristan and Isolde* music is used on the soundtrack. Their thwarted love turns into a passion that is neither of the flesh nor of the spirit but that draws its destructive energy from impulses and subsequent frustration. Alejandro ruins Ricardo through gambling and drink, and finally seduces Eduardo's sister Isabel into marrying him.

Isabel suffers badly for her love for Alejandro and remains trapped in her marriage to Alejandro while his fiendish, sadistic nature rules over her with a disregard for conventional morality. In Buñuel's version, neither Eduardo not Isabel may be described as passive or timid. Eduardo suffers as he sees Alejandro as a rival in his love for Catalina.

When Catalina tells Eduardo that he cannot love her more than Alejandro does it is partly because Catalina and Alejandro share a close affinity in nature with each other. William Wyler, more than Buñuel, juxtaposes their closeness with the two contrasting worlds of Wuthering Heights and Thrushcross Grange quite early on in the film. High on the barren moorland, Wuthering Heights is the land of storm. It had been the natural home of the Earnshaw family and Catherine and Heathcliff are the wild, untamed children of the storm.

In Wyler's film, Edgar is the child of a sheltered leafy valley home below, Thrushcross Grange, which is the appropriate home of the children of the calm, gentle, if not passive or timid, Lintons. Together, each group—the Earnshaws and the Lintons, Wuthering Heights and Thrushcross Grange—following its own nature in its own sphere, combine to compose a cosmic harmony. It is the destruction and reinstatement of this cosmos that is the theme of Emily Brontë's novel and Wyler's film.

Buñuel's vision of conflict builds itself on a series of conflicts and oppositions, not just human conflicts but at a larger scale—between the outer and inner world, storm and poise, childhood and maturity, passion and reason, the mundane and the sublime, chaos and cosmos, death and life. An agnostic and an atheist, Buñuel manifested a recurrent fascination for plots bordering on supernatural and paranormal experiences. Being a director who was also affiliated with the surrealists, Buñuel focuses on visual motifs and keeps alive the "spirit" of Brontë's ambivalent, gothic tale.

Nature in both Wyler's and Buñuel's films is not a background but an intimate part of the action—violent, fruitful, animating, destroying. In Buñuel's version, its importunate reality registers most immediately in the suffering, desiring, perishing bodies of its characters. Brutal animal imagery is used throughout as animals are killed and displayed as trophies.

Buñuel successfully changed the ending of the novel, suggesting that passion in its world is asserted, often by an appeal to elemental energy, rather than analysed. It appears that the gothic melodrama of Brontë's genre makes way for a "pervasive sense of the precariousness of bodily life" (Glen 185) in Buñuel's film. The final scene's central focus is on a passion that seems to transcend mortality, which ultimately points toward the chaotic, tempestuous world of Wuthering Heights.

The ambivalence related to Cathy's ghost is here left open-ended, unlike in Robert Fuest's adaptation of *Wuthering Heights* (1970). This version literally shows the ghost of Cathy haunting Heathcliff (Timothy Dalton) for quite some time. He hallucinates Cathy (Anna Calder-Marshall) dispersed throughout his world. At Cathy's grave he clutches and clenches his fist, crying out in sheer despair, "Catherine Earnshaw, I say one prayer, may you not rest while I'm living." The more Heathcliff (Dalton) attempts to grasp the ghostly yet earthy Cathy's form, the more he fails to grasp her. The suggestive ambiguity and Brontë's pervasive hints concerning Cathy's ghost are probably lost—especially because her ghost is filmically shown. In Fuest's version, Brontë's frustrated lovers reunite in the grave and defy the possibility of extinction.

Buñuel's interpretation of the final scene is radically different from Hollywood adaptations, providing a rather invigorating perspective. Here Catalina is placed in an underground crypt after her death. As Alejandro breaks the fetters and enters the crypt, a gunshot is heard. Wounded, Alejandro climbs down the dark stairs, uncovers Catalina, and stoops to kiss her. Immediately afterwards, for a very brief moment, he has a vision of a living Catalina appearing to him as a bride. The hallucinatory presence of Catalina soon dissolves into an image of the scheming Ricardo/Hindley who fires a shot and kills Alejandro. The audience is left to wonder whether the lovers reunite in death.

Other than reconfirming a surrealist director's lifelong preoccupation with the supernatural and the *danse macabre*, Buñuel's final scene perhaps suggests that like Brontë, he believed that even death does not lead to fulfilment. Through this scene, Buñuel not only gives outlet to his gothic, melodramatic fantasy but also like Brontë reconfirms the notion of a love that outlives death. Buñuel's surrealist version excels as an adaptation because it recreates its source novel's ambivalence. Like Brontë, Buñuel through his final scene suggests events beyond interpretation.

In Wyler's and Buñuel's adaptations, like Brontë's much revered classic, there is an enticing refusal of closure, where haunting tales of the unquiet dead continue to baffle us ceaselessly. In 2020, as we fondly remember Brontë on her bicentenary, let us not forget the multiple film adaptations that have paid their homage and made the cultural afterlife of *Wuthering Heights* so memorable.

Works cited

Abismos de Pasión. Directed by Luis Buñuel, performances by Irasema Dylan and Jorge Mistral. Plexus, 30 June 1954.
Apter, T. E. "Romanticism and Romantic Love in *Wuthering Heights*." *The Brontë Sisters*, edited by Harold Bloom. Chelsea House Publishers, 2002, 65–79.
Eagleton, Terry. *Myths of Power: A Marxist Study of the Brontës*. Palgrave Macmillan, 2005, 97–121.
Glen, Heather. "Emily Brontë." *The Cambridge Companion to English Novelists*, edited by Adrian Poole, Cambridge University Press, 2009, pp. 180–90.
Fragola, Anthony. "Buñuel's Re-vision of 'Wuthering Heights': The triumph of 'L'Amour Fou' over Hollywood Romanticism." *Literature/Film Quarterly* 22, no. 1 (1994): 50–56.
Jones, Julie. "Fatal Attraction: Buñuel's Romance with *Wuthering Heights*." *Society of Spanish and Spanish-American Studies* 22, no. 1/2 (1997): 149–63.
Wheeler, Michael. *English Fiction of the Victorian Period, 1830–1890*, 2nd edition. Longman, 1994.
Winnifrith, Tom, and Edward Chitham. *Charlotte Brontë and Emily Brontë: Literary Lives*. Macmillan Press, 1989.
Wright, Terry R. "Film Adaptation: The Case of *Wuthering Heights*." *Teaching Nineteenth Century Fiction*, edited by Andrew Maunder and Jennifer Phegley, Palgrave Macmillan, 2010.
Wuthering Heights. Directed by William Wyler, performances by Laurence Olivier and Merle Oberon. Samuel Goldwyn Productions, 24 March 1939.

Chapter 13

"Ceaselessly into the Past"— In Search of Fitzgerald's Gatsby and the American Dream on Celluloid

Fiction and film share several common grounds. They share not only the same narrative patterns and many of the same storytelling strategies, but also a familiar aesthetic appeal. Critics tend to identify film with the form it most frequently assumes, and in which we usually experience it—that is the fictional narrative. This article takes into consideration one such fictional narrative, *The Great Gatsby*.

As is well known, classics and popular literature have often been turned into films. In a similar vein, F. Scott Fitzgerald's classic *The Great Gatsby* has witnessed multiple film adaptations over several decades. Major adaptations of *The Great Gatsby* include Herbert Brenon's 1926 silent film, the "Alan Ladd version" of 1949, Jack Clayton's adaptation with Robert Redford and Mia Farrow in the leads, a made-for-television version in 2000, an opera in 2000 composed by John Harbison, and most recently Baz Luhrmann's 2013 production.

The directors of such fiction-to-film adaptations are caught between two different art forms. While the film-maker must show devotion to the original literary work, he or she must also create a new work of art in terms of the language of film. It goes without saying that whatever may be the similarities between two differing sister arts or to be more specific, prose fiction and film, and whatever may be the parallels in their languages, to appropriate a book to film, words to images, requires an immense act of creative imagination and interpretation on the part of the director.

This chapter discusses and assesses the success or failure of the 1974 film adaptation by the British director Jack Clayton. It also analyses Baz Luhrmann's 2013 adaptation with Leonardo DiCaprio as Jay Gatsby and Tobey Maguire as Nick Carraway. The chapter attempts to read closely the result of such artistic collaboration between literature and cinema. In analysing such an interface between two different art forms that share the same mode of communication, the chapter hopes to unravel the very language of adaptation.

Both fiction and film, as we all know, share a kind of mutually reciprocal relationship. For when a film is made of a novel, it tends to encourage rather than discourage reading it. We are all aware that after the film *Jurassic Park* was a big success at the box office, the sale of the book, by Michael Crichton, increased rapidly and the book became a bestseller overnight. But, while dealing with the adaptation angle, we should remember that a film is itself a work of art, it is the result of a director's vision; it has a language and content of its own; it develops a narrative of its own. A particular adaptation if it lacks ingenuity and follows its source book blindly, may become a "literal adaptation"; however, there is nothing called a "straight adaptation."

The Great Gatsby centres on the decadent mores of the American dream and the spoilt recklessness of the age. The 1920s in America or the Jazz Age is a period that is usually identified with money and gaiety. Gatsby's flashy cars, his lavish parties, the over-adventurous conduct of his guests, and the thoughtlessness of the Buchanans are all part of this atmosphere of gaiety and untamed enjoyment. The beauty and splendour of Gatsby's parties masks the decay and corruption that lay at the heart of the Roaring Twenties.

> [. . .] gaudy with primary colours and hair shorn in strange new ways, and shawls beyond the dreams of Castile [. . .] the air is alive with chatter and laughter, and casual innuendo and introductions forgotten on the spot, and enthusiastic meetings between women who never knew each other's names. [. . .] The party has begun. (Fitzgerald 50)

This was the time of jazz music, the Charleston, and the motor car. For Fitzgerald, the popular music of the twenties—jazz—embodied the modern spirit of the roaring decade. The novel is replete with musical references both to popular 1920s jazz and to romantic musical metaphors that are deeply embedded in its narrative.

The society of the Jazz Age, as observed by Fitzgerald, is morally bankrupt, and thus continually plagued by a crisis of character. Fitzgerald ties the expressions of jazz to cultural anxieties within the modernisation of American society. Jay Gatsby, though he struggles to be part of this world, remains unalterably an outsider. His life is a tremendous irony, in that it is a parody of twenties-style pretentiousness: his closet overflows with custom-made shirts; his lawn is alive with "the right people," all engaged in the serious work of absolute triviality; his mannerisms (his fake British accent, his old-boy friendliness) are ludicrously affected. As

Weinstein states: "the book seems to be imbued with excess: the tawdry excesses of the Flapper Age, the wild parties, the flashy and not-so-flashy materialism of Gatsby, the excesses of capitalism, the sentimental and blinding excesses of the rags-to-riches story itself, the American Dream" (22).

Despite all this, Gatsby can never be truly a part of the corruption that surrounds him: he remains intrinsically "great." The classic, unreliable narrator, Nick Carraway, reflects upon the fact that Gatsby's determination, his lofty goals, and most importantly the grand character of his dreams, set him apart from his vulgar contemporaries. Fitzgerald constructs Gatsby as a true American dreamer, set against the decay of American society during the 1920s. His devotion to and single-minded pursuit of Daisy is not just a story of unrequited love but symbolic of the evanescent and essential emptiness of the American dream.

In the 1920s, jazz was a new, edgy style carrying deep-seated social meanings. The 1974 film adaptation directed by Jack Clayton portrays the Jazz Age. The scenes of Gatsby's parties, though less wild, seem almost real because of suitable costumes and well-trained dancers. The parties include the Charleston, dancing, drinking, and many other things that were common in the 1920s. Yet the scenes of dancing at Gatsby's parties are deliberately graceless. We start wondering whether this is the same world that produced what Gertrude Stein called the "Lost Generation"? Is it the same world that T. S. Eliot condemned in *The Waste Land*?

Fitzgerald denounces 1920s America as an age of blindness and greed, an age hostile to the work of dreaming; therefore, its dreamers meet a tragic fate. The society of the Jazz Age is presented as possessing the unlimited potential of their great new nation; however, their response is to allow themselves to be carried "like boats against the current, borne back ceaselessly into the past" (Fitzgerald 42). Their work is a recreation of European historical grandeur, a fact that the film is keen to demonstrate.

Jack Clayton's adaptation puts costume design and art direction above the intricacies of character. It seems that the director fell in love with the flapper dresses, the party scenes, and the Jazz Age tunes, ending up with a classic illustrated version of a great book rather than a fresh, organic take on the text. Unsurprisingly, the film won two Oscars for its costume and musical score.

In the film Gatsby is shown holding court in a neo-classical mansion complete with a glass-fronted ballroom, mirrors, and chandeliers that recall the excesses of Versailles rather than the east coast of twentieth-century America. When Nick and Daisy are shown around Gatsby's house, their feet echo in the vast empty spaces of the rooms. Francis Ford Coppola, co-writer of the 1972 film *The Godfather*, wrote the screenplay for the production of *The Great Gatsby*. Consequently, Gatsby's dubious past and possible gangster background are emphasised in the film. The scene where Nick first meets Gatsby has been mysteriously changed, ruining one of the most interesting parts of the novel. In the novel, Nick introduces himself to a stranger at Gatsby's party only to discover later that the man had been none other than the host himself.

Despite this, Clayton's film has a subtlety about it, especially in Mia Farrow's portrayal of Daisy's fickle and inconstant character. Farrow gives us a hollow Daisy in stark contrast to Gatsby's expectations of depth of character. Nevertheless, the principal characters seem unsuited to their assigned roles. Mia Farrow is not alluring enough to explain Gatsby's focused dedication towards her, while Robert Redford is both unstable and lacking in the characteristic Redford charisma.

The focus becomes sharper when the film visits the miserable gas-station home of Tom Buchanan's lover Myrtle. Here, amongst the dirt "where ashes grow like wheat" (Fitzgerald 36), the colour drains from the film, in sharp contrast to the rainbow spectrum of Gatsby's world. In the book, Myrtle was supposed to be ugly, overweight, and dirty, almost like a binary opposite of Daisy. In the film, Myrtle is dressed in white, is skinny, and is not ugly. In portraying her so, they take away from the viewer the opportunity to realise that Tom was interested in a woman who was so unlike Daisy.

Important parts of Gatsby's past are left out of the film, such as the omission of the figure of Dan Cody; in this example, we are therefore not shown that Gatsby was once a working man. The figure of Dan Cody exemplifies the hardships faced by the dreamer. Cody is a miner, "a product of the Nevada silver fields, of the Yukon, of every rush for metal since seventy-five" (Fitzgerald 97). He becomes a millionaire through hard work, ambition, and a little bit of fine American luck. Despite these qualities, he dies alone, drunk and betrayed. Through Dan Cody, Fitzgerald suggests that 1920s society manipulated its visionaries, milking them for their hard-earned money, and then promptly forgot them. This formula is reiterated through the story of Gatsby as well. To appropriate Cody, however, the film would have to take recourse to a flashback again, though flashbacks in the novel are frequent. For example, we get to know Gatsby's childhood only towards the end of the novel.

Fitzgerald's novel is structurally dense and involves a complex handling of time. Again, the novel describes a moment of stasis when Daisy and Gatsby meet for the first time after a gap of five years. But the question is how to show this in the film. The medium of film demands that it should move forward. These are complex issues any adaptation has to deal with. An important character, Owl Eyes, is never shown in the film. One of the important scenes in the novel occurs when Daisy runs over Myrtle. The film leaves out this gruesome yet crucial scene completely. The loss of this scene also adds to the confusion regarding the plot. The 2000 version, directed by Robert Markowitz, has a dramatic accident scene, something that was necessary in the 1974 film to make it more dramatic.

Scott Fitzgerald's works—*Tender Is the Night, The Beautiful and the Damned, Babylon Revisited*—were all adapted for the screen. Here was a writer whose works demanded cinematic translation—and none perhaps so much as his delicate masterpiece, *The Great Gatsby*. One might wonder why *The Great Gatsby* has received so much attention from film-makers. Of course, it is the magnetic, paradoxical figure of Jay Gatsby and his mystique: the fabulous "rags to riches hero" obsessed with his dream of Daisy. Yet the millionaire bootlegger Gatsby, who in the summer of 1922 lives at West Egg, is not the central character in Baz Luhrmann's film. Instead, it is the elusive, self-effacing Nick Carraway, aged thirty, who is Daisy's cousin, played by Tobey Maguire, who is the central focus.

In Luhrmann's version, Nick has taken a cottage next door to Gatsby's mansion while he attempts to establish himself as a stockbroker; Gatsby uses him as a means to reconnect with Daisy. Every single detail in this adaptation is presented to the audience from Nick's perspective; Nick narrates the incidents from a sanatorium as a form of therapy on the advice of a psychiatrist. The framing device sets the film explicitly in the context of the Wall Street bubble and a nation's collective breakdown—the economic collapse as well as the rampant gangsterism are all brought into purview.

Gatsby's dream of rising out of the poverty of his childhood and securing wealth and social standing to attain Daisy's love is a romantic, utopian one that is often read as a representation of the American dream. It is perhaps the doomed romance of Gatsby and Daisy that film-makers have found romantic. It is also the world of the novel that has attracted film-makers: a world of alluring riches and gaudy, loud parties populated with wealthy people.

In Clayton's film, as Boyum has noted, all of Fitzgerald's novel is richly visualised: "the novel is filled with striking individual images (the poster featuring the eyes of Dr. Eckleburg; the green light at the end of Daisy's dock) and marked by a strongly scenic presentation," like the "breeze-swept living room where Daisy and Jordan Baker lounge on a summer's afternoon: the 'valley of ashes' where Wilson's garage is located" (98). Boyum further observes:

> There is also Fitzgerald's prevailing mode of characterization in the Clayton film—characterization not by lengthy summary or extended internal musing, but by speech (Gatsby's "old sport": Meyer Wolfsheim's "I understand you are looking for a business gonnegtion [sic]") and action (Tom breaking Myrtle's nose; Daisy sobbing over Gatsby's beautiful shirts). And lastly there is the novel's slimness and economy of structure. There is little cutting and compression needed here. In fact, the novel reads much as if it were a scenario for a film. (98–99)

Fitzgerald at times uses Daisy as an emblem of "old money's" pompous hypocrisy: it can never be equal to Gatsby's dreams. However, such subtle nuances are missed in Clayton's adaptation. As Daisy is tainted by her association with the brutal and uncouth Tom, she is in fact more like him than she is like the idealistic Gatsby. During the first meeting, Fitzgerald focuses on the fact that she is no longer dressed completely in white: "her brass buttons glint in the sunlight" (Fitzgerald 85).

On the other hand, Daisy Buchanan is one of the most enigmatic characters in American literature. Daisy represents something indefinable: an idealised love. Daisy herself, however, is not Gatsby's goal. Gatsby's goal is to keep hold of the love that she once inspired, the memory of her, which is coloured by his idealisation of her. Luhrmann's adaptation catches the real essence of the not-so-hollow Daisy. His pop culture references gel with Fitzgerald's classic love story. Luhrmann's bravura film-making techniques, in a postmodern style, try to flesh out an innovative approach towards its literary source.

Gatsby's unwavering optimism is sometimes at odds with Fitzgerald's social critique of American materialism during the modernisation of the 1920s. These cultural anxieties are lost in Clayton's translation. Clayton's film is slow-paced. All the other people are mere shadows of Gatsby and so only come to life after his arrival in the film. However, the Clayton-Coppola film begins at a leaden pace with shots that are supposed to indicate Gatsby's suspicious past. Right from the beginning, there is an over-reliance on Redford's iconic screen presence. Redford is wooden and unreal, playing his "star persona" image. It seems that the choice of Robert Redford and Mia Farrow was in large measure dictated by their iconicity as popular actors rather than for any inherent affinity they may have had with Fitzgerald's characters.

Boyum observes:

As reviewers noted at the time, almost everything seems wrong with the Clayton film and out of sync with the novel to boot: its pacing is languorous, verbose and lacking in visual innovation whereas the novel is tight, fast-paced and visually both rich and promising. The economy of expression and swift pacing of the original novel are missed in the film. In the novel much of what we see is characterised by an "ineffable gaudiness"; in the Clayton adaptation the parties are less wild and vulgar than they seem in the book and are populated not by a mix of nouveau-riche West-Eggers and elegant East-Eggers, but with all the same type of people. (100)

Despite the grand intentions of David Merrick, the producer, Jack Clayton, the director, and Francis Ford Coppola, the film almost violated most of the key intentions of Fitzgerald's mysterious and resistant text. It failed to present a dramatic and suspenseful story. Luhrmann's adaptation of *Gatsby* with its lavish *mise en scène*, layers of intertextuality, and musical anachronisms is more dramatic and suspenseful. Luhrmann's blockbuster adaptation parallels Fitzgerald's novel through the musical styles chosen for the film, which include jazz, hip-hop, and a romantic instrumental underscore.

Yet if the Clayton-Coppola film is a little too restrained and sensitive, it is the sheer loudness, both visual and aural, that drowns Luhrmann's postmodern pastiche. Luhrmann's non-naturalistic, unrestrained style revels in artifice, exaggerated acting, fast cutting between images, quick camera movements, elaborate set designs, lavish costuming, and special effects. Wolfsheim, Gatsby's partner in crime, whom Nick meets, has been turned from a Jew into an Indian to fend off the charge of anti-Semitism. Luhrmann still manages to deploy effective visual metaphors, one of which is the shooting star seen during the flashback to Gatsby's first meeting with Daisy at her parents' home in Louisville, Kentucky. The star symbolises all that he ever wished his relationship with Daisy could be. In the novel, the shooting star is metaphorical; in the film, it is literal. The image of the star motif is repeated in other visuals. The light at the end of Daisy's dock is unmistakably star-like.

We may look out too for some effective use of metaphor employed by Jack Clayton. The distorting effect of reflection in mirrors and pools play an important part in his version. Spectacles, not least those on the face in the menacing billboard advertisement for Dr T. J. Eckleburg, seem to stand as a metaphor for obscured vision and poor judgement. Blindness is one of the novel's central themes: it is populated almost entirely with people who wish not to see. They seek out blindness in the form of drunkenness: Daisy binges on alcohol the night before her wedding, in order to obliterate her vision of a miserable future. Jordan, Daisy, and Tom and the other jet-setters of the 1920s drive recklessly; they remain blind to danger, so caught up are they with the selfish pursuit of pleasure. They thoughtlessly risk their own lives and the lives of others. Nick says to Jordan, "You're a rotten driver. Either you ought to be more careful, or you oughtn't drive." Jordan responds, "They'll keep out of my way. It takes two to make an accident" (Fitzgerald 138). The crucial confrontation between Gatsby and Tom Buchanan in front of Nick, Daisy, and Jordan in a suite at the Plaza Hotel is worked out well by Luhrmann.

For Fitzgerald, twenties society was driving toward death through the cooling twilight, which is truly seen only by Nick, who is above all else an observer (the novel is in some sense his memoir, and thus a collection of his observations). He is Fitzgerald's representative and alter ego within the narrative. But, as is interestingly observed by Boyum, Clayton's film reveals a crucial flaw: its "mishandling of point of view" (100). Boyum states:

> the film may open and close with Nick Carraway and even grant him more screen time than Gatsby; it may make clear that he is our storyteller, allowing him to comment in voice-over on the soundtrack. But, it nevertheless fails to establish the perspective of the film as his own, to show us the world as if it were filtered through his eyes and consciousness. . . . For not only are we restricted here to what Nick sees and what Nick hears; not only are even his reports of what others have told him dominated by his sensibility; it is also that, however one reads Nick . . . as ironic narrator . . . or straightforward storyteller and true moralist, his perceptions and judgements stand at the story's very heart, not on its periphery. (100)

Nick's vision alters in the course of the novel. His attitude evolves as the story unfolds. Much mystery surrounds Gatsby's character in the novel. He is a shady underworld man, an ornate, clumsy snob, a socially awkward, unrefined liar. But as the fiction comes to its close, Fitzgerald portrays him in a different light. He is more idealistic, more generous, and full of indestructible aspirations. However, it is the perception of Nick that is at the heart of the novel: his perception of Gatsby, his way of looking at the Buchanans. The workings of Nick's mind, his consciousness, defines the novel.

It is this narrative voice that goes missing in the Clayton adaptation, which is a huge loss. In the film an all seeing, omniscient point of view prevails that destroys the beauty and mystery of Gatsby and Daisy's relationship because it has access to every aspect it. In the novel, Nick admits to being aware that he may be giving a partial account. Hypocrisy and the ability of people to manipulate the way they are perceived by others are important themes in the novel. In Clayton's film, the Fitzgerald novel is stripped of several layers of meaning. It should have been Nick's perspective that denied us such proximity to Gatsby. In which case, Gatsby's aura could have been retained.

As Boyum remarks, "Gatsby is Fitzgerald's most quixotic and troublesome creation" (101). Whether it is Gatsby's amazing accumulation of riches, or the manner of his articulation, or his single-minded undying affection for Daisy, Fitzgerald's Gatsby remains an unsolved riddle. Whether it is Gatsby's belief in the "green light," or his desire to "recreate the past," there is something unconvincing yet magnificent about him. Interestingly, such a Gatsby is well represented by Leonardo DiCaprio in Luhrmann's adaptation.

Luhrmann's Gatsby, like Fitzgerald's, is a marvellous character in the most literal sense of the word: more symbolic or representative of a class than an individualised personality. We see him directly but we see him only from Nick's perspective. Nick's perspective in Luhrmann's version, unlike Clayton's, never deprives Gatsby of his mystery and distance. In Clayton's film, Gatsby has a reality, and to our disappointment there is a complete breakdown of distance. There, Gatsby is a more sketchy character whose presence simply cannot hold; under the film's dissection, his obsession for Daisy is reduced from tragedy to mere self-indulgent tenderness.

Clayton's film ends up by showing Gatsby more unambiguously, unequivocally, which thereby shrinks Gatsby to someone ordinary. As a result, Nick is also significantly diminished. In Fitzgerald's novel, multi-layered projections have come into play. It is indeed difficult to recreate Fitzgerald's Gatsby on screen. In the book "we cannot be certain whether Nick is projecting his fantasies on to Gatsby, or is instead the only person to see past Gatsby's façade to the grandeur of the real man" (Churchwell).

However, as viewers we must be sensitive to what a film cannot accomplish but that literature can, about dissimilarities in the structure, and the effects of the two media. In "reading" an adaptation, we are never really juxtaposing a book with a film, but a novelist's vision with a film-maker's vision—the novel that we ourselves have re-enacted/recreated in our minds, out of which we have contrived our own individualised "film." The film-maker too has done something similar. His or her work of art has worked out a parallel act of transformation.

For, just as we are readers, so implicitly is the film-maker, offering us, through his or her vision, a particular rendition and deciphering of a source text. An adaptation is always, whatever else it may be, a transcreation. If this is one way of understanding the nature of adaptation and the relationship of any given film to the book that inspired it, it is also a way of understanding what may give rise to this kind of a filmic recreation in the first place: the opportunity to nurture, value, and treasure one work of art through another.

Works cited

Boyum, Joy Gould. *Double Exposure/Fiction Into Film*. New American Library, 1985.

Churchwell, Sarah. "*The Great Gatsby* and the American Dream." https://www.theguardian.com/books/2012/may/25/american-dream-great-gatsby.

Clayton, Jack, director. *The Great Gatsby*. Performances by Robert Redford, Mia Farrow, and Karen Black. Paramount, 1974.

Coppola, Francis Ford, director. *The Godfather*. Performances by Marlon Brando and Al Pacino. USA, 1972.

—, director. *The Godfather Part II*. Performances by Al Pacino and Robert Duvall. USA, 1974.

Fitzgerald, F. Scott. *Babylon Revisited and Other Stories*. Scribners, 1996.

—. *Tender Is the Night*. London: Scribners, 1995.

—. *The Beautiful and the Damned*. Oxford World's Classics, 1998.

—. *The Great Gatsby*. Wordsworth Classics, 1993.

Luhrmann, Baz, director. *The Great Gatsby*. Performances by Leonardo DiCaprio, Tobey Maguire, and Carey Mulligan. Australia, USA, Warner Bros, 2013.

Markowitz, Robert, director. *The Great Gatsby*. Performances by Mira Sorvino and Toby Stephens. A and E Entertainment, 2000.

Sontag, Susan (1961). "A Note on Novels and Films." *Against Interpretation*. Doubleday, 1990.

Weinstein, Arnold. "Fiction as Greatness: The Case of Gatsby." *Novel: A Forum on Fiction* 19, no. 1 (1985), pp. 22–38.

PART 3

UNLOCKING THE TROUBLED MIND: AESTHETICS OF HITCHCOCK AND KUBRICK

CHAPTER 14

VERTIGO'S AFTERLIFE: A TRAVEL THROUGH SIX DECADES

In 1958 Alfred Hitchcock's *Vertigo* had a solidly crafted script in the thriller/detective genre, but the manner in which the director effortlessly blended a range of genres like thriller, romance, mystery, horror, and drama makes it a fascinating watch. Structurally, like Hitchcock's other masterpiece *Rear Window*, *Vertigo* resembles a "thriller," a generic term that has come to include a wide range of films—detective films, police procedural films, spy films, political thrillers, courtroom thrillers, erotic thrillers, or psycho-thrillers, that is to say all films dealing with the enactment, execution, or prevention of crime; all also share another crucial characteristic: suspense.

Generally, thrillers focus on plot over character and emphasise intense physical action over the character's psyche. Psychological thrillers tend to reverse the formula to a certain degree, emphasising the characters just as much. Usually crime thrillers are organised around an innocent victim wrongly accused; in *Vertigo*, it is Scottie (James Stewart) who unintentionally lands up in a world of intrigue and deceit.

Scottie is here deceived by his old schoolmate Gavin Elster into believing that his wife Madeleine (Kim Novak) has developed suicidal tendencies. He believes that a long-dead maternal ancestor named Carlotta Valdes has come to possess her and lead her to a repetition of the ancestor's suicide.

Elster takes advantage of Scottie's acrophobia, vertigo, a psychosomatic illness, as Elster decides to use him in his plan to murder his wife. As suggested by Wells, Scottie may be compared to Norman Bates in *Psycho*. In several ways "the obsessed Scottie, in his sincere attempts to refashion the dead Madeleine, through his insistent transformation of Judy and the subsequent suggestion of necrophiliac fulfilment anticipates the psycho-sexual perversion of Norman Bates" (Wells 77). Up to a certain point, then, *Vertigo* resembles both the psycho-thriller and the crime thriller.

Along with *Vertigo*, Hitchcock started a trilogy of films from this period that focused on the need to conceal aspects of someone's disturbed character, the other two being *Psycho* and *Marnie*. Gradually we start questioning whether his films focus on obsession or are exorcisms of the same overtly destructive longings for certainty and fantasy.

Unlike the psycho-thriller *Psycho*, or other 1980s or early 1990s films, *Vertigo* does not show the presence of a stalking "monstrous" (because mentally disturbed) figure, a psycho-killer lurking at the centre of the film. Yet, like any psychological thriller, *Vertigo* indulges in deceptive mind games and delves deeper into the complexity of the human mind and its fatal obsession. Hitchcock, it seems, was obsessively trapped in his dedication to "pure cinema," a director who was in awe of aberration and yet found it tantalisingly attractive.

Again, in many respects *Vertigo* is a quintessential film noir. Based on French pulp novel *D'entre les morts* (*From Among the Dead*), it features an unofficial investigator investigating a mysterious woman, a carefully planned and executed murder, a voice-over and a flashback, San Francisco as a subjective labyrinth, expressionistic moments, and reminiscences of gothic suspense and melodrama.

Organised around the psychotic effects of trauma on a protagonist's current involvement in a lone affair and a crime or intrigue, Scottie in *Vertigo*, is a victim of some past trauma and of a real villain (Gavin Elster), who takes advantage of his friend's masochist guilt. The villain makes the female protagonist acquire an unaccustomed identity to serve the murderous plot.

Judy takes on the identity of Madeleine, Elster's wife, to dupe Scottie. As Scottie is made to investigate Madeleine's moves and follow her everywhere she goes, Scottie's role is that of a private investigator making this film akin to the detective thriller. Scottie's frighteningly dark, harrowing, and extreme obsession with Madeleine grows.

Abandoning the boyish Midge, he falls desperately in love with the "possessed" woman, only to witness her fake a spectacular suicide by intentionally leaping into San Francisco bay. He dramatically saves her and takes her to her place. In its greatest moments, a "dark and romantic fable" (Spoto 56) like *Vertigo* undeniably invokes the mood of film noir. It is a quintessential film noir.

Profoundly influential on neo noir, particularly the erotic thriller (Bould 18), the film privileges the woman's story in a way no film noir had ever done before. Hitchcock stylistically deviates from the genre's characteristic absorption in the man's dilemma (falling in love with a villainous woman) and intelligently does away with the typically convoluted plots found in film noirs.

The phenomenal rooftop sequence in *Vertigo*, the chase, and Madeleine's fall from the rooftop repeated twice in the film make this psycho/crime/erotic thriller a horror film too. Interestingly enough, both *Vertigo* and Hitchcock's *Rebecca* tell the tale of a dead (absent/absence as presence) woman's grip on a living "daughter" figure. Kim Novak, in *Vertigo* is a *femme fatale*, presented as a mysterious and seductive woman whose beauty and charm ensnares Scottie in bonds of irresistible desire leading to Scottie's insane obsession. Its major focus on Scottie's romantic obsession for Madeleine, the essential theme of love at first sight, infidelity, the love story, and the search for love are at the heart of the film.

Vertigo's ultimate ending in tragic love make it a romance film that may be seen as a sub-genre of the drama film. It brilliantly manifests the features of the romantic thriller where the master of suspense explores the depths of his own abilities that had never been captured on screen before.

Scottie though initially reluctant to accept the assignment of following Madeleine to save her from her illusions and detect the truth, fails to rescue her when she hurls herself from a church tower. Overwhelmed by guilt and sadness for the woman he has fallen madly in love with, he is duped into believing that he has witnessed the woman (Elster's wife) committing suicide.

It is the villainous Elster who uses Madeleine in his murderous plot to exploit her beauty, charm, and sexual allure. She is disguised, her identity altered, but she is not entirely a cunning enchantress or simply a manipulator of male desire. She is not represented entirely in negative or perverse terms. For in Kim Novak the director projects the *femme fatale* as a victim and victimiser; and from a feminist perspective this binary of victim/victimiser originates from a fatal male aggressiveness in the film. In the dual Madeleine/Judy role, her character is a tragic victim of the men who fashion her into a sexual object. Judy is ultimately made to atone for the man's visual and narrative pleasure. Judy's troubled childhood, her distancing from her own mother, precipitates Judy's move to the big city in search of a man who will love her for herself, but she ends up in the arms of the cunning Elster who entraps her.

Novak's portrayal of Madeleine and Judy presents brilliant contrasts: Madeleine is a well-bred, sophisticated super aristocrat; Judy is a warm-hearted, insecure commoner. The concept of Kim Novak's character duelling with herself has led to significant feminist debates in the film for decades. For if Madeleine/Judy is made into an object of deception and desire which the hero is attracted to and repulsed by, it is also a conflict within the self of the tormented lover.

The complex dualities of Novak's character, the damsel in distress and the scheming seductress, is the key to the suspense and success of the film. Scottie, who is enraged at the end of the film on realising the double deception, tells her:

> You played the wife very well, Judy. . . . He made you over, didn't he, he made you over just as I made you over, only better, not only the clothes and the hair, but the looks and the manner and the words and those beautiful phoney trances . . . (*Vertigo*)

It is Novak's objectification and fetishisation in the film by the male characters and the camera that actually contribute to the cinema's signifiers of voyeuristic pleasure. Madeleine is Scottie's object of obsessive desire. The mystification of female beauty may be apparent in the film, aided by Bernard Herrmann's emotionally gripping score that creates a sense of haunting, perturbed yearning.

Novak's position as a "manufactured romantic idol" as a "love goddess" (Wexman 34), as the mysterious otherworldly icon of beauty, is one of the major reasons for the film's phenomenal success. François Truffaut in his interview with Hitchcock in 1962 said to Hitchcock: "I take it, from some of your interviews, that you weren't too happy with Kim Novak, but I thought she was perfect for the picture . . . I can assure you that those who like *Vertigo* like Kim Novak in it. Very few American actresses are quite as carnal on the screen" (58).

Scottie's romantic pursuit of the female is tragic, for his underlying purpose is to distance the maternal ghostly presence from the daughter's mind, which Madeleine resists even when she is in love with Scottie. The film works through a "female Oedipal drama, the desire for unity with the powerful maternal presence (Carlotta) and in the process subverts its masculinist premises" (Hollinger 22).

Tania Modleski reads *Vertigo* as narrating a story of female desire for unity with a mother "who assumes unlimited power in death" (Modelski 93). Scottie falls in love with an image of Madeleine as an etherealised, aestheticised beauty.

Interestingly then, the film offers a view through a kaleidoscope of genres, challenging the viewer to go beyond a single-genre approach. It playfully features one genre against another—overshadowing one over the other—an approach that promotes creative and productive comparisons to be made across formal generic boundaries. Hitchcock was perhaps trying to explore the nature and complexities of obsessive love in this film—that love and beauty are associated with something appalling, with the idea of pain, fear, guilt, and ultimately the unobtainable.

What actually glued filmgoers to *Vertigo* was its ability to body forth and externalise the romantic concepts of unattainability, atonement, and damnation that were the sources of its appeal and strength. For reasons quite obvious, Hitchcock's glorious masterpiece has progressed from a thriller to a classic love story.

Works consulted

Bould, Mark. *Film Noir: From Berlin to Sin City*. Wallflower, 2005.
Hollinger, Karen. "'The Look,' Narrativity and the Female Spectator in *Vertigo*." *Journal of Film and Video* 39, no. 4 (Fall 1987): 18–27.
Modleski, Tania. *The Women Who Knew Too Much*. Routledge, 2005.
Spoto, Donald. *The Dark Side of the Genius: The Life of Alfred Hitchcock*. Da Capo Press, 1999.
Truffaut, Francois. *Hitchcock/Truffaut*. Simon & Schuster, 1985.
Wells, Paul. "Configuring the Monster." *The Horror Genre: From Beelzebub to Blair Witch*. Wallflower, 2000.
Wexman, Virginia Wright. "The Critic as Consumer: Film Study in the University, *Vertigo* and the Film Canon." *Film Quarterly* 39, no. 3 (Spring 1986): 32–41.
Vertigo. Dir. Alfred Hitchcock. Paramount Pictures, 1958. Film.

CHAPTER 15

CROSSWINDS OF FEAR AND DESIRE: HITCHCOCK'S ADAPTATION OF *THE BIRDS*

The Birds (1952) a long short story written by Daphne du Maurier narrates the story of a farmer named Nat and his family who struggle very hard to resist the attack of a flock of savage, predatory birds. Throughout the story reverberates a sense of impending doom and a foreboding of a coming disaster. Hitchcock's film *The Birds* (1963) is based on du Maurier's short story.

Deviations and points of departure from the classic du Maurier story are countless and one may as well avoid detailing the same in this reassessment of translating a short story into film. Rather this chapter goes back to du Maurier's original story in relation to its film adaptation only to fathom how the writer and director's vision converge in portraying a nature-rebellion narrative or a community-under-threat narrative. A narrative of how the literary precursor and its visual counterpart foreground humanity's struggle or endurance against predatory birds/nature.

In the short story, du Maurier tells how on 3 December the winter weather changes overnight and the birds appear to be restless and uneasy. The first bird attack in the story takes place when Nat hears a bird tapping at his window pane at night while they are sleeping. He opens the window to locate the cause of tapping:

> He opened it [the window], and as he did so something brushed his hand, jabbing at his knuckles, grazing the skin. Then he saw the flutter of the wings and it was gone, over the roof, behind the cottage. It was a bird; what kind of bird he could not tell. The wind must have driven it to shelter on the sill. He shut the window and went back to bed, but feeling his knuckle wet put his mouth to the scratch. The bird had drawn blood. Frightened, he supposed, and bewildered, the bird, seeking shelter, had stabbed him in the darkness. . . . (du Maurier 87)

The bird attacks continue throughout the night. When Nat hears a second tapping at his window, he alone must resist the attack of half a dozen birds flying at his face. After a while, the birds are heard in the children's bedroom, as they have entered the room through the open window. Nat struggles in the darkness to ward off the attack of these predatory creatures. He passes the night silently, wounded and bleeding.

As morning creeps in, he is utterly disturbed at the sight of the dead birds that he combated the previous night:

> They were all small birds, none of any size; there must have been fifty of them lying there upon the floor. There were robins, finches, sparrows, blue tits, larks and bramblings, birds that by nature's law kept to their own flock and their own territory . . . (du Maurier 89).

Du Maurier shows strong ornithological knowledge in her story for she mentions several species of birds that have strangely flocked to attack humans. There are blackbirds, thrushes, house sparrows, pigeons, starlings, black-headed gulls, crows, rooks, gannets, robins, wrens, and other species. Nat and his family realise that what they have experienced is something unnatural. Nat tries to rationalise the unnatural event to his family as well as to himself. He tries to believe that the weather is responsible for what has happened, that these birds must have been "driven down from upcountry" because of the hard weather.

The fierce struggle that ensued the night before must have been a fright that made the birds act the way they did. Yet after all this rationalising, the bird assaults escalate and Nat finds himself at a loss, while the violent nature of the birds spreads all over the country. The birds defy all human attempts to decipher or resist their attacks. To build an aura of inexorable dread, the story's plot circles around Nat's efforts to protect his family amid the dreariness of the English countryside.

Hitchcock's adaptation takes the focal point of du Maurier's story and intelligently weaves it in the film's diegesis: as to how the characters in the story search for meaning in the face of the unknown, how they struggle for human survival. Both the story and the film are survival narratives of weaker mortals trying to brave all odds when nature takes revenge. Both the short story and the film possess an uncompromising ambiguity and blend fantasy with day-to-day elements of everyday life. Unlike the short story, the great upheaval is not a national disaster but a localised event in the film.

What du Maurier's story does not contain is the romantic intrigue and love triangle that is at the heart of the film adaptation. Fear of isolation and abandonment, however, feature as integral themes of both the story and film. In the adaptation, the theme is extended to personal human relations, where each character has unknowingly placed his or her own self in a state of emotional isolation from the others. The leading characters, Melanie and Mitch, the schoolteacher Annie, and Mitch's mother Lydia, are all engulfed by a fearful loneliness. So it is the terror and the imperative to survive that governs both the story and the film.

It serves no purpose, however, to try to detail what Hitchcock retains of du Maurier's story, for the differences are too many to enumerate and the process of doing so would be quite unrewarding. The director even changes the basic plot and story, bringing in new characters and new relationships in a completely new setting. Hitchcock also sets the film in Bodega Bay, a dreamy, picturesque seaside town sixty miles from San Francisco. He perhaps believed that the pastoral loveliness of Bodega Bay, presented in soft colour, would make the audience feel more attached to the location when it is abruptly threatened by thousands of attacking gulls and crows: it is such a beautiful little town to witness such a savage attack.

Hitchcock's film is indebted to Frank Baker's novel *The Birds*. Other bird attack fiction that may have influenced the director's version include Melville Davisson Post's *The Revolt of the Birds* (1927) and Philip MacDonald's short story *Our Feathered Friends* (1931). The question now is, which of these texts were Hitchcock's source texts? Or were his sources multiple in number? The ensuing debate could be endless, but I will discuss the primary argument as to why the film rightfully acknowledges du Maurier in its opening credits.

But before I do that I would like to highlight that Hitchcock's film is able to express ideas and thoughts that are integral to the meaning and value of the literary text it is adapting. The film adaptation is the director's own interpretation of the text. Secondly, the film showcases a collaborative effort of good film-making as we know that film is the most collaborative of all mediums. Thirdly, Hitchcock's film demonstrates audacity in creating a work that stands as an independent entity, as a separate work of art in its own right, and at the same time draws its source and inspiration from du Maurier's short story in such a way that a self-reliant, but related, aesthetic creation is born out of it.

Fourthly, Hitchcock's film is never so self-governing as to be completely independent of or antithetical to the source material. What makes this film interesting as an adaptation of a literary work is that it demonstrates why a film-maker would want to take up the particular challenge of turning a short story into a film: to develop the integral ideas that the story raises and to cultivate complexities of character and human relationships that the originating literary text may not have touched upon.

Du Maurier's short story posed significant issues to Hitchcock, who made a film not to resolve them but to use the expanse of the feature film to expound upon them. In elaborating the survival narrative and other related themes of du Maurier's tale, Hitchcock's film attempts to reflect and meditate upon the major issue of the short story. The unquestioning tone evoked by the writer in her gothic tale foregrounds a sense of the apocalypse, also emphasising struggle to a great extent in the face of the unknown. It is this sense of doom or apocalypse in the short story that Hitchcock translates into a film about a community in crisis, making this process of adaptation an instance of intertextual dialogism.

Certain sections of du Maurier's story happen to be unfilmable. One may quote a particular passage to suggest this:

> Then he [Nat] saw them. The gulls. Out there, riding the seas.
> What he had at first thought to be the white caps of the waves were gulls. Hundreds, thousands, tens of thousands.... They rose and fell in the trough of the seas, heads to the wind, like a mighty fleet at anchor, waiting on the tide. To eastward, and to the west, the gulls were there. They stretched as far as his eye could reach, in close formation, line upon line. Had the sea been still they would have covered the bay like a white cloud, head to head, body packed to body. Only the east wind, whipping the sea to breakers, hid them from the shore. (Du Maurier 95)

Towards the end of the story Nat believes the navy at last is coming to their rescue; however, he is soon disillusioned:

> He paused, his work on the bedroom chimney finished, and looked out to sea. Something was moving out there. Something grey and white amongst the breakers.
> "Good old Navy," he said, "they never let us down. They're coming down channel, they're turning in the bay."
> He waited, straining his eyes, watering in the wind, towards the sea. He was wrong, though. It was not ships. The Navy was not there. The gulls were rising from the sea. The massed flocks in the fields, with ruffled feathers, rose in formation from the ground, and wing to wing soared upwards to the sky.
> The tide had turned again. (Du Maurier 121)

In the story, with the coming of the tide, the birds attack. Hitchcock invents his own method of bird attacks through the language of cinema. The film begins with a chance encounter in an urban pet shop. A wealthy lady, Melanie Daniels, deceives a lawyer, Mitch Brenner, who believes that Melanie is an employee of the pet shop. Very soon, we discover that Mitch was aware of the lady's identity and it was he who was actually deceiving her. In the scene, sharp words are exchanged between the two characters and as the lawyer Mitch leaves, Melanie decides to pursue him. The mutual attraction between the two is evident and is established in the sequence. Melanie decides not only to buy the lovebirds Mitch has been looking for but also to make the long drive to secretively deliver the caged birds to Mitch's doorstep at Bodega Bay. The action is indicative of her impulsive nature and Melanie's budding desire for Mitch.

Right after delivering the birds through the back door of Mitch's home, the first bird attack takes place. As Melanie furtively tries to escape by sailing her boat across the bay, Mitch spots her through binoculars. The bird-related images of watching and spying begin. As Melanie is about to reach her destination, a seagull suddenly dives and pecks her forehead leaving her wounded and bleeding. If Melanie's secretive entry to the lawyer's house was a violation of etiquette, the film-maker almost mutes the sense of violation that the sequence evokes. Rather, the focus is on building up the suspense and tension.

Melanie's first intrusion leads to further intrusions as she decides to stay on at Bodega Bay at Mitch's request. As Melanie and Mitch become involved in a romantic relationship, Melanie ultimately intrudes into Mitch's family, which is considered to be a mother's territory by Mitch's over-possessive mother. The "revenge of nature" is aroused by the mother's resistance to her son's relationship. Though Melanie is loved and made to feel at home by Mitch's young sister, Melanie remains an outsider: firstly, because the mother's domain leaves no space for her in the Brenner family; secondly, because of her high social ranking as a very wealthy and well-groomed lady.

In her sudden decision to visit Bodega Bay, Melanie carries no luggage and wears an elegant fur coat and finely tailored attire that she does not change for the rest of the film. The dress is systematically destroyed in the course of the film. Her aristocratic but unselfish and affectionate nature restricts her outsider status as a visitor from town and almost thrusts upon her the role of a marginal insider. At the age of eleven, she was deserted by her own mother. Consequently, Melanie was an abandoned child who had not known the love of a mother.

On the other hand, the local schoolteacher Annie Hayworth was earlier involved in a serious relationship with Mitch; however, it is revealed in conversation between Annie and Melanie that now Annie and Mitch have broken up. Annie blames Lydia, Mitch's mother, for the break-up. Mitch for certain unspecified reasons of his own has remained a bachelor. Never in the film does Annie show any dislike or fear because of

Melanie's presence; although she is a very refined and intelligent lady herself, she realises that Melanie may have conquered the eligible bachelor's heart. She tells Melanie that she did share a great relationship with him in the past but as far as she is concerned she is not yet "over" the relationship. It is clear from her politeness and subtlety that the relationship is something she still fondly cherishes.

Unlike David Humbert, who believes that "Hitchcock reminds us that the rivalry (between Annie and Melanie), which could have far more violent consequences, is there, lurking. Melanie and Annie are rivals for Mitch" ("Desire and Monstrosity in the Disaster Film" 93), I believe Annie knows Mitch is over this past relationship and is now in love with Melanie entirely. She never actually therefore considers Melanie to be her rival. Her affection for Mitch is unconditional and her desire for Mitch is never subsumed by Melanie's presence.

Going back to du Maurier's story we see that if the birds represent an irresistible natural force, the writer cleverly suggests this by allying her birds with the ebb and flow of the tides; Hitchcock's film also hints at the connection.

The deadly creatures depicted in *The Mist* (2007), an adaptation of the Stephen King novella of the same title, are strikingly similar to Hitchcock's and du Maurier's winged creatures that are instruments of destruction and vengeance.

In Hitchcock's film, Melanie is staying at Annie's place the night before Mitch's daughter Cathy's birthday party when a gull flies ominously into the entrance of the house with a deathly thud. The women stand together and silently contemplate the reason for such aggressive behaviour. When Annie suggests the bird must have lost its way in the dark, Melanie's reply, that it is a full moon, strikes an ominous note. Then, at Cathy's birthday party, a violent bird attack on the children by a coordinated flock disrupts a game of blind man's bluff. Later in the day, hundreds of sparrows enter the Brenner home through the chimney.

Similarly, there is no way one can explain why the birds attack the schoolchildren at Bodega Bay and why the winged creatures direct their rage against them. There is something sinister and ugly about the nature of the attacks in both the story and the film. The scene is a much-studied sequence of the film, primarily for documenting how Hitchcock uses editing to enhance suspense. McCombe observes, "what deserves even more attention is how Hitchcock connects elements of the *mise-en-scène* and sound to the film's ideology" (74).

As Melanie waits for the school hour to be over so that she may collect Cathy, the audience sees what is happening behind her. The birds gathering one after the other is indicative of forthcoming violence. By the time Melanie spots an ominous crow heading in the same direction, she is taken aback by the sight of a large number of crows that have gathered at the park just adjacent to the main school building. Sensing great danger, for these birds are no longer ordinary birds but creatures with sharp beaks and tearing claws, she decides not to delay a moment longer to save the children. Quietly but quickly she heads towards the classroom and informs Anne, the schoolteacher, about the situation.

As Melanie and Anne both look outside through the window they see the crows that have gathered to wreak havoc. For the viewer, the birds here represent the threatening Other. What the sight inscribes is a sense of plundering/marauding that goes back to a primal sense of panic towards the unpredictable and uncontrollable in nature. This is where the vision of the writer and the director converge. In the film, the schoolchildren who have earlier practised a fire drill, end up as the target of vicious bird attacks in the film's most famous sequence. As the killer birds make the children their prey, one realises that the outbreak signifies some great upheaval of nature where order has given way to chaos. The relentless nature of the attacks and the rapid-fire editing contribute to the film's violent atmosphere.

Melanie, a romantic *femme fatale*, is believed to have caused the disaster. In the town restaurant a group of inhabitants of Bodega Bay do not believe Melanie and Mitch's version of the bird attacks at Bodega Bay school. An elderly ornithologist, Mrs. Bundy, utterly refutes the claim of the birds' aggressive behaviour. She believes that the brains of birds do not permit the coordination of a mass attack and that, secondly, birds do not indulge in mixed species flocking. As a natural scientist, she refuses to accept Melanie's claim. In another corner, a town drunk prophetically announces that it is the "end of the world."

Other religious interpretations make the birds the agents of a benign superpower that is taking revenge for the unknown crimes of mankind. Meanwhile, an anxious and almost hysterical mother attempts vehemently to silence everyone. Soon after this exchange, the town square witnesses a disastrous eruption of violence as people are attacked, windows are smashed, and a petrol station explodes in flames. Though people try to extinguish the flames, their attempts are in vain.

Hitchcock here uses an aerial point-of-view shot showing Bodega Bay devastated as the birds seem to coordinate another mass attack. The high angle and the extreme long shot are suggestive of the birds seeking revenge on humanity for disrupting the delicate balance of nature. It is as if through their coordinated mass attacks that the birds are now expressing the desire to punish mankind for their brutal crimes of destroying nature.

The brutal attack of the birds signifies that they are defying humanity's ability to defend itself. The film's most visually shocking moment is when an elderly man is discovered dead in his bedroom with his eyes pecked out. As Kendrick observes: "Hitchcock draws us directly into the gruesome imagery with three rapid cuts, each of us brings us in closer until we are staring directly into the empty sockets" (59).

Moments after the attack on the town square, Melanie is left trapped in a phone booth where she is almost on the verge of being destroyed by birds. She even has a traumatic vision of a man pecked to death. After a while, Mitch saves her and both soon experience the eerie silence of the place, where a group of women have huddled together at the corner out of extreme fear. They almost seem to be representing the community of Bodega Bay.

Melanie is obviously an outsider in the community: according to Camille Paglia, "she [Melanie] has become the ritual scapegoat" (Paglia 73). The hysterical mother in the restaurant seems to be speaking on behalf of the entire community: "They said when you got here the whole thing started. Who are you . . . what are you? Where did you come from? I think you're the cause of all this. I think you're evil . . . evil!" (*The Birds*). However, the audience knows that there is nothing to prove that there is some relation between Melanie and the attack of the birds. Melanie's presence in Bodega Bay, just when the bird attack begins, is a matter of chance and coincidence.

Coming now to the ending of du Maurier's story, we are informed the bird attacks continue until morning. Meanwhile, the radio has stopped broadcasting programs altogether. "We've got to depend upon ourselves" is Nat's terse comment. The family heads to the farm. Birds watch on either side. Now Nat's worst fears are confirmed. Mr. Trigg lies dead by the telephone, his wife's legs protruding from the bedroom doorway upstairs. The tide again is soon to turn and sure to bring another attack. Nat plans to return to the cottage with his family. Whether they can withstand another siege is left uncertain.

Towards the end of the film, after Melanie has suffered another traumatic bird attack in the attic, she is rescued by Mitch and his mother. The trauma makes her so vulnerable that she almost suffers a nervous breakdown. The final scene therefore represents the destruction of Melanie's independent identity. Her final rescue by the son and mother emphasise the imposing power of a patriarchal structure. The family cautiously leaves the house and plans to head towards the city.

Although we expect another bird attack, in a kind of doomsday fantasy of escape, the family does manage to get away. Hundreds of quietly clucking gulls sit all around the house and watch the four depart. It is clear that the Brenner family will survive, but whether peace will be restored in Bodega Bay is left open-ended.

The Birds explores the frailty of human relations combined with a fear of depletion and desertion. Donald Spoto in Hitchcock's biography *The Dark Side of Genius* states, "The bird attacks seem in fact to be symbolic manifestations of fragile human relations—or, more accurately—the attacks exteriorize the failure of human relations" (461). No one is spared: not the heroine, Melanie, not the elderly, and certainly not the school children.

Each incident or episode immediately after the bird attacks is followed by a scene describing a character's fear of being alone or abandoned. Yet one striking characteristic of any Hitchcock film that never goes unnoticed is that he had a great talent in projecting the subtlety and beauty of romantic relationships.

The complex web of desires in *The Birds* is exemplary of this particular streak of his creative genius. In both the story and film, birds become signifiers of apocalyptic destruction, a devastating reversal in which humans end up as prey in a horrifying subversion of order, or what we believe is "order." The quiet, almost inconclusive turbulence of nature remains disturbingly threatening in its horror.

Works cited

Humbert, David. "Desire and Monstrosity in the Disaster Film: Alfred Hitchcock's *The Birds.*"
www.jhu.edu/journal/contagion/summary/.humbert.html.

Kendrick, James. *Film Violence: History, Ideology, Genre.* Wallflower, 2009.

McCombe, John P. "Oh I See . . . *The Birds* and the Culmination of Hitchcock's Hyper-Romantic Vision." *Cinema Journal* 44, no. 3 (Spring 2005).
www.muse.jhu.edu/journal/cinema_journal/mccombe.html.

The Birds. Directed by Alfred Hitchcock, performances by Tippi Hedren and Rod Taylor. United, 1963.

Maurier, Daphne du. *The Apple Tree.* Gollancz, 1952.

Paglia, Camille. *The Birds.* BFI, 1998.

Spoto, Donald. *The Dark Side of Genius: The Life of Alfred Hitchcock.* Da Capo Press, 1999.

Works consulted

Andrew, Dudley. *Concepts in Film Theory*. Oxford University Press, 1984.

Agee, James. *Film Theory and Criticism*. Oxford University Press, 1974, pp. 333–36.

Aycock, Wendell, and Michael Schoenecke, eds. *Film and Literature: A Comparative Approach to Adaptation*. Texas Tech University Press, 1988.

Callenbach, Ernest. *The Birds*. Review. *Film Quarterly* 16, no. 4 (Summer, 1963): pp. 44–46.

Sellors, Paul C. *Film Authorship: Auteurs and Other Myths*. Wallflower, 2010.

Sinyard, Neil. *Filming Literature*. Croom Helm, 1986.

CHAPTER 16

A WORLD UNTO ITSELF: HITCHCOCK'S MASTERY OF SUSPENSE

Born in 1899, Alfred Hitchcock directed fifty-seven films in a career that gives a comprehensive glimpse of the moving image, from the silent era to the sound era, black and white to Technicolor, from Britain to Hollywood. The gripping Hitchcock classics often contain the ingredients of a grand spy thriller or an espionage film involving a wild chase and a harrowing portrait of an innocent man struggling to prove his innocence while the outside world is absolutely unwilling to believe that he is anything less than a murderer.

Often repeating this uniquely Hitchcockian motif of a chase, the heroes of *The 39 Steps* (1935) and *Spellbound* (1945), namely Richard Hannay and John Ballantine, set out to solve a perplexing, life-threatening mystery. *The 39 Steps*, a heart-racing spy thriller from his British period, is often credited with being the first really successful "Hitchcock" film, the one that brought together for the first time all the dramatic potentials of mystery, exciting escapism, and suspense for which Hitchcock became justly famous. Richard Hannay (Robert Donat) stumbles upon a conspiracy as Annabella Smith is knifed to death in his London apartment. This conspiracy involves a double chase in which Hannay is both the pursuer and the pursued.

The innocent Hannay has to clear himself of the charge of murder lodged against him by those conspiring against him. This wild chase later became a template that Hitchcock used time and again for his other successful films. Adapted from the novel by John Buchan, *The 39 Steps* is interesting in its representation of an overtly political intrigue in its primarily sexual thematic matrix. The film anticipates Hitchcock's later films like *North by Northwest*.

A paranoid melodrama is unleashed in the spy thriller *The Lady Vanishes* (1938) as the elderly, ever-spirited Miss Froy mysteriously disappears in a train compartment and everyone present denies her very existence except the leading lady, Iris Henderson (Margaret Lockwood).

As the train speeds on its way, this romantic thriller makes way for denial, concealment, and substitution, which rapidly unfold in its plot while at the same time striking the right balance of suspense and humour. An iconic scene in the film that adds substantial tension to the drama occurs when the film's hero, Gilbert (Michael Redgrave), tries to unravel the mystery, ultimately hanging out of the moving train while another train speeds from the other direction and blows by.

Hitchcock's entire filmic oeuvre is a study of his engagement with romance and sexuality and on a larger scale the art of cinema itself. In 1940, Hitchcock collaborated with Anglophile producer David Selznick to make his first American film, *Rebecca*. The story of *Rebecca* is adapted from Daphne du Maurier's celebrated gothic novel of the same name. A classic Hitchcock suspense thriller, *Rebecca* tells the story of a rich aristocrat and wealthy widower, Maxim de Winter (Laurence Olivier), with a dark secret, whose deceased wife, Rebecca, the first Mrs. De Winter, is felt to have an uncanny hold on the gothic mansion, Manderley, and on its characters.

The absent Rebecca figure exhibits an uncanny charm over the naïve and modest second wife of de Winter (Joan Fontaine) and Manderley's menacingly rigid housekeeper, Mrs. Danvers (Judith Anderson). The housekeeper looks after the manor and attempts to keep the first Mrs de Winter's memory alive in an almost obsessive way. The socially unaccomplished, shy, sweet, but timid second wife of de Winter is much in love with and in awe of the lord of the manor, the enigmatic, mysterious dark melancholist, Maxim de Winter (Laurence Olivier). She is placed in stark contrast to the assertive, equally awe-inspiring, dead Mrs. De Winter who is never shown on screen. Such is her strange, unearthly hold on the Manderley mansion that Mrs. Danvers in her devotion to her former mistress provokes the second Mrs. de Winter to suicide (which she resists). Evocative of a fearful and imposing mood, *Rebecca* established Hitchcock as the "Master of Suspense" in the forties. In 1939, he adapted Daphne du Maurier's Gothic fiction *Jamaica Inn* into a whodunnit and in the 1960s he was to return to du Maurier again in his famous filmic rendition of *The Birds* (1963).

In *Spellbound*, (1945) Gregory Peck (John) plays the role of a "paranoid impostor" apparently believed to be guilty of dispatching Dr Edwardes. Irresistibly drawn to John, a potential madman-murderer, is the cool, rational psychiatrist Dr Constance Peterson (Ingrid Bergman), who tells us "I couldn't feel this way about a man who was bad, who had committed a murder" (*Spellbound*). Through his "metasceptical" narrative, the director at once asserts and subverts the possibility and promise of romance.

Hitchcock's grand mystery thriller *Spellbound* is one of his richest, most perfectly conceived films; centring on uncovering the subconscious, it is a psychological drama on repressed memory and unwarranted guilt. As we begin to undermine the director's own remark on *Spellbound* as "just another manhunt story wrapped up in pseudo-psychoanalysis" (Spoto 185), we tend to focus our attention on the famous surrealist dream sequence in the film, based on the drawings of Salvador Dalí, to resolve the mystery.

Hitchcock's credentials as the master of suspense were established in thrillers like *Blackmail, Sabotage, Suspicion, Shadow of a Doubt, Strangers on a Train, Rear Window*, and *Vertigo*. These films engage with psychopathic, murderous imperatives as the drama unfolds in an apparently amoral world. From *Strangers on a Train* (1951) to *Dial M for Murder* (1954), we see the full flowering of Hitchcock's mature art. The plan to exchange murders in *Strangers on a Train* is so fascinating because of the underlying assumption of the film that subversive or even destructive desires exist in all of us, waiting for a momentary relaxing of our vigilance. At Senator Morton's party, Mrs Cunningham unknowingly shows interest in the villain Bruno's fantasies and Bruno takes a chance with her by demonstrating a mock strangulation game in public. The comic exchange of dialogue on murder methods in the scene fearfully culminates in Bruno's demonstration of silent strangling.

When Bruno engages in a menacing strangulation game, his hands are wrapped around Mrs Cunningham's neck but he actually stares at Barbara, Anne's sister. From a distance, Bruno imagines he is strangling not Mrs Cunningham but Barbara. Barbara resembles Guy's adulterous wife, Miriam, because of her physical appearance and her glasses. In this game of strangulation, Bruno in a trance revisits his earlier murder of Miriam in the amusement park. The scene is a marvellous example of the Hitchcockian "spectator trap." As the subjective shots force us to share Bruno's subject position, we are uncomfortably and disturbingly situated in the suppressed underworld of desire.

Critics have noted that *Strangers on a Train* draws together several motifs already adumbrated in earlier films, which will be taken further in later ones: the motif of the "sickening assumption of common guilt" developed especially in *Psycho* (1960); the theme of the search for identity in *Vertigo* (1958); the theme of the struggle of a personality torn between order and chaos in *The 39 Steps* and *North by Northwest* (1959); or the use of a train to depict entrapment and escape in *Number Seventeen*

(1932), *The 39 Steps* and *Secret Agent* (1936), *The Lady Vanishes* (1938), *Suspicion* (1941), *Saboteur* (1942), and *North by Northwest*.

That the director's American period is in general richer than his British period can doubtless be attributed as much to a complex set of signifying determinants as to personal development. Any film from Hitchcock's oeuvre is to be seen as a product of an intricate network of influences, circumstances of production, collaborations, and happy and/or unhappy confluences, and, last but not least, an expression of the auteur director's darkest desires. At the centre of this network is the director's creative personality, his unparalleled genius.

In *Dial M for Murder* (1954), Tony Wendice, the stylish, upper-class villainous husband of Margot (Grace Kelly), hires an agent named Swann to murder his wife. The murder scene of *Dial M for Murder* significantly adds to the suspense, partly through camera movement and editing and particularly through constant cross-cutting. Close-ups from Tony's point of view of the casement window beside which Swann will hide, the latch of the internal door by which the murderer will enter, the latch key in Tony's hand, Margot's handbag from which Tony must steal the key, and the place under the stair carpet where the key will be hidden all establish Hitchcock's brilliant camera placement for extraordinary point of view shots.

From *Dial M for Murder* to *Notorious* (1946) a key is often used as a structuring device to successfully generate tension. Through close-ups, the key to the wine cellar and the staircase become elaborate motifs in *Notorious*. The cellar defines a dangerous space for Alicia (Ingrid Bergman), the daughter of a Nazi spy who decides to work as an American agent. The circulation of the cellar key at Alex's residence locks and unlocks dangerous secrets. Bergman's outstanding performance reminds us of her performances in films like *Gaslight* and *Casablanca*. We also find Alex's formidable mother compelling. Leopoldine Konstantin's performance may be compared to Judith Anderson's as the housekeeper Mrs Danvers in *Rebecca*. It is Madame Konstantin who sees through the deceptive Alicia from the beginning.

In films like *Notorious, Foreign Correspondent, North by Northwest, Torn Curtain,* and *Topaz*, Hitchcock often projects his hero's dangerous and compulsive thrill-seeking behaviour. He often focuses on his hero's dilemma in having to choose between personal love and international duty, which renders complexity to his heroes.

In 1954 Hitchcock directed his phenomenal film *Rear Window*, a brilliant visual study of obsessive human curiosity based on Cornell Woolrich's novella *It Had to be Murder*. The film set was built entirely at

Paramount Studios: a realistic courtyard composed of thirty-two apartments. All the events take place either in the apartment of the main protagonist, a photojournalist, Jefferies, or in the courtyard or in neighbouring apartments. Temporarily immobilised by an accident, Jefferies (James Stewart) voyeuristically uses his binoculars to spy on his neighbours through his rear window, thereby becoming the all-observing spectator.

Audience members share Jefferies's controlling and curious gaze and become voyeurs as they pry on the private lives of his neighbours. Jefferies's fiancé, the excessively glamourised Lisa Carol Fremont (Grace Kelly), for whom Hitchcock too shared a great fascination in real life, accuses Jeff of being an immoral voyeur. Gradually, "looking" itself becomes a source of pleasure and the "scopophilia" (or "pleasure in looking") is shared by the audience too. The film evolves as a gripping murder mystery as it explores the sexual politics of looking.

Rear Window highlights self-referential allusion and cinematic illusion. Calling attention to the cinematic apparatus itself, the binoculars and telephoto lens facilitate a multiplicity of perspectives foregrounding the metacinematic dynamic and self-reflexivity of the film. *Rear Window* evolves as a critique of voyeurism by making the audience aware of itself as spectators of a film, and of the film as artifice.

Often to understand the relation between form and content in Hitchcock's films one has to see his indebtedness to the traditions of Soviet montage and German expressionist cinema. For instance, to exemplify Hitchcock's image-centred view of cinema, one need not look beyond the first shot of *Marnie* (1964). Each precisely calculated detail in the action, décor, and *mise en scène* conveys an exact idea or represents a strategy in Hitchcock's game of audience manipulation.

The auteur's desire to control and the terror of losing control: such phrases not only describe Hitchcock's conscious relationship to technique and to his audiences but also signify the crux of his oeuvre. The personal relationships that fascinated Hitchcock invariably involve the exercise of power, or its obverse, impotence—in many cases, a dangerous repressive desire that seeks to conceal or deny or compensate for a dreaded impotence, the perfect metaphor for which is provided by the "double" of Norman Bates (Anthony Perkins) in *Psycho* (1960): the young man terrified of women and the exaggeratedly "potent" monster wielding the "phallic" deadly weapon of murder. This relationship pattern, with its possible variations and permutations, is traceable in films as apparently diverse as *Notorious*, *Rear Window*, *Rope*, *Vertigo*, *Psycho*, and *Marnie*.

Psycho is much nearer to being a masterpiece. In the film, menacingly transgressive events are placed in an everyday context. It challenged accepted notions in relation to sex, sexuality, violence, and social identity and did so with an aesthetic sensibility. The vicious shower murder of Marion Crane (Janet Leigh) is remarkable for its impressionist brutalities. The shower scene where the murderer's silhouette is visible through the shower curtain seems to be influenced by German expressionist cinema, particularly F. W. Murnau's silent film *Nosferatu*. Hitchcock employs his considerable skill to shock us past the spectacle of horror amusement to something much more artistic. The "shower scene" as a cinematic moment undeniably to a great extent shaped and transformed the horror genre for generations to come.

Hitchcock's towering success in shocking audiences did not result in resentment but only fuelled a desire for more such horror films. Film markets were flooded in subsequent years with so many *Psycho*-inspired films—*Homicidal*, *Maniac*, *Paranoiac*, *What Ever Happened to Baby Jane?*, *Nightmare*, and *Strait Jacket*, most of which increased the violence but none except Roman Polanski's *Repulsion* or *The Tenant* could perhaps equal Hitchcock's mastery of technique. In terms of graphicism and in matters of tone, *Psycho* redefined the horror genre. *Psycho* is continually cited by critics as a film that was genuinely shocking, disturbing, and clearly different from previous horror films. Through its stylistic bravura, *Psycho* redefines the parameters of the text and subtext of a modern horror film.

Psycho foregrounds the chaos that underpins modern existence and relentlessly threatens to ensure its subsequent collapse. Wells remarked that Norman Bates (Anthony Perkins) "both is and is not mother, both is and is not dead, is neither masculine nor feminine, mother nor son, fetish, corpse, nor living body. Rather it is all these steps amalgamated into one phantastic body, into whose presence Hitchcock has drawn us" (Wells 30). With *Psycho*, Hitchcock frighteningly domesticates the modern monster in horror films. Norman Bates is not unknowable but someone familiar from our everyday lives. The core meanings of the horror genre—"psychosexual and psychosomatic angst" (Wells 76)—and the stifling omnipresence of death are remarkably present in *Psycho*.

The first half of *Psycho* up to the point where Marion's car sinks into the swamp is regarded to be among the most extraordinary achievements of American cinema. However, it is ultimately Hitchcock's black humour—the suspense as the car containing Marion's body initially fails to sink into the swamp—that has been much imitated and considered remarkably brilliant. Running through all Hitchcock's films is a fascinating vein of black humour that itself presents a moral position: it is the expression of his idea of impersonality in art, of his detached and impersonal attitude to themes that clearly obsessed him. This black humour is carefully deployed in other films like *Shadow of a Doubt*, where two characters obsessed with their love for crime fiction relentlessly discuss ways to murder one another while being blissfully unaware that a murderer may be living in their house.

Certain enigmatic scenes from Hitchcock's films have undeniably left a lasting impact on our minds: the much discussed shower murder in *Psycho*, the crop-duster scene in *North by Northwest*, the traumatic bird attack in the attic on Melanie or hundreds of destructive sparrows entering the Brenner home through a chimney in *The Birds*, or the rooftop chase in *Vertigo*, to suggest only a few.

Works consulted

Bronfen, E. *The Knotted Subject: Hysteria and its Discontents.* Princeton University Press, 1998.
Kelvan, Andrew. *Film Performance: From Achievement to Appreciation.* Wallflower, 2005.
Mercer, John, and Martin Shingler. *Melodrama: Genre, Style, Sensibility.* Wallflower, 2004.
Spoto, Donald. *The Dark Side of the Genius: The Life of Alfred Hitchcock.* Da Capo Press, 1999.
Wells, Paul. "Configuring the Monster." *The Horror Genre: From Beelzebub to Blair Witch.* Wallflower, 2000.

Chapter 17

From Gothic Romance to Horror Text: Problematising Genre in *Rebecca*

Since its first publication in 1938, Daphne du Maurier's *Rebecca* has found enduring popularity but little critical acclaim. It was dismissed as a gothic romance—gothic being a kind of fiction considered to have a special appeal to women—and subsequently, as "women's fiction." Yet this most famous of Du Maurier's quintessential Cornish novels continues to perplex a new class of readers even today. Several aspects of the author's split personality are mirrored or doubled in the portrayal of the two female antagonists of the novel: the unnamed narrator who is the living, docile, and submissive second wife of Maxim de Winter, and the rebellious, dead, yet indestructible first wife, Rebecca.

A reassessment of this angry, strange, and almost bizarre novel is long overdue. Any discussion of this intriguing text could begin with du Maurier's style and how the novel's generic elements have been absorbed into mainstream horror thrillers through its film adaptation by Alfred Hitchcock in the 1940s. From popular fiction and bestseller to cult classic, the journey of *Rebecca* has indeed been fascinating.

Daphne du Maurier had often been categorised as a "romance" writer during her lifetime, a category she resented. The reasons for her resentment could have been many. Critics above all believe that romance fiction deals with the doubts and delights of heterosexuality. Romances are seen as coercive and stereotyping narratives that invite the reader to identify with a passive heroine who only finds true happiness in submitting to male authority. Romance thus emerges as a form of oppressive ideology, which works to keep women in their socially and sexually subservient position. Since Rebecca dealt with women-centric issues and focused on the experiences of a female protagonist, it has often been labelled as "women's fiction."

Transcending limited stylistic categorisations, even today, *Rebecca* continues to enthral public imagination in various shapes: as romance, gothic melodrama, family drama, crime novel, thriller, a gothic

Bluebeard tale, and French family romance that has finally triumphed as a classic of popular romance fiction. Therefore du Maurier's novel is not to be read as a traditional romance or a romance written for women.

Interestingly, in Hollywood the prominent genres of the 1940s were the literary adaptation, the women's film (a studio-created genre of the 1930s and 40s with a female first-person voice-over narration), and the film noir. Traditionally marketed as a gothic romance, the narrative of *Rebecca* deals with the threat and anxiety a woman suffers under the patriarchal control of her husband. The gothic, noirish, and brooding melodrama, with its theme of a menaced, terrorised, or sheltered, woman (or wife) threatened by a deranged man (often a husband) was one of a number of similar films made in the 1940s. There are many films of this type: Thorold Dickinson's *Gaslight* with Diana Wynyard; Hitchcock's *Suspicion* (1941), with Joan Fontaine; Robert Stevenson's *Jane Eyre* (1943), with Joan Fontaine; Hitchcock's *Shadow of a Doubt* (1943), with Teresa Wright; Otto Preminger's *Laura* (1944) with Gene Tierney; George Cukor's *Gaslight* (1944) with Ingrid Bergman; William Castle's *When Strangers Marry* (1944) (aka *Betrayed*), with Kim Hunter; Joseph H. Lewis's *My Name is Julia Ross* (1945), with Nina Foch; and several other such films.

What makes the second Mrs de Winter insecure about "romance" in *Rebecca* is not simply her young and inexperienced self but the class difference between her and her husband (Maxim de Winter), and her and Rebecca, now dead. As a gothic love story it tells the story of a virtuous woman (the unnamed, second Mrs de Winter) who triumphs over an evil one (the first Mrs de Winter/Rebecca) by winning the love of her rich, aristocratic husband. The husband, Maxim, then is the hero, the father figure and protector. For those who identify the novel as a reworking of the Bluebeard fairy tale, it is the story of a suave gentleman-hero (Maxim) who actually turns out to be a villain for unjustifiably murdering his first wife (Rebecca).

Traditionally, the gothic refers to a set of traditional literary conventions. These include set characters like a dark but courageous hero and a leading lady with sexual anxiety, together with a collection of assorted demons, ghosts, uncanny creatures, and the like. The remote Manderley mansion in *Rebecca* with its irresistible melancholy creates an atmosphere of doom. The large family estate, with its dark interiors, harbours a fearful secret. The dark corridors, doors, and staircases of the enchanting mansion have an aura of foreboding and menace.

What is more formal and characteristic of the gothic is the production of suspense, terror, and, at its most intense, horror. As the

British novel progressed during the nineteenth century, the gothic took on an implication of an alternative aesthetic idiom that countered mainstream classical styles. In self-conscious examples, the gothic was linked with notions of repression, taboo, and terror. *Rebecca* gradually becomes a thriller that goes behind the scenes of the romance drama.

Just as du Maurier's classic has transcended the traditional boundaries of "women's fiction," similarly Alfred Hitchcock's adaptation of *Rebecca* in the 1940s has transcended the limitations of a "woman's film" or the limitations of its sub-genre, the "paranoid gothic." One must not forget that the gothic was a style popular with women in Hollywood in the 1940s. Yet in its filmic transcreation, *Rebecca* has evolved from a gothic romance film of the 1940s or an ordinary psychological thriller/suspense film to a more discursive horror film.

Though *Rebecca* begins as a woman's film, a, subversion soon occurs as the narrative voice is undermined by male authority. The female voice-over is abruptly terminated mid-film. Such an abrupt termination interrogates the female heroine's perspective in the film. The focus of the film is not entirely on the female narrator/protagonist but the female protagonist's investigation of a male character. *Rebecca* is also about a female protagonist who faces impediment in establishing a fulfilling romantic relationship.

Problematically, the horror film genre has no clearly defined boundaries and overlaps with aspects of science fiction, murder mystery, and fantasy films. In *Rebecca*, the motif of the uncanny—the deep-rooted fear of the unknown—is a projection of particular threats, fears, and contradictions that refuse coexistence with the prevailing paradigms and consensual orthodoxies of everyday life. It is closely linked to other primal anxieties. Anxiety arises from the conceptualisation of an imaginary presence. Unlike popular horror films from *Nosferatu* (1922), *Frankenstein* (1931), *Dracula* (1931), to *The Wolf Man* (1941), in *Rebecca* there is no central image of a monster, a vampire, the undead, or a corpse to remind the viewer of threat or extinction. Rebecca, almost a phantom villain, now dead, vivid, and vengeful, never appears (on screen). It is the fear of the unknown—our primal anxieties combined with a deep crisis of identity—that the director plays with in his innovative treatment of the horror genre. In the Manderley mansion, Rebecca's eerie absence is a reminder of her haunting presence. Rebecca is all in the mind. It is a film about how the past affects the present.

Mrs Danvers, the housekeeper of Manderley, enjoys a crucial position in both the fiction and the film versions as she demonstrates an apparent indifference towards the second Mrs de Winter combined with her vicarious pleasure in perceiving the painful outcome of threat to the second wife. This threat is due to the overpowering, imaginary presence of the beautiful, upper-class Rebecca or the pressure to live up to her standards created upon the second Mrs de Winter by Mrs Danvers. She tries to maintain the status quo by keeping the dead Rebecca's memories alive; the second Mrs de Winter loses control of her life in the face of such profound disruptions. As the absent/dead Rebecca becomes more alive in the second Mrs de Winter's troubled mind, Hitchcock's treatment of the horror represents a conflict between competing sexualities, gender orientations, and repressed desires, and a more obvious, confrontational antithesis between the powerful and the powerless.

Both Rebecca and the second Mrs de Winter, in the novel, reflect aspects of du Maurier's complex personality: she divided herself between them. Both the novel and its adaptation expose the two competing sides of the individual—one obedient and submissive, the other uncontrolled and transgressive. The unnamed second wife fantasises about Rebecca, about the other woman. Rebecca is everything the second wife would like to be. Rebecca's class difference makes her appear more mature, more adult, both socially and sexually. Rebecca is that icon of womanhood the second Mrs de Winter aspires to be. However, her idealisation of Rebecca is fraught with anxiety and effeminacy. The rivalry persists until she can resolve the duality/conflict with the envied, powerful other. Rebecca is one of the mysteries she must solve in order to achieve a more mature sexual identity.

Along with extraordinary sexual anxiety, the second Mrs de Winter begins to perceive that Maxim would love her if she emulated Rebecca. Yet the couple are distanced from one another the more this unnamed narrator, the naïve, inexperienced young woman, tries to merge with Rebecca. Maxim later reveals to his second wife that beneath the exterior image of a dedicated wife, Rebecca was actually trying to conceal her unacceptable sexual behaviour. The aristocratic, larger-than-life Rebecca comes to signify a confident, seductive, but tabooed expression of femininity. Rebecca's aristocratic lineage made way for a more passionate sexuality that is at odds with the second Mrs de Winter's own middle-class version of womanhood with emphasis on companionship and responsibility.

The dark, disturbing presence of Rebecca in the film has an aura of threatening mystery. She reminds us of the beautiful Mrs. Paradine in Hitchcock's *The Paradine Case*. Both films are variations of the "vicious woman" theme that dominated Hollywood during the era. Later, films such as Billy Wilder's *Double Indemnity* (1944) and *Sunset Boulevard*

(1950), or Orson Welles's *The Lady from Shanghai* (1974), delved deeper into this theme of "vicious womanhood."

Rebecca's imaginary presence articulates images of abjection in the horror film as a particular model of "the return of the repressed" in which, paradoxically, the absent Rebecca is a relentless reminder of the collapse of the illusory. In Rebecca's illusory presence emerges a threat of sublime excess. Like *Rebecca* the novel, Hitchcock's adaptation straddles film styles and its success is due in no small measure to the fact that it contains elements from several overlapping styles—from women's film, the female gothic film, and the psychological thriller, to the horror film. Its stylised features anticipate a classic film noir.

Works consulted

Bould, Mark. *Film Noir: From Berlin to Sin City*. Wallflower, 2005.
Edwards, Kyle Dawson. "Literature Film Adaptation and Selznick International Pictures: *Rebecca*." *Cinema Journal* 45, no. 3 (Spring 2006): 32–58.
Harbord, Janet. "Between Identification and Desire: Rereading *Rebecca*." *Feminist Review* 53, Speaking Out: Researching and Representing Women (Summer 1996): 95–107.
Hutcheon, Linda. *A Theory of Adaptation*. Routledge, 2006.
Johnson, David T. "After Adaptation." *Literature/Film Quarterly* 36, no. 3 (2008): 162–63.
McFarlane, Brian. *Novel to Film: An Introduction to the Theory of Adaptation*. Clarendon Press, 1996.
Pons, Auba Llompart. "Patriarchal Hauntings: Re-reading Villainy and Gender in Daphne du Maurier's *Rebecca*." *Atlantis* 35, no. 1 (June 2013): 69–83.
Pyrhonen, Heta. "Bluebeard's Accomplice: *Rebecca* as a Masochistic Fantasy." *Mosaic: An Interdisciplinary Critical Journal* 38, no. 3 (September 2005): 149–65.
Wells, Paul. "Configuring the Monster." *The Horror Genre: From Beelzebub to Blair Witch*. Wallflower, 2000.

CHAPTER 18

CHAOS AND COLLAPSE: FORTY YEARS INTO THE MAGNIFICENT ENIGMA OF *THE SHINING*

One of the most disturbing, surreal shots in *The Shining* (1980) is that of a young boy cycling through a huge hotel corridor. Almost caught in an enormous maze, the director's Steadicam follows him everywhere. It is while cycling that young Danny (Danny Lloyd) sees the mysterious twin sisters appearing in front of him at a distance and blocking his way. Their sinister, ominous presence is mixed up with a vision of their mutilated bodies. Danny is terrified but his alter ego reminds him what Halloran said: "it's just like pictures in a book, Danny. It isn't real." Wendy (Shelley Duvall), his loving mother, is genuinely petrified when she starts realising that her husband, Jack Torrance (Jack Nicholson), is gradually descending into madness. The anxiety is palpable as young Danny and his mother start anticipating that Jack will hurt them eventually as his insanity gets the better of him.

The setting is a classic, luxurious resort—the deserted Overlook Hotel. Stanley Kubrick's horror film begins with Jack being appointed as the winter caretaker of the Overlook Hotel. Winter being off-season, the hotel will soon be deserted and the Torrance family, we are told, will be the ones to stay back to take care of the property. The Overlook, built on top of a sacred Indian burial ground, is a huge space for the Torrance family. Separation and isolation take a strong hold over the fragile family, Jack, Wendy, and Danny, who are now the only inhabitants of a haunted hotel with an eerie past. Jack at his job interview is informed by the manager that, some years ago, the previous caretaker of the hotel went insane and killed his wife and two daughters with an axe before killing himself. Though Jack laughs at the grisly story and convinces the manager, Mr Ullman, that nothing of this sort will happen to him, it is precisely what Jack will attempt to do to his family as he gradually transforms into the axe murderer.

Kubrick's self-reflexive *mise en scène* in *The Shining* gets fearful and scary when Jack as a writer isolates himself from his wife and son to finish his manuscript. With no spooky jump scares in a deserted mansion, Kubrick's film language reads very differently from conventional gory horror flicks. At its release, *The Shining,* however, received only a lukewarm response, with films like *The Omen* (1976) and *Alien* (1979) being more commercially successful at the time.

It is well known that Kubrick's adaptation did not get the nod of approval from Stephen King, from whose novel of the same name *The Shining* is adapted. In fact, King expressed strong disapproval of Kubrick's version. Yet Kubrick being an auteur director could not be convinced to budge an inch to satisfy its author. His film version was not a faithful rendition of the story: Kubrick left out many supernatural themes and scenes from King's story. He did what he felt was right; here was a director who with sufficient confidence was directing a horror film for the first time. The result was a Kubrickian version: his own take on King's story. Critics have also stated that Kubrick drew his real inspiration from Stephen Crane's story *The Blue Hotel* (Baxter 301). Kubrick's film generated a gamut of ambiguity as he left it for the audience to interpret its multiplicity of meanings.

Kubrick took multiple takes of each scene, finally accepting one amongst many as the final shot. Much has been discussed about the 127 takes he shot of a single scene with Shelley Duvall. He made his actors Jack Nicholson and Shelley Duvall go through this ordeal to such an extent that it is believed that he drew them to the brink of madness. When, seemingly, that happened, the actors could deliver their best and Kubrick waited for that moment—the moment where his actors would start believing they were actually trapped in a deserted hotel. That was the level of his perfectionism. He desired to be excessively or rather obsessively perfect.

Now, the question that this essay tries to address is what makes *The Shining* such an iconic horror film? Didn't the film almost change the way we looked at horror films in the 1980s? Rather than focusing entirely on external ghosts or paranormal activity, the director plays on our ideas of horror lurking within the human mind. In a way, it reminds us of *The Innocents*, Jack Clayton's adaptation of Henry James's *The Turn of the Screw*.

Kubrick's ground-breaking approach to horror is very different in its style and treatment of the paranormal. On its fortieth anniversary we revel at Kubrick's masterpiece and his film language continues to intrigue us. That something is not right about the place, that something ominous is about to happen, is familiar from most horror films. In this respect, Kubrick's theme is nothing revolutionary; and yet he projects it in his unique style, his own film language. He never overdoes its scary effects and preserves the subtlety of his scares. Though this carries *The Shining* forward, it never fully explains its enduring effectiveness.

Kubrick draws on specific motifs to escalate the gothic horror: the word "Redrum" (murder) spelt on the bedroom wall, the encounter with the dead twin sisters who coax Danny to play with them while he cycles, Danny's vision of the twin sisters' mutilated bodies strewn along the hotel corridor, the lobby's ornate carpet design with geometric shapes on which Danny rides on his tricycle or plays with toy trucks, the blood gushing out of the elevator, and the phenomenal room 237 that opens on its own. These motifs, along with the disquieting music of Béla Bartók, heighten the iconic moments in Kubrick's film. They sound an ominous note, but Kubrick uses these motifs only to escalate the tension. The real horror is psychological and it is the psychological state of mind of his characters that the film focuses on so exquisitely.

In his mind, Danny speaks to Tony, his imaginary friend, quite often. Tony is actually a personification of Danny's psychic powers or his unconscious self. Tony converses with Danny and tells him that his father has the job and a while later shows him a future vision of an elevator with blood gushing forth. The paranormal activities have set in; or are they just snippets of Danny's imagination? One of the greatest appeals of *The Shining* is the way it examines the tension between materiality and imagination. Imaginative constructs test the recognisable limits of the concrete, objective, and normative codes of the material world.

Dick Halloran, a very important character in the film, who also possesses psychic powers, engages in a telepathic link with Danny. Dick will try to save the family in distress when Jack's insanity threatens their existence. It is Dick who hears Danny's cry for help across the country in Florida; he undertakes a perilous journey to Colorado to help Danny and his mother. Even the recent sequel, *Doctor Sleep* (2019), appropriates the telepathic link among characters possessing the shining. Shockingly, Mike Flanagan's film came nowhere close to *The Shining*.

The labyrinthine outdoor hedge maze where Danny throws snowballs with his mother and where Jack chases Danny towards the end of *The Shining* is indeed a psychological maze. We start wondering whether the erratic Jack's encounter with a ghost in room 237 is just a figment of his tormented mind? When Jack is about to sexually engage with the woman in the bathroom of room 237, he is terrified to see that the naked woman he fancies is actually a decomposing corpse, now living and making an ugly joke of Jack's desire for her. Jack's fantasy of the woman in room 237 is immediately changed from attraction to horror as he sees her terrifying reflection in the mirror. The ghost woman's beauty and allure had ensnared Jack, but now he shudders. He realises she is a rotten hag. Kubrick here plays on the idea of the human mind encountering the grotesque, the ugly, the shocking, and the repulsive. This is perhaps Kubrick's distinctive sense of the paranormal.

Kubrick's bleak tone and unforgettable iconographies are alluded to by director Mike Flanagan in the sequel *Doctor Sleep*. Flanagan's film version is perhaps more faithful to King's classic, and Flanagan blends King and Kubrick, all the while paying homage to Kubrick's inimitable dread of filmic iconographies. While the sets of the Overlook are painstakingly recreated, Flanagan's film fails to come anywhere close to Kubrick. Driven by intense violence towards children, the film's diffused suspense can never compare to Kubrick's brilliance.

It was Kubrick's slow build-up of an atmosphere of dread and his emphasis on symbolism and iconographies that made his film inimitable. Interpretations and theories abound; in *Room 237*, a documentary on *The Shining*, critics cite how the film refers to the holocaust and genocide. Critics have commented how one among many of its iconographies reveals the Minotaur in the background while the camera frames the twin sisters staring at Danny.

Combined with innovative camera angles and subsequently developing his unique film language for a horror film, Kubrick succeeds in making *The Shining* outstanding. The film begins with an extreme long shot that develops into medium shots, dissolves, and superimpositions; these shots are accompanied by unsettling music. He uses wide-angle shots to capture the slightly distorted facial expressions of his characters throughout, and towards the end of the film uses a lot of close-ups.

Shock receives a rather innovative treatment in the hands of Kubrick. *The Shining*'s ability to shock the human mind is accomplished in myriad, intriguing ways. Something of this kind happens when we start sharing Wendy's subject position as she suspects that her moody husband is going insane. The climax of this exploratory journey we undergo with Wendy is reached when we, along with her, discover that Jack has been typing the aphorism "all work and no play makes Jack a dull boy" in his study endlessly for all the days since their arrival at the Overlook. Kubrick gives us a disturbing revelation of Jack's perversion; however, the suspense is all the more palpable throughout because we had no inkling that Jack had kept himself locked up in his study so seriously doing nothing—that his mental derailment has gone to this frightening extent.

The trivial can be alarmingly and shockingly serious. Reality gapes at us with such shocking intensity in the scene in which Wendy discovers Jack's type-written manuscript that we are left with a feeling of a void that is difficult to overcome. It is heightened as Wendy realises that her husband/protector/family could now be her destroyer. It is a fear lurking within the family—an isolated family with no one to reach out to. Jack's insanity has changed the entire family dynamics. Jack will resort to domestic violence. Fear is not something external Wendy should be scared about now. Jack, the symbol of patriarchal authority in the family, can harm her, ruin her, and kill her. That danger comes from someone she loves and trusts, her husband.

With his violent villainous impulses, Jack, now transformed into the "axe" murderer, is almost like a monster (abject): violence in the film is wielded by him. His role is crucial in this regard because the monster within him functions literally and metaphorically. The evil we see in him is not unproblematic; being the father figure in the family, his role is that of a protector and care-giver. We do not desire his absolute destruction. When the film begins, there is no insanity in Jack. Once the Torrances start inhabiting the Overlook, Jack's disturbing yet calm demeanour is replaced by a feeling that he is someone who will end up as a mental wreck.

The chase begins with Jack hunting down both son and wife to murder them. They unproblematically evolve as his victims. Wendy is victimised but is initially sympathetic towards Jack, even though he poses the threat of violence. The scene where Wendy tries to ward off Jack's attack with Danny's baseball bat swinging in her hand is a scene where "horror violence" is shaped tonally and visually to transgressive ends.

One of the most oft-cited assertions about the horror film is that it is structured around male violence against female victims, an argument that seems to be illustrated again and again by images of shrieking, terrified women cowering from a physically masculine monstrosity (Kendrick 84). In *The Shining*, such simplistic assertions are problematised with Jack being the knife-wielding killer from within the family who poses a threat not only to his female victim (wife) but also to his young son (Danny). Given the extraordinary nature of gory, sadistic horror films, with their onslaught of realistically rendered blood spurts, torn flesh, and fragmented and mutilated bodies, it might appear that violence and the horror genre are inextricably related. This is well refuted by *The Shining*.

Though the paranormal has a strong presence in the film, in *The Shining* the real threat is human. Since the relationship between horror and violence has been a contested issue for so long, it is interesting to observe how Kubrick visualises the violence. Kubrick made it clear to his audience that "horror violence" need not always be gory to generate that spine-chilling effect. He very deftly balances his craft upon the fine line between direct and indirect horror films. By indirect horror films, I mean films that rely on the interplay of light and shadow, foreboding music, slanted camera angles, and other traditional means of generating suspense. By direct horror films, I mean especially the "slasher" films that revel in visually graphic representations of violence. Kubrick manipulates both categories to his desired effect, just as he manipulates King's novel to give us his ambivalent take on the source material.

We see Kubrick's multi-layered approach to its literary predecessor in this appropriation. The horror film in general as a genre has earned a lot of disrepute, not unsurprisingly, for giving birth to a variety of cheap pulp flicks. A genre-redefining horror film, the complex subtlety and ambiguity of *The Shining* appeals at a much more profound level.

Works cited

Baxter, John. *Stanley Kubrick: A Biography*. Harper Collins, 1998, 301.
Kendrick, James. *Film Violence: History, Ideology, Genre*. Wallflower, 2009.

INDEX OF FILM TITLES

Abismos de Pasión (dir. Luis Buñuel, 1954), 136, 138–43
Achyut Kanya (dir. Frank Osten, 1936), 85
Agneepath (dir. Mukul Anand, 1990), 70
Alexander Nevsky (dir. Sergei Eisenstein, 1938), 102
Alien (dir. Ridley Scott, 1979), 184
Amanush (dir. Shakti Samanta, 1975), 45n1
Amazing Spider-Man, The (dir. Marc Webb, 2012), 67
Amrapali (dir. Lekh Tandon, 1966), 24
Angoor (dir. Gulzar, 1982), 70
Année dernière à Marienbad, L' (*Last Year at Marienbad*) (dir. Alain Resnais, 1961), 124
Aparajito (dir. Satyajit Ray, 1956), 86
Apocalypse Now (dir. Francis Ford Coppola, 1979), 108
Arshi Nagar (dir. Aparna Sen, 2015), 17
As You Like It (dir. Kenneth Branagh, 2006), 109
Awaara (dir. Raj Kapoor, 1951), 71, 86

Bend It Like Beckham (dir. Gurinder Chadha, 2002), 96
Bicycle Thieves (dir. Vittorio De Sica, 1948), 86
Birds, The (dir. Alfred Hitchcock, 1963), 161–69, 172, 177
Black Friday (dir. Anurag Kashyap, 2004), 72, 74

Blackmail (dir. Alfred Hitchcock, 1929), 173
Blue (dir. Anthony D'Souza, 2009), 23
Bobby (dir. Raj Kapoor, 1973), 70
Bollywood/Hollywood (dir. Deepa Mehta, 2002), 96
Boys from Syracuse, The (dir. A. Edward Sutherland, 1940), 110
Bride and Prejudice (dir. Gurinder Chadha, 2004), 96
Brief Encounter (dir. David Lean, 1945), 66

Casablanca (dir. Michael Curtiz, 1942), 174
Catch My Soul (*Santa Fe Satan*) (dir. Patrick McGoohan, 1974), 110
Chimes at Midnight (dir. Orson Welles, 1965), 101, 108
Chinnamul (dir. Nimai Ghosh, 1950), 7n2
Citizen Kane (dir. Orson Welles, 1941), 101
Cleopatra (dir. Raja Nawathe, 1950), 101
Clockwork Orange, A (dir. Stanley Kubrick, 1971), 105
Cocktail (dir. Homi Adajania, 2012), 93
Company (dir. Ram Gopal Verma, 2001), 72, 74

Dangal (dir. Nitesh Tiwari, 2016), 96
Dangerous Liaisons (dir. Stephen Frears, 1988), 20

Deewana (dir. Raj Kanwar, 1992), 75
Deewar (dir. Yash Chopra, 1975), 71, 73, 95
Dev D (dir. Anurag Kashyap, 2009), 44–45n1, 54–56, 93
Devdas (dir. Naresh Mitra, 1927), 44n1
Devdas (dir. P. C. Barua, 1935), 44n1
Devdas (dir. P. C. Barua, 1936), 44n1
Devdas (dir. P. C. Barua, 1937), 44n1
Devdas (*Devadasu*) (dir. Vedantam Raghavaiah, 1953), 44n1
Devdas (dir. Bimal Roy, 1955), 44n1, 45–50, 53–54, 56
Devdas (*Debdas*) (dir. Dilip Roy, 1979), 44n1
Devdas (dir. Sanjay Leela Bhansali, 2002), 44n1, 45, 47–54, 56, 87, 92
Devdas (dir. Shakti Samanta, 2002), 44n1
Devdas (dir. Chachi Nuzrol Islam, 2010), 45n1
Devdas (dir. Iqbal Kasmiri, 2010), 45n1
Dharti Ke Lal (dir. Khwaja Ahmad Abbas, 1946), 86
Dheepan (dir. Jacques Audiard, 2015), 89
Dhoom (dir. Vijay Krishna Acharya, 2004), 22
Dhoom 2 (dir. Sanjay Gadhvi, 2006), 22
Dial M for Murder (dir. Alfred Hitchcock, 1954), 173, 174
Dil Chahta Hai (dir. Farhan Akhtar, 2001) 62, 70, 93–94
Dil Dhadakne Do (dir. Zoya Akhtar, 2015), 22, 25–26
Dil Farosh (dir. M. Udvadia, 1927), 85

Dilwale Dulhaniya Le Jayenge (dir. Aditya Chopra, 1995), 89, 90–92
Dirty Picture, The (dir. Milan Luthria, 2011), 30, 36–39, 41
Do Bigha Zameen (dir. Bimal Roy, 1953), 86
Doctor Sleep (dir. Mike Flanagan, 2019), 185–86
Dolce Vita, La (dir. Federico Fellini, 1960), 9
Dolly Kitty Aur Woh Chamakte Sitare (dir. Alankrita Shrivastava, 2020), 16
Don (dir. Farhan Akhtar, 2006), 91, 93, 94
Donnie Brasco (dir. Mike Newell, 1997), 76
Dostana (dir. Tarun Mansukhani, 2008), 92, 93
Double Indemnity (dir. Billy Wilder, 1944), 181
Dracula (dir. Tod Browning, 1931), 180
D: Underworld Badshah (dir. Vishram Sawant, 2005), 72, 73
Dushman (dir. Tanuja Chandra, 1998), 21

Earth (dir. Deepa Mehta, 1998), 5, 96
Eklavya (dir. Vidhu Vinod Chopra, 2007), 70
English Vinglish (dir. Gauri Shinde, 2012), 22

Family (dir. Raj Kumar Santoshi, 2005), 74
Fashion (dir. Madhur Bhandarkar, 2008), ix, 30–35, 36, 41, 93
Fatal Attraction (dir. Adrian Lyne, 1987), 20
Firaaq (dir. Nandita Das, 2008), 24, 25
Fire (dir. Deepa Mehta, 1996), 27, 96

Foreign Correspondent (dir. Alfred Hitchcock, 1940), 174
Frankenstein (dir. James Whale, 1931), 180
French Lieutenant's Woman, The (dir. Karel Reisz, 1981), 123–34

Gangster (dir. Anurag Basu, 2006), 80
Garam Hawa (dir. M. S. Sathyu, 1973), 10–13
Gaslight (dir. Thorold Dickinson, 1940), 174, 179
Gaslight (dir. George Cukor, 1944), 179
Ghajini (dir. A. R. Murugadoss, 2008), 76n6
Godfather, The (dir. Francis Ford Coppola, 1972), 75–76, 148
Good Morning, Vietnam (dir. Barry Levinson, 1987), 108
Great Gatsby, The (dir. Herbert Brenon, 1926), 145
Great Gatsby, The (dir. Elliott Nugent, 1949), 145
Great Gatsby, The (dir. Jack Clayton, 1974), 145, 147–53
Great Gatsby, The (dir. Robert Markowitz, 2000), 145, 149
Great Gatsby, The (dir. Baz Luhrmann, 2013), 145, 149–53

Haath Ki Safai (dir. Prakash Mehra, 1974), 44n1
Haider (dir. Vishal Bhardwaj, 2014) 67, 70, 96
Hamlet (dir. Laurence Olivier, 1948), 100–101, 106, 107
Hamlet (dir. Kishore Sahu, 1954), 101
Hamlet (dir. Grigori Kozintsev, 1964), 105
Hamlet (dir. Franco Zeffirelli, 1990), 107, 108
Hamlet (dir. Kenneth Branagh, 1996), 109

Henna (dir. Randhir Kapoor, 1991), 70
Henry V (dir. Laurence Olivier, 1944), 106, 108
Henry V (dir. Kenneth Branagh, 1989), 107–8
Heroine (dir. Madhur Bhandarkar, 2012), 30, 35–36, 41
Hey Ram (dir. Kamal Haasan, 2000), 5
Hindi Medium (dir. Saket Chaudhary, 2017), 67
Homicidal (dir. William Castle, 1961), 176
Hum Aapke Hain Koun . . ! (dir. Sooraj Barjatya, 1994), 89, 92
Hum Saath Saath Hai (dir Sooraj Barjatya, 1999), 89

Inferno (dir. Ron Howard, 2016), 64
Innocents, The (dir. Jack Clayton, 1961), 184
In the Bleak Midwinter (dir. Kenneth Branagh, 1995), 109
Irma la Douce (dir. Billy Wilder, 1963), 76n6
Ishaqzaade (dir. Habib Faisal, 2012), 96
Issaq (dir. Manish Tiwary, 2013), 96
Iti Mrinalini (dir. Aparna Sen, 2010), ix, 16–17, 31, 39–41

Jaane Tu Ya Jane Na (dir. Abbas Tyrewala, 2008), 59–62
Jamaica Inn (dir. Alfred Hitchcock, 1939), 172
Jay Vejay (dir. L. V. Prasad, 1977), 24
Joe Macbeth (dir. Ken Hughes, 1955), 73
Julius Caesar (dir. Joseph Mankiewicz, 1953), 104
Jurassic Park (dir. Steven Spielberg, 1993), 146

Jurassic World (dir. Colin Trevorrow, 2015), 64

Kaagaz Ke Phool (dir. Guru Dutt, 1959), 45n1
Kabhi Alvida Na Kehna (dir. Karan Johar, 2006), 87, 91
Kabhi Khushi Kabhie Gham (dir. Karan Johar, 2001), 27, 89, 90–92
Kaho Naa . . . Pyaar Hai (dir. Rakesh Roshan, 2000), 93
Kal Ho Na Ho (dir. Nikhil Advani, 2003), 90, 92
Karma (dir. J. L. Freer Hunt, 1933), 85
King Is Alive, The (dir. Kristin Levring, 2000), 118–19
King Lear (dir. Peter Brook, 1971), 117–18, 119
King Lear (dir. Jean-Luc Godard, 1987), 119
Kiss Me Kate (dir. George Sidney, 1953), 110
Kites (dir. Anurag Basu, 2010), 23, 93
Komal Gandhar (dir. Ritwik Ghatak, 1961), 3, 7
Korol Lir (dir. Grigori Kozintsev, 1970), 113–14, 115, 116–17, 118
Kuch Kuch Hota Hai (dir. Karan Johar, 1998), 87, 91, 92, 95

Lady from Shanghai, The (dir. Orson Welles, 1947), 182
Lady Vanishes, The (dir. Alfred Hitchcock, 1938), 171–72, 174
Lagaan (dir. Ashutosh Gowariker, 2001), 87, 94, 95
Laura (dir. Otto Preminger, 1944), 179
Layla Majnu (dir. Harnam Singh Rawail, 1976), 56n6
Life in a . . . Metro (dir. Anurag Basu, 2007), 66
Life of Pi (dir. Ang Lee, 2012), 64
Love's Labours Lost (dir. Kenneth Branagh, 2000), 109
Lunchbox, The (dir. Ritesh Batra, 2013), 66

Macbeth (dir. Orson Welles, 1948), 101–2
Macbeth (dir. Roman Polanski, 1971), 105–6, 107
Magnificent Seven, The (dir. John Sturges, 1960), 109
Mammo (dir. Shyam Benegal, 1994), 10
Maniac (dir. Michael Carreras, 1962), 176
Maqbool (dir. Vishal Bhardwaj, 2004), 65, 69–70, 72–81, 96, 104
Marnie (dir. Alfred Hitchcock, 1964), 157, 175
Meghe Dhaka Tara (*The Cloud-Capped Star*) (dir. Ritwik Ghatak, 1960), 3–7
Memento (dir. Christopher Nolan, 2000), 76n6
Men of Respect (dir. William Reilly, 1990), 73
Midsummer Night's Dream, A (dir. Adrian Noble, 1996), 110
Midsummer Night's Dream, A (dir. Michael Hoffman, 1999), 110
Mist, The (dir. Frank Darabont, 2007), 166
Monsoon Wedding (dir. Mira Nair, 2001), 96
Mother India (dir. Mehboob Khan, 1957), 86
Much Ado About Nothing (dir. Kenneth Branagh, 1993), 107, 109
Muqaddar Ka Sikandar (dir. Prakash Mehra, 1978), 45n1, 95
Murder (dir. Anurag Basu, 2004), 93

My Name is Julia Ross (dir. Joseph H. Lewis, 1945), 179
My Name Is Khan (dir. Karan Johar, 2010), 92

Namastey London (dir. Vipul Amrutlal Shah, 2007), 27
Namesake, The (dir. Mira Nair, 2006), 27, 64–65, 67, 96
Neecha Nagar (dir. Chetan Anand, 1946), 85
New York (dir. Kabir Khan, 2009), 92
Nightmare (dir. Freddie Francis, 1964), 176
North by Northwest (dir. Alfred Hitchcock, 1959), 20, 171, 173, 174, 177
Nosferatu (dir. F. W. Murnau, 1922), 176, 180
Notorious (dir. Alfred Hitchcock, 1946), 174, 175
Number Seventeen (dir. Alfred Hitchcock, 1932), 173

Omen, The (dir. Richard Donner, 1976), 184
Omkara (dir. Vishal Bhardwaj, 2006), 70, 96, 103–4
Om Shanti Om (dir. Farah Khan, 2007), 24, 62
Othello (dir. Orson Welles, 1951), 100–103
Othello (dir. Sergei Yutkevich, 1955), 103

Paan Singh Tomar (dir. Tigmanshu Dhulia, 2012), 66
Paradine Case, The (dir. Alfred Hitchcock, 1947), 181
Paranoiac (dir. Freddie Francis, 1963), 176
Pardes (dir. Subhash Ghai, 1997), 27, 92
Parinda (dir Vidhu Vinod Chopra, 1989) 73

Pather Panchali (dir. Satyajit Ray, 1955), 4, 86
Peepli Live (dir. Anusha Rizwi, 2010), 25, 95
Piku (dir. Shoojit Sircar, 2015), 66, 67
Pinjar (dir. Chandraprakash Dwivedi, 2003), 5
PK (dir. Rajkumar Hirani, 2014), 96
Platoon (dir. Oliver Stone, 1986) 108
Psycho (dir. Alfred Hitchcock, 1960), 105, 156, 157, 173, 175–77
Pyaasa (dir. Guru Dutt, 1957), 45n1

Qarib Qarib Singlle (dir. Tanuja Chandra, 2017), 21, 22, 66
Qayamat Se Qayamat Tak (dir. Mansoor Khan, 1998), 70

Raazi (dir. Meghna Gulzar, 2018), 24
Rab Ne Bana Di Jodi (dir. Aditya Chopra, 2008), 76n6
Ram-Leela (*Goliyon Ki Raasleela Ram-Leela*) (dir. Sanjay Leela Bhansali, 2013), 96
Ran (dir. Akira Kurosawa, 1985), 105, 114–16, 117, 199
Rear Window (dir. Alfred Hitchcock, 1954), 156, 173, 174–75
Rebecca (dir. Alfred Hitchcock, 1940), 101, 158, 172, 178–82
Reluctant Fundamentalist, The (dir. Mira Nair, 2012), 96
Repulsion (dir. Roman Polanski, 1965), 176
Richard III (dir. Laurence Olivier, 1955), 101
Richard III (dir. Richard Loncraine, 1995), 101
Romeo and Juliet (dir. Renato Castellani, 1954), 104

Romeo and Juliet (dir. Franco Zeffirelli, 1968), 106–7, 109
Room 237 (dir. Rodney Ascher, 2012), 186
Rope (dir. Alfred Hitchcock, 1948), 175
Rosemary's Baby (dir. Roman Polanski, 1968), 105

Sabotage (dir. Alfred Hitchcock, 1936), 173
Saboteur (dir. Alfred Hitchcock, 1942), 174
Sachaa Jhutha (dir. Manmohan Desai, 1970), 24
Salaam Bombay (dir. Mira Nair, 1988), 64, 96
Sarkar (dir. Ram Gopal Verma, 2007), 72, 74–76, 80
Sati (dir. Aparna Sen, 1989), 16
Satya (dir. Ram Gopal Verma, 1997), 72, 73, 74n4
Secret Agent (dir. Alfred Hitchcock, 1936), 174
Shadow of a Doubt (dir. Alfred Hitchcock, 1943), 173, 177, 179
Sholay (dir. Ramesh Sippy, 1975), 71, 76, 86
Shri 420 (dir. Raj Kapoor, 1955), 71
Shining, The (dir. Stanley Kubrick, 1980), ix, 183–88
Singin' in the Rain (dirs. Gene Kelly and Stanley Donen, 1952), 109
Slumdog Millionaire (dir. Danny Boyle, 2008), 64, 74
Snow White and the Seven Dwarfs (prod. Walt Disney, 1937), 102
Sohni Mahiwal (dirs. Umesh Mehra and Latif Faiziyev, 1984), 56n6
Some Like It Hot (dir. Billy Wilder, 1959), 109
Spellbound (dir. Alfred Hitchcock, 1945), 171, 172–73
Strait Jacket (dir. William Castle, 1964), 176

Strangers on a Train (dir. Alfred Hitchcock, 1951), 173
Subarnarekha (dir. Ritwik Ghatak, 1962), 3, 7–10
Sunset Boulevard (dir. Billy Wilder, 1950), 181
Suspicion (dir. Alfred Hitchcock, 1941), 173, 174, 179

Taal (dir. Subhash Ghai, 1999), 92, 93
Talaash (dir. Reema Kagti, 2012), 18–21
Talwar (dir. Meghna Gulzar, 2015), 24, 65
Tamas (dir. Govind Nihalani, 1987), 10–11
Taming of the Shrew, The (dir. Franco Zeffirelli, 1966), 109
Tenant, The (dir. Roman Polanski, 1976), 176
39 Steps, The (dir. Alfred Hitchcock, 1935), 171, 173, 174
36 Chowringhee Lane (dir. Aparna Sen, 1981), 16
Thoda Pyaar Thoda Magic (dir. Kunal Kohli, 2008), 23
3 Idiots (dir. Rajkumar Hirani, 2009), 62, 96
Throne of Blood (dir. Akira Kurosawa, 1957), 104–5
Titus (dir. Julie Taymor, 1999), 108
Topaz (dir. Alfred Hitchcock, 1969), 174
Torn Curtain (dir. Alfred Hitchcock, 1966), 174
Train to Pakistan (dir. Pamela Rooks, 1998), 5
Twelfth Night (dir. Trevor Nunn, 1996), 110

Vaastav (dir. Mahesh Manjrekar, 1999), 74
Vertigo (dir. Alfred Hitchcock, 1958), 20, 156–60, 173, 175, 177

Warrior, The (dir. Asif Kapadia, 2001), 64, 67
Water (dir. Deepa Mehta, 2005), 27, 96
West Side Story (dirs. Robert Wise and Jerome Robbins, 1961), 110
What Ever Happened to Baby Jane? (dir. Robert Aldrich, 1962), 176
When Strangers Marry (*Betrayed*) (dir. William Castle, 1944), 179
William Shakespeare's Romeo + Juliet (dir. Baz Luhrmann, 1996), 106
Wolf Man, The (dir. George Waggner, 1941), 180
Wuthering Heights (dir. William Wyler, 1939), 136–38, 140, 142, 143
Wuthering Heights (dir. Robert Fuest, 1970), 143

Yeh Jawani Hai Deewani (dir. Ayan Mukerji, 2013), 93

Zindagi Na Milegi Dobara (dir. Zoya Akhtar, 2011), 22–23, 93, 94

General Index

Work titles listed by director or author

Abbas, Khwaja Ahmad
  Dharti Ke Lal, 86
abject, 20–21, 182, 187
Acharya, Vijay Krishna
  Dhoom, 22
acting, 6, 16, 39, 65, 67, 104, 151
Adajania, Homi
  Cocktail, 93
adaptation, ix, 44–45, 55–56, 64, 69–70, 85, 93, 94, 96, 100, 107–10, 113–19, 123–25, 134, 136–38, 141, 143, 145–47, 150, 153–54, 161–63
Adenauer, Konrad, 8
Advani, Nikhil
  Kal Ho Na Ho, 90, 92
aesthetics, ix, 3, 6, 9, 11, 30, 54, 80–81, 94, 104, 122, 145, 159, 163, 176, 180
agency, 5, 24, 26, 31, 52, 54, 90
Akhtar, Farhan, 22, 25, 70, 93
  Dil Chahta Hai, 62, 70, 93–94; "Jaane Kyu Log Pyar Karte Hai" (song), 94; "Woh Ladki Hai Kahan" (song), 62
  Don, 91, 93, 94
Akhtar, Zoya, 16, 22–23, 94
  Dil Dhadakne Do, 22, 25–26
  Zindagi Na Milegi Dobara, 22–23, 93, 94
Aldrich, Robert
  What Ever Happened to Baby Jane?, 176
Ali, Mohammed (gangster), 73
Althusser, Louis, 30
Ambani, Anil, 89

Amitabh Bachchan Corporation Ltd., 95
Anand, Chetan, 85
  Neecha Nagar, 85
Anand, Mukul, 70
  Agneepath, 70
Anderegg, Michael, 102
Anderson, Judith, 172, 174
Anderson, Wes, 64
Annis, Francesca, 106
archetypes, 3–5, 7–9, 23, 24, 45, 56, 70
architecture, 12, 103
Arnold, Andrea, 136
Ascher, Rodney
  Room 237, 186
art (fine art), 13
atomic bombs, 8
Audiard, Jacques, 89
  Dheepan, 89
Azmi, Kaifi, 10

Bachchan, Amitabh, 75, 91, 95
Bajpai, Manoj, 73
Baker, Frank, 163
  Birds, The, 163
Balan, Vidya, 36
Bangla, viii
Barjatya, Sooraj, 89
  Hum Aapke Hain Koun . . !, 89, 92
  Hum Saath Saath Hai, 89
Barnouw, Eric, 46
  See also Barnouw, Eric, and S. Krishnaswamy, works by,
Barnouw, Eric, and S. Krishnaswamy, works by,

Indian Film, 46
Bartók, Béla, 185
Barua, P. C., 44n1
  Devdas (1935), 44n1
  Devdas (1936), 44n1
  Devdas (1937), 44n1
Basu, Anurag, 23, 66, 74
  Gangster, 80
  Kites, 23, 93
  Life in a . . . Metro, 66
  Murder, 93
Basu, Bipasha, 103
Batra, Ritesh
  Lunchbox, The, 66
Beckett, Samuel, 59
  Waiting for Godot, 59
Bedi, Monica, 80
Benegal, Shyam, 10
  Mammo, 10
Bengal Famine, 5, 86
Benjamin, Walter, 76–77
Bergman, Ingrid, 172, 174, 179
Bhandarkar, Madhur, 31, 32, 35, 93
  Fashion, ix, 30–35, 36, 41, 93
  Heroine, 30, 35–36, 41
Bhansali, Sanjay Leela, 44n1, 47, 48, 49, 50, 52, 53, 87
  Devdas, 44n1, 45, 47–54, 56, 87, 92; "Dola Re, Dola Re" (song), 50–51
  Ram-Leela (*Goliyon Ki Raasleela Ram-Leela*), 96
Bhardwaj, Vishal, 65, 69–70, 73, 74n4, 77–78, 100, 103
  Haider, 67, 70, 96
  Maqbool, 65, 69–70, 72–81, 96, 104
  Omkara, 70, 96, 103–4
Bharti, Divya, 75
Bhatia, Vanraj, 11
Bhaumik, Kaushik, 71
Birmingham Centre for Contemporary Cultural studies, viii
Biswas, Moinak, 7n2
body, 15, 30–33, 35, 42, 143

Boileau-Narcejac, works by
  D'entre les morts (*From Among the Dead*), 157
Bollymadrid, 92
Bolt, Robert, 130
Bonham Carter, Helena, 107, 110
Bose, Rahul, 25
Botticelli, Sandro, 106
Boyle, Danny, 64, 74
  Slumdog Millionaire, 64, 74
Boyum, Joy Gould, 149–50, 151, 152, 153
Branagh, Kenneth, 69, 100, 107–10
  As You Like It, 109
  Hamlet, 109
  Henry V, 107–8
  In the Bleak Midwinter, 109
  Love's Labours Lost, 109
  Much Ado About Nothing, 107, 109
Brando, Marlon, 75, 104
Brecht, Bertolt, 3, 9, 117, 118
Brenon, Herbert, 145
  Great Gatsby, The, 145
Brontë, Emily, 136–38, 140–43
  Wuthering Heights, 136–38, 140–43
Brook, Peter, 100, 117–18, 119
  King Lear, 117–18, 119
Browning, Tod
  Dracula, 180
British Film Institute, 92
Buchan, John, 171
  39 Steps, The, 171
Buñuel, Luis, 9, 136, 138–43
  Abismos de Pasion, 136, 138–43
Butler, Judith, 17
Byron, Lord (George Gordon Byron), 139

Calder-Marshall, Anna, 143
Cannes Film Festival, 85, 89
Carpaccio, Vittore, 102
Carreras, Michael
  Maniac, 176
Carrière, Jean-Claude, 127, 129

caste, 8, 9, 25, 55, 96, 103
Castle, William, 179
    Homicidal, 176
    Strait Jacket, 176
    When Strangers Marry (Betrayed), 179
Castellani, Renato, 104
    Romeo and Juliet, 104
Cavanah, Robert, 136
Chadha, Gurinder, 95
    Bend It Like Beckham, 96
    Bride and Prejudice, 96
Chandra, Tanuja, 16
    Dushman, 21
    Qarib Qarib Singlle, 21, 22, 66
Chaplin, Charlie, 71
Chatman, Seymour, 125
Chatterjee, Sarat Chandra, 44, 56
    Devdas (novel), 44–46, 55–57, 93
Chaudhary, Saket
    Hindi Medium, 67
China, 96–97
Chopra, Aditya, 89–90
    Dilwale Dulhaniya Le Jayenge, 89, 90–92
    Rab Ne Bana Di Jodi, 76n6
Chopra, Priyanka, 25, 32, 93
Chopra, Vidhu Vinod, 70, 73
    Eklavya, 70
    Parinda, 73
Chopra, Yash, 27, 71, 90
    Deewar, 71, 73, 95
Chugtai, Ismat, 10
cinema
    American, 87
    art, viii, ix, 2, 7, 9, 37, 67, 86, 102, 107, 146
    Bangla, 16
    Bengali, 17
    Bollywood, viii, 20, 39, 45, 48, 55, 59, 62, 67, 69–77, 79–81, 86–89, 91–97
    commercial, ix, 3, 7, 30, 37, 42, 55, 65, 79, 86–87, 107
    European, 85, 102
    Hindi, viii, 10, 16, 18, 20, 22–24, 31, 62, 85, 86, 87–88, 92, 94–95
    Hollywood, 19, 20, 59, 67, 76, 85, 91, 94, 96, 107, 109, 118, 119, 136, 138, 171, 179, 180
    Indian, 42, 45–46, 52, 69–70, 74, 85–89, 94–95, 97
    industry, 35–36, 88–89, 94, 97
    Kannada, 16
    Maratha, 16
    meta-, 118, 123
    Mumbai, 16, 65
    regional, 16
    South Indian, 36, 39, 93
    Tamil, 93
    task of, 31
    Telegu, 16
    Western, 4, 17, 71, 72, 76, 86, 96
    women's 15–16, 18
    world, 86
cinemas, 88
Cixous, Hélène, 26
class, 25, 27, 48, 51, 57, 130, 136, 181
Clayton, Jack, 145, 147–53, 184
    Great Gatsby, The, 145, 147–53
    Innocents, The, 184
Climan, Bernice W., 105
Close, Glenn, 20, 107
communication, ix, 146
control, 20, 21, 31, 33–34, 37, 45, 51, 73, 75, 91, 121, 137, 140, 175, 179, 181
Coppola, Francis Ford, 76, 148, 150, 151
    Apocalypse Now, 108
    Godfather, The, 75–76, 148
Crane, Stephen, 184
    Blue Hotel, The, 184
Crichton, Michael, 146
    Jurassic Park, 146
Crowl, Samuel, 107, 108

Cukor, George, 179
Gaslight, 179
Curtiz, Michael
Casablanca, 174

Dal, Oleg, 116, 117
Dalí, Salvador, 173
Dalton, Timothy, 136, 143
Darabont, Frank
Mist, The, 166
Darwin, Charles, 121
Das, Nandita, 16
Firaaq, 24, 25
de Gaulle, Charles, 8
de Lauretis, Teresa, 30
Dench, Judi, 17
Deol, Sunny, 56n6
Depp, Johnny, 76
Desai, Manmohan
Sachaa Jhutha, 24
De Sica, Vittorio, 86
Bicycle Thieves, 86
desire, 18–20, 26, 37, 38, 41, 46, 47–54, 59, 78, 88, 90, 100, 102, 104, 115, 123, 124, 141, 158–59, 165–66, 169, 173–76, 181, 186
Devgan, Ajay, 103
Devi, Arundhati, 16
Dhillon, Poonam, 56n6
Dhuila, Tigmanshu
Paan Singh Tomar, 66
DiCaprio, Leonardo, 145, 153
Dickinson, Thorold, 179
Gaslight, 174, 179
discourse, viii, 11, 18–19, 26, 28, 30, 31, 36, 37, 54, 70, 80, 81, 85, 121, 126
Disney, Walt, 101, 102
Snow White and the Seven Dwarfs, 102
Dogme 95, 118
Donaldson, Peter S., 104
Donat, Robert, 171
Donner, Richard
Omen, The, 184

dream sequences, 60–61, 173
D'Souza, Anthony, 23
Blue, 23
D'Souza, Genelia, 60
Du Maurier, Daphne, 161–64, 166, 167, 168, 172, 178–81
Birds, The, 161–64, 166, 168, 172
Jamaica Inn, 172
Rebecca, 172, 178–82
Durga, 5, 7, 47, 48
Dutt, Guru, 45n4
Kaagaz Ke Phool, 45n1
Pyaasa, 45n1
Dutt, Sanjay, 74n4, 75
Dutt, Sunil, 24
Dutta, Bisakha, 39
Duvall, Shelley, 183, 184
Dwivedi, Chandraprakash, 5
Pinjar, 5

Eagleton, Terry, 137
editing, 54, 103–5, 118, 166–67, 174
Eisenstein, Sergei, 9, 102
Alexander Nevsky, 102
Eliot, George, 121
Eliot, T. S., 147
Waste Land, The, 147
empiricism, viii
epics, 3, 7, 9, 46, 56n6, 89, 109
expressionism, 3, 6, 102, 103, 157, 175, 176, 175, 176

Faisal, Habib
Ishaqzaade, 96
Farrow, Mia, 145, 148, 150
Fellini, Federico, 9–10
Dolce Vita, La, 9
femininity, 3, 18, 20–21, 23, 25, 27, 36, 45, 48–49, 51, 181
feminism, 15, 26, 30, 54, 124, 158
femmes fatales, 4, 20–21, 124, 158, 167
Fiennes, Ralph, 136
Film France, 89

film industry. *See* cinema: industry
film-makers, ix, 3, 10, 27, 69, 71, 89, 145, 149, 153, 163
  female, 15–18, 20, 22, 27–28, 64, 95–96
  See also cinema; *names of specific film-makers*
films. *See* cinema
Finch, Jon, 106
Fitzgerald, F. Scott, 145, 147–53
  Babylon Revisited, 149
  Beautiful and the Damned, The, 149
  Great Gatsby, The, ix, 145–53
  Tender Is the Night, 149
Flanagan, Mike, 185, 186
  Doctor Sleep, 185–86
Foch, Nina, 179
Fontaine, Joan, 172, 179
Ford, John, 86
Fowles, John, ix, 121–25, 130–35
  French Lieutenant's Woman, The, ix, 121–26, 130–34
frame, viii, 4–5, 8, 11, 13, 30–31, 38, 39, 42, 59–62, 75, 113, 127, 186
Francis, Freddie
  Nightmare, 176
  Paranoiac, 176
Frears, Stephen
  Dangerous Liaisons, 20
Freer Hunt, J. L.
  Karma, 85
Fuest, Robert, 136, 143
  Wuthering Heights, 143

Gadhvi, Sanjay
  Dhoom 2, 22
Gaston, Georg, 134
Gawli, Arun, 73
gaze, 7, 21, 42, 55, 93, 102
  female, 18, 21, 34, 45–53, 56, 141
  male, 20–22, 34, 45, 51, 52, 54

gender, viii, ix, 5, 11, 15–21, 23–25, 27, 30–31, 36, 42, 45, 55, 79, 96, 110, 115, 121, 136, 181
  See also femininity, film-makers: female; masculinity; women on screen
genres, viii, 110, 156, 158–59, 179
  costume drama, 39, 114
  crime, 65, 71–73, 103
  drama, 25, 59, 70, 87, 89, 95, 101, 158, 126, 156, 158, 159, 172, 173, 178, 180
  film noir, 71, 79, 100, 103, 107, 157, 179, 182
  gangster film, 65, 69–76, 80–81, 110
  horror, 20, 71, 156, 158, 176, 179, 180, 182, 184–85, 187–88
  masala, 70, 72, 79, 87, 94–95
  melodrama, 45, 56, 71, 72, 178
  romance, 48, 55, 59–62, 66, 70, 71, 87, 156, 158, 178–80
  science fiction, 180
  thriller, 156–58, 159, 171–72, 178, 182
Ghai, Subhash, 27, 90, 92
  Pardes, 27, 92
  Taal, 92, 93
Ghatak, Ritwik, ix, 2–10
  Komal Gandhar, 3, 7
  Meghe Dhaka Tara (*The Cloud-Capped Star*), 3–7
  Subarnarekha, 3, 7–10
Ghosh, Nimai, 7n2
  Chinnamul, 7n2
ghungru (dancing bells), 52
Gibson, Mel, 107
globalisation, 23, 27, 32, 34, 37, 55, 57, 62, 81, 85–97, 100
Godard, Jean-Luc, 2, 9, 118, 119
  King Lear, 119
Gopalkrishnan, Adoor, 3
gothic, 100, 136–38, 142–43, 157, 164, 172, 178–80, 182

Govindan, Padma, 39
Gowariker, Ashutosh, 87
   Lagaan, 87, 94, 95
Gulzar (Sampooran Singh Kalra), 10, 70
   Angoor, 70
Gulzar, Meghna, 16
   Raazi, 24
   Talwar, 24, 65

Haasan, Kamal,
   Hey Ram, 5
Hanks, Tom, 64
Harbison, John, 145
   Great Gatsby, The, 145
Hardy, Thomas, 121
Hardy, Tom, 136
Hashmi, Emraan, 37, 39
Heer Ranjha (epic poem), 56n6
Herrmann, Bernard, 159
Hirani, Rajkumar
   PK, 96
   3 Idiots, 62, 96; "Zooby Dooby" (song), 62
Hitchcock, Alfred, ix, 101, 105, 156, 158–60, 161–69, 171–77, 178–82
   Birds, The, 161–69, 172, 177
   Blackmail, 173
   Dial M for Murder, 173, 174
   Foreign Correspondent, 174
   Jamaica Inn, 172
   Lady Vanishes, The, 171–72, 174
   Marnie, 157, 175
   North by Northwest, 20, 171, 173, 174, 177
   Notorious, 174, 175
   Number Seventeen, 173
   Paradine Case, The, 181
   Psycho, 105, 156, 157, 173, 175–77
   Rear Window, 156, 173, 174–75
   Rebecca, 101, 158, 172, 178–82
   Rope, 175
   Sabotage, 173
   Saboteur, 174
   Secret Agent, 174
   Shadow of a Doubt, 173, 177, 179
   Spellbound, 171, 172–73
   Strangers on a Train, 173
   Suspicion, 173, 174, 179
   39 Steps, The, 171, 173, 174
   Topaz, 174
   Torn Curtain, 174
   Vertigo, 20, 156–60, 173, 175, 177
Hitler, Adolf, 101
Hoffman, Michael, 110
   Midsummer Night's Dream, A, 110
honour killing, 57
Howard, Ron
   Inferno, 64
Howard, Trevor, 66
Howlett, Kathy, 102
Howson, James, 136
Hughes, Ken, 73
   Joe Macbeth, 73
Humbert, David, 166
Hunter, Kim, 179
Hussain, Akhtar, 101
Hussey, Olivia, 106

Ibrahim, Dawood, 72–74
Independence, 46n3, 71; post-Independence, 7, 9, 86
Indian People's Theatre Association (IPTA), 10
Irons, Jeremy, 125
Islam, Chachi Nuzrol, 45n1
   Devdas, 45n1

Jackson, Russel, 107
Jagadhatri, 5
James, Henry, 184
   Turn of the Screw, The, 184
jazz, 94, 146–47, 151
Johar, Karan, 27, 87, 89, 91, 92, 95
   Kabhi Alvida Na Kehna, 87, 91

Kabhi Khushi Kabhie Gham, 27, 89, 90–92
Kuch Kuch Hota Hai, 87, 91, 92, 95
My Name Is Khan, 92
Johnson, Celia, 66
Jonson, Ben, 78
Jorgens, Jack, 118
Jung, Carl, 3

Kagti, Reema, 16, 18–19, 20, 25
  Talaash, 18–21
Kaif, Katrina, 22
Kali, 3, 8
Kanwar, Raj
  Deewana, 75
Kapadia, Asif
  Warrior, The, 64, 67
Kapoor, Kareena, 35, 104
Kapoor, Pankaj, 72
Kapoor, Raj, 70, 71, 86
  Awaara, 71, 86
  Bobby, 70
  Shri 420, 71
Kapoor, Randhir, 70
  Henna, 70
Kapoor, Rishi, 56n6
Kapur, Pankaj, 65, 75
Karanth, Prema, 16
Kasarvalli, Girish, 3
Kashyap, Anurag, 44n1, 54, 55, 72, 93
  Black Friday, 72, 74
  Dev D, 44–45n1, 54–56, 93
Kasmiri, Iqbal, 45n1
  Devdas, 45n1
Kaul, Mani, 3
Kaur, Nimrat, 66
Kaur, Rajneeta, 56n6
Kelly, Gene, and Stanley Donen, works by
  Singin' in the Rain, 109
Kelly, Grace, 174, 175
Kendrick, James, 168
Khan, Aamir, 18, 76n6, 96
Khan, Arbaaz, 33

Khan, Farah, 16, 24
  Om Shanti Om, 24, 62; "Dhoom Taana" (song), 62
Khan, Imraan, 60
Khan, Irrfan, 21, 64–67, 73
Khan, Kabir
  New York, 92
Khan, Mansoor, 70
  Qayamat Se Qayamat Tak, 70
Khan, Mehboob
  Mother India, 86
Khan, Saif Ali, 103
Khan, Shah Rukh, 76n6, 90
Khanna, Rajesh, 24
Khosla, Raj, 71
King, Stephen, 166, 184
  Mist, The, 166
  Shining, The, 184
Kline, Kevin, 110
Kohli, Kunal, 23
  Thoda Pyaar Thoda Magic, 23
Konstantin, Leopoldine, 174
Kosminsky, Peter, 136
Kott, Jan, 117
Kozintsev, Grigori, 100, 105, 113–14, 115, 116–17, 118
  Hamlet, 105
  Korol Lir, 113–14, 115, 116–17, 118
Krishnaswamy, S., 45
  See also Barnouw, Eric, and S. Krishnaswamy, works by
Kristeva, Julia, 20
Kubrick, Stanley, ix, 105, 183–88
  Clockwork Orange, A, 105
  Shining, The, ix, 183–88
Kumar, Gulshan, 75
Kurosawa, Akira, 86, 100, 104, 106, 114–16, 119
  Ran, 105, 114–16, 117, 199
  Throne of Blood, 104–5

Ladd, Alan, 145
Lahiri, Jhumpa, 64
Lakdawala, Ejaz, 73

language, viii, 5, 16, 44, 69, 74, 77, 80, 91, 92, 96, 102, 105, 108, 119, 145–46, 164, 184–86
"Layla and Majnun" (story), 56n6
Lean, David, 66
  Brief Encounter, 66
Lee, Ang, 64
  Life of Pi, 64
Leigh, Janet, 176
Leone, Sergio, 86
Levinson, Barry
  Good Morning, Vietnam, 108
Levring, Kristin, 118–19
  King Is Alive, The, 118–19
Lewis, Joseph H., 179
  My Name is Julia Ross, 179
Lockwood, Margaret, 171
Loncraine, Richard, 101
  Richard III, 101
Lorsch, Susan E., 133
Luhrmann, Baz, 69, 106, 145, 149–153
  Great Gatsby, The, 145, 149–53
  William Shakespeare's Romeo + Juliet, 106
Luthria, Milan, 36
  Dirty Picture, The, 30, 36–39, 41
Lloyd, Danny, 183
Lyne, Adrian
  Fatal Attraction, 20

MacDonald, Philip, 163
  Our Feathered Friends, 163
Madden, John, 69
Maguire, Tobey, 145, 149
Manjrekar, Mahesh, 74
  Vaastav, 74
Mankiewicz, Joseph, 100, 104
  Julius Caesar, 104
Mansukhani, Tarun
  Dostana, 92, 93
Markowitz, Robert, 149
  Great Gatsby, The, 145, 149
Marsden, Jean, 78

Marx, Karl, 121, 130
Marxism, 9, 10, 130
masculinity, 18–21, 23, 26–28, 47, 55, 60–61, 95
Mastaan, Haaji, 73–74
McCombe, John P., 166
McGoohan, Patrick
  Catch My Soul (Santa Fe Satan), 110
McHale, Brian, 124
  Postmodernist Fiction, 124
McKellen, Ian, 101
media, 30–38, 40, 41, 55, 59, 93, 96
Mehra, Kamal, 25
Mehra, Prakash, 45n1
  Haath Ki Safai, 44n1
  Muqaddar Ka Sikandar, 45n1, 95
Mehra, Umesh, and Latif Faiziyev, works by
  Sohni Mahiwal, 56n6
Mehta, Deepa, 16, 27, 95
  Bollywood/Hollywood, 96
  Earth, 5, 96
  Fire, 27, 96
  Water, 27, 96
Mehta, Vijaya, 16
Meman, Tiger, 72, 73, 74
Menon, Kay Kay, 75
Merrick, David, 151
metafiction, 121–23
Mills & Boon, 59, 60, 62
mise en abyme, 61
mise en scène, 4, 6, 11, 12, 61, 70, 71, 100, 103, 106, 109, 114, 117, 151, 166, 175, 184
Mitra, Naresh, 44n1
  Devdas, 44n1
Modleski, Tania, 159
modernism, 7
modernity, 4, 93
Mohanlal, 74
Moi, Toril, 26
montage, 3, 9, 118, 175
Mōri Motonari, 115
motherhood, 33

movies. *See* cinema
MTV, 87
Mughal empire, 12
Mukerji, Ayan
   Yeh Jawani Hai Deewani, 93
Mulvey, Laura, 45
   "Visual Pleasure and Narrative Cinema," 45
Mumbai terrorist attacks
   1993 bombings, 72, 74, 75
   2008 attacks (26/11), 72
Murnau, F. W., 176
   Nosferatu, 176, 180
Murugadoss, A. R.
   Ghajini, 76n6
music (musical film soundtrack), 50, 79–80, 103, 109, 137
   Baul, 6
   by Bhatia, 11
   classical (Indian), 3, 4, 6
   film (Indian), 24, 93–94
   folk, 3, 6–7
   by Herrmann, 159
   in Luhrmann's *Great Gatsby*, 151
   qawwali, 12, 13
   Rabindrasangeet (Tagore songs), 6
   by Rahman, 62
   in *Shining, The*, 185
   by Shostakovich, 116
mythology, 3, 7, 9, 12, 19, 45–46, 56, 64

Nair, Mira, ix, 16, 27, 64, 95
   Monsoon Wedding, 96
   Namesake, The, 27, 64–65, 67, 96
   Reluctant Fundamentalist, The, 96
   Salaam Bombay, 64, 96
Nargis, 86, 101
Nawathe, Raja
   Cleopatra, 101
Neeta, 7
neorealism (Italian), 8, 106

Newell, Mike, 76
   Donnie Brasco, 76
new wave (French), 106, 117, 118
new wave (Indian), 10, 16
Nicholson, Jack, 183, 184
Nihalani, Govind, 10–11
   Tamas, 10–11
Nirmala, Vijaya, 16
Noakhali riots, 5
Noble, Adrian, 110
   Midsummer Night's Dream, A, 110
Nolan, Jeanette, 102
Nolan, Christopher, 76n6
   Memento, 76n6
Novak, Kim, 20, 156, 158–59
NRIs (non-resident Indians), 26, 70, 85, 87–88, 90–94, 96
Nugent, Elliott
   Great Gatsby, The, 145
Nunn, Trevor, 110
   Twelfth Night, 110

Oberoi, Vivek, 74, 103
Oberon, Merle, 137
Olivier, Laurence, 100–101, 106, 107, 108, 109, 136, 137–38, 140, 172
   Hamlet, 100–101, 106, 107
   Henry V, 106, 108
   Richard III, 101
Osten, Frank, 85
   Achyut Kanya, 85

Pacino, Al, 76, 108
Paglia, Camille, 168
Paranjape, Sai, 16
Partition, 2–12, 86
Patekar, Nana, 73
Pathak, Ratna, 62
patriarchy, 6, 19–21, 26, 27, 33, 34, 37, 39, 54, 56, 115, 119, 131, 136, 168, 179, 187
Peck, Gregory, 172
Peckinpah, Sam, 86
performativity, 17–19, 21, 24, 136

Perkins, Anthony, 175, 176–77
Piatek, Beata, 134
Pinter, Harold, 123–33
Polanski, Roman, 100, 105–6, 107
   Macbeth, 105–6, 107
   Repulsion, 176
   Rosemary's Baby, 105
   Tenant, The, 176
Post, Melville Davisson, 163
   Revolt of the Birds, The, 163
postcolonialism, 2, 11, 69, 81, 95, 104
Prasad, L. V.
   Jay Vejay, 24
Preminger, Otto, 179
   Laura, 179
Pre-Raphaelites, 121
Progressive Writers Association, 10
Pudovkin, Vsevolod, 9
Puri, Om, 65

Raghavaiah, Vedantam, 44n1
   Devdas (*Devadasu*), 44n1
Rahman, A. R., 62
Rai, Bina, 101
Rai, Himanshu, 85
Rajadhyaksha, Ashish, 3
Rajan, Chota, 74
Ramayana, 9
Ranaut, Kangana, 32
Rao, Narsimha, 89
Rawail, Harnam Singh, 56n6
   Layla Majnu, 56n6
Ray, Satyajit, 2–4, 86
   Aparajito, 86
   Pather Panchali, 4, 86
Redford, Robert, 145, 148, 150
Redgrave, Michael, 172
refugees, 2–5, 7–9, 89, 113
Reilly, William, 73
   Men of Respect, 73
Reisz, Karel, 123–27, 130
   French Lieutenant's Woman, The, 123–34
religion, 11, 12, 24, 25, 92, 93
Renoir, Jean, 86

Resnais, Alain, 124
   Année dernière à Marienbad, L' (*Last Year at Marienbad*), 124
Rizwi, Anusha, 25
   Peepli Live, 25, 95
Robbe-Grillet, Alain, 124
romance, 26–27, 44, 48, 54–55, 57, 59–62, 65, 66, 71, 94, 172, 178–80
Rooks, Pamela
   Train to Pakistan, 5
Roshan, Hrithik, 22
Roshan, Rakesh
   Kaho Naa ... Pyaar Hai, 93
Rothwell, Kenneth S., 102, 118
Roy, Amitava, 70
Roy, Bimal, 44n1, 45, 47, 48, 49, 50, 53, 54, 86
   Devdas, 44n1, 45–50, 53–54, 56
   Do Bigha Zameen, 86
Roy, Dilip, 44n1
   Devdas (*Debdas*), 44n1

sacred, 5, 183
Sahni, Balraj, 10, 11
Sahu, Kishore, 101
   Hamlet, 101
Saint, Eva Marie, 20
Salem, Abu, 72, 80
Samanta, Shakti, 44–45n1
   Amanush, 45n1
   Devdas, 44n1
Sanders, Julie, 77
Santoshi, Raj Kumar, 74
   Family, 74
Sathyu, M. S., ix, 10–13
   Garam Hawa, 10–13
Sawant, Vishram, 72
   D: Underworld Badshah, 72, 73
scopophilia, 51, 175
Scott, Joan, 17
Scott, Ridley
   Alien, 184
screenplays, 25, 76, 81, 101, 108, 110, 124–29, 132–33, 140, 148
secular, 5, 13

Selznick, David O., 172
semiotics, viii, ix, 8, 17
Sen, Aparna, ix, 16–17, 31, 39
   Arshi Nagar, 17
   Iti Mrinalini, ix, 16–17, 31, 39–41
   Sati, 16
   36 Chowringhee Lane, 16
Sen, Mrinal, 3
Sen, Suchitra, 17
sexuality, 11, 18, 22–24, 27, 33, 35–39, 45n1, 48, 49, 54–56, 115, 172, 176, 178, 181
Shah, Naseeruddin, 36, 61, 65
Shah, Vipul Amrutlal
   Namastey London, 27
Shahani, Kumar, 3
Shakeel, Chhota, 73
Shakespeare, William
   adaptations of, ix, 17, 69–70, 72, 73, 77–81, 85, 94, 96, 100–111, 113–19
   As You Like It, 109
   Comedy of Errors, The, 70, 110
   Hamlet, 70, 96, 100–101, 105, 107, 109, 118
   Henry V, 106, 107
   Julius Caesar, 104
   King Lear, 100, 105, 113–19
   Love's Labours Lost, 109
   Macbeth, 65, 69, 73, 75, 76–81, 101–2, 104–6, 107, 109
   Merchant of Venice, The, 85
   Midsummer Night's Dream, A, 110
   Much Ado About Nothing, 70, 94, 107, 109
   Othello, 70, 96, 101, 102–4, 110
   Richard III, 101
   Romeo and Juliet, 17, 70, 96, 101, 104, 106–7, 110
   Taming of the Shrew, The, 109, 110
   Titus Andronicus, 108
   Twelfth Night, 110
Shanti, Disco, 36
Sharma, Anushka, 25
Sharma, Konkona Sen, 16–17, 39, 66, 104
Shelley, Percy Bysshe, 139
Shinde, Gauri, 22
   English Vinglish, 22
Shiva, 7, 9
Shostakovich, Dmitri, 116
Shrivastava, Alankrita
   Dolly Kitty Aur Woh Chamakte Sitare, 16
Sidney, George
   Kiss Me Kate, 110
sign, ix
Singh, Manmohan, 89
Singh, Ranveer, 25
Sinha, Mala, 101
Sippy, Ramesh, 71
   Sholay, 71, 76, 86
Sircar, Shoojit
   Piku, 66, 67
Sivanandan, D., 74
Smitha, Silk, 36–39, 41
"Sohni Mahiwal" (story), 56n6
sound (diegetic soundtrack), viii, 6, 12, 13, 23, 80, 104, 166
soundtrack (musical soundtrack). *See* music
Spielberg, Steven, 89
   Jurassic Park, 146
Spoto, Donald, 169
   Dark Side of Genius, The, 169
Srivastava, Babloo, 73
Stanislavski, Konstantin, 9
stars (film stars), 16, 31–32, 35–38, 40–41, 55, 67, 73
Stein, Gertrude, 147
stereotypes, 15, 20, 21, 23, 25, 31, 42, 45n1, 54, 115, 123, 178,
Stewart, James, 156, 175
Stone, Oliver
   Platoon, 108
Streep, Meryl, 17, 124–25
Stubbs, Imogen, 110
studios, 86–87, 179

Sturges, John, 109
  Magnificent Seven, The, 109
subjectification, 22
subjectivity, viii, 24, 40, 95
Sutherland, A. Edward
  Boys from Syracuse, The, 110
symbology, 3, 9

Tabu, 65, 75
Tagore, Rabindranath, 3, 6
  Je raate mor duwaar guli bhanglo jhore, 6
  See also music: Rabindrasangeet (Tagore songs)
Taj Mahal, 12
Tandon, Lekh
  Amrapali, 24
Tate, Sharon, 106
Taymor, Julie, 108
  Titus, 108
television; cable, 87; satellite, 87
text, viii
Thiruvothu, Parvathy, 21
Tierney, Gene, 179
Tiwari, Nitesh
  Dangal, 96
Tiwary, Manish
  Issaq, 96
Todd, Richard, 136
tradition, 3, 7, 9, 18, 19, 25–27, 34, 36, 48n4, 50, 54, 55, 61, 65, 69, 80, 90–93, 100, 102, 115, 123, 125, 175, 179–80, 188
Trevorrow, Colin
  Jurassic World, 64
Trivedi, Poonam, 77
Truffaut, François, 159
Tyrewala, Abbas, 59
  Jaane Tu Ya Jane Na, 59–62; "Kabhi Kabhi Aditi" (song), 62; "Pappu Can't Dance" (song, 62)

Udvadia, M.
  Dil Farosh, 85
Uma. *See* Durga

uncanny, 172, 179, 180

Vasudevan, Ravi, 47
  "Addressing the Spectator of a 'Third World' National Cinema," 47
Venice Film Festival, 86
Verma, Ram Gopal, 71, 72, 74, 76
  Company, 72, 74
  Sarkar, 72, 74–76, 80
  Satya, 72, 73, 74n4
violence, 2, 5–6, 11, 13, 19, 25, 32, 65, 69–70, 74, 77–81, 92, 104–8, 116–18, 167, 176, 186–88
Virdi, Jyotika, 71
  "Deewar/Wall (1975)," 71
voyeurism, 23, 37, 93, 159, 175

Waggner, George
  Wolf Man, The, 180
Wagner, Richard, 141
  Tristan and Isolde, 141
Wajda, Andrzej, 86
Webb, Marc
  Amazing Spider-Man, The, 67
Weinstein, Arnold, 147
Welles, Orson, 100, 101–3, 106, 108, 109, 117, 182
  Chimes at Midnight, 101, 108
  Citizen Kane, 101
  Lady from Shanghai, The, 182
  Macbeth, 101–2
  Othello, 100–103
Wells, Paul, 156
Whale, James
  Frankenstein, 180
Wheeler, Michael, 139
Whiting, Leonard, 106
Wilder, Billy, 181
  Double Indemnity, 181
  Irma la Douce, 76n6
  Some Like It Hot, 109
  Sunset Boulevard, 181
Winterbottom, Michael, 64

Wise, Robert, and Jerome Robbins, works by
   West Side Story, 110
womanhood, 30–32, 36, 41–42, 90–91, 181–82
   Indian womanhood, depiction of, 23, 25, 36, 46, 54, 94
Woolrich, Cornell, 174
   It Had to be Murder, 174
Wright, Teresa, 179
Wyler, William, 136–38, 140, 142, 143
   Wuthering Heights, 136–38, 140, 142, 143
Wynyard, Diana, 179

Yarvet, Yuri, 113–14, 117
Yash Raj Films, 95
youth culture, 55, 60, 62, 93
Yutkevich, Sergei, 103, 106
   Othello, 103

Zaidi, S. Hussain, 72
   Black Friday, 72
Zeffirelli, Franco, 69, 100, 106–7, 108, 109
   Hamlet, 107, 108
   Romeo and Juliet, 106–7, 109
   Taming of the Shrew, The, 109